Diary of a Decade

1. Costy our golden retriever and Martin his successor

Diary of a Decade

More Memoirs of a Bishop's Wife

by

Cicely Williams

LONDON
GEORGE ALLEN & UNWIN LTD
RUSKIN HOUSE MUSEUM STREET

FIRST PUBLISHED 1970

© *George Allen & Unwin Ltd* 1970

ISBN 0 04 920030 5

PRINTED IN GREAT BRITAIN
in 11 *on* 12 *point Plantin*
BY BLACKFRIARS PRESS LTD
LEICESTER

FOR DIANA
*on her twenty-first
birthday*

Give us
courage
and
gaiety
and the
quiet
mind.

R.L.S.

FOREWORD

I must say a very big thank you to Mr Philip Unwin for his kindness in asking me to write a fourth book – but for him I should never have fulfilled my ambition to become an author. The Prologue explains the reason for the book, and the purpose of it. Readers of my first book may remember that I am always known as Bim to my friends; I mention this to give validity to the captions under the photographs. My thanks are due to John Fortune, Editor of the *Leicester Mercury* who took endless trouble to provide me with some of the photographs, and also to the *Leicester Graphic* who were very helpful in this respect too. Last of all a very special thank you to Jill England and Angela Pollard – former secretaries at Bishop's Lodge – who between them typed the script, in spite of rapidly increasing families.

CICELY WILLIAMS
Bishop's Lodge
Leicester

PROLOGUE

If this book links on to anything else I have written, it is to my first real book, *Bishop's Wife – but still myself*. Indeed, the writing of it is a direct consequence of events stemming from that book, although it is not necessary to have read that in order to read this.

Since that first book was published, nine years ago, I have received nearly a thousand letters from readers; they still arrive at the rate of about one a week. The theme is repetitive – 'Do write a sequel to *Bishop's Wife*'. I cannot do exactly that; not just now anyhow. Perhaps in years to come, if we live to be elderly and retire, I might try; assuming that I still have the power to write and that there are still people who want to read what I write. The ifs and buts are numerous. Of course, many authors produce second and even third instalments of their autobiographies. I love such books and pounce on them in the library. But not being either Somerset Maugham or Mrs Robert Henrey I cannot see my inconspicuous story lending itself to that kind of treatment.

My second book, *Zermatt Saga*, was a labour of love – a tribute to all that one village and its people have meant to me over the years. I have discovered that there are hosts of Zermatt fanatics in the world; they want to hear more and tell me so in no uncertain terms. Alas, there is not sufficient material; there is a limit to what can be written about one small village, however greatly loved.

Dear Abroad, published more recently, is the story of the travels of my husband and myself over many years. The writing of it brought back a flood of happy memories; it seemed to touch a chord in my readers too and all the letters insisted, 'Do write another travel book soon.' I should like to – but travel takes time. In a busy life it takes quite a while to accumulate enough travel experience on which to write a book.

After these negative meanderings, what exactly *is* this book? It is a scrap-book; a pot pourri of events and an anthology of reflections on, and reactions to, those events. It is, too, a token of gratitude to all the kind friends, known and unknown, who have asked for more. It tries to show something that I have discovered, something hinted at in the title of my first book, *Bishop's Wife – but still myself*. Then I was struggling to retain my individuality in a new and strange rôle in life; in this book I try to show that the acceptance of duty has enhanced my sense of individuality.

It is not a travel book but it covers a good many journeys because, during the last few years, our travels have suddenly widened and become more exciting; we have had to travel for official purposes as well as purely for pleasure; that adds a dimension.

It tells too of how I have been involved in some recent historic and moving events in the life of Zermatt; I should, in any case, find it hard to write a book that did not include Zermatt in some form and addicts will be brought up to date with events in this beloved place.

More than anything else, perhaps, the book picks out the recent highlights in my life and in that of my husband. Many things have happened to us; some have brought deep sadness; one, at least, black tragedy. But these are part of life; hazards that must be dealt with and overcome because they cannot be avoided. As a keen mountaineer, I tend to think of life as a continuous climb on a mountain which, like all mountains, sometimes brings one to the depths of despair, sometimes provides sublime experiences. Occasionally on a big mountain it is necessary to climb down into the darkness of a crevasse in order to work one's way up on the other side where the next bit of the route lies. Thus when I find myself in one of life's deep crevasses I try to persuade myself that, beyond my vision, I shall find a sunlit slope again. It is often a stern test of faith but so far I have not been disappointed. That is why these experiences appear in this scrap-book.

But if we have had rather more than our full share of sorrow during these last few years we have also had our full share of happiness. Not only the joy of great events and exciting adventures, although we have had these, but the sheer satisfaction of the daily round; of work in which we are very happy, performed among people whom we love and by whom we feel we are loved.

It takes several years to become thoroughly established in our kind of life; especially for the wife – at any rate for me. For so long one feels so new; there is so much to learn; so many people to get to know; life is full of pitfalls and unwary types like me make endless mistakes. But, inevitably, the day dawns when we are no longer new; when most of the people around us are later arrivals than ourselves and our responsibilities towards them are correspondingly greater. There is still, there always will be, much to learn; one still makes mistakes, but at least one is no longer 'on approval'. Some of the early struggles have been resolved; the foundation stone has been laid and dedicated; one begins to build at last.

We have also the constant background of a happy home. We have come to love the great Victorian villa which is our official residence, which at first seemed so strange and entirely unlike anything we had experienced before. Perhaps this is because it is now the only home we have; the glowing embers of the parental firesides which we enjoyed for so long have slowly died away. Some of the treasures from those homes, familiar from our childhood, have come to us and have provided that sense of continuity that we have sometimes felt was lacking.

Readers of my first book will have realized how very much my friends, and especially my closest friends, mean to me – on the end papers of that book are printed the signatures of some of them. My friends played a large part in the book; incidentally this infuriated one reviewer who took the greatest offence that anyone should be referred to by a Christian name. However, so many readers have told me that they feel my friends are now their friends and they would like to hear more about them, that I make no excuse for re-introducing them in this book, nor for adding some new ones as well. In this rapidly changing world the friends whom one can trust implicitly, whom one can rely on in any circumstances, whose love and loyalty are unchanging, give a security to life that nothing else can give

We are more than fortunate in our little household – especially in these days of almost non-existent domestic help. Our caretakers, Mr and Mrs Bell, who came to us early in 1960 are still with us*. They retired to a lovely country cottage in 1965 but in 1967 we decided to join forces again and they returned to Bishop's Lodge. Other members of the household are new and take their place in the story as it unfolds. Needless to say, there is always more than enough for all of us to do but we regard our helpers as friends and *confidantes*: they never betray the trust we put in them; they seem to find a true vocation in helping us and, through us, the Church and the community.

All Bishops, I think, find their work gradually extending beyond

*But see p.255

the boundaries of their own diocese; they are caught up in the wider work of the Church throughout the world. This has repercussions for the wives; it is possible to opt out if you feel you must, but most do not. I certainly enjoy to the full my tiny part in these affairs. People and places and institutions of which I had scarcely heard a few years ago have become part and parcel of my lot in life. With the work in the diocese and commitments in the Church at large, almost every day, except for our precious summer holiday, seems to be mortgaged. But we would not have it otherwise; it is fascinating and exhilarating – above all it is a caring job. I would not change places with anyone else in the world.

The loss of parents, of the heroes of one's youth, and even of the friends of our own generation, is an unavoidable accompaniment of middle age. Often one feels strangely defenceless; there is no one to turn to; the final decision, the ultimate responsibility, must rest with you alone. But the example and tradition of those who have gone come to one's aid; we take our feebly flickering torches and relight them from those which have been laid down; they burn more brightly as a result and we carry them more proudly and with greater purpose.

And life is not all labour and responsibility and decision; life is for living and includes all the fun that can be got out of it. Our increased commitments have taken nothing from our pleasures; there are still books and music to enjoy; there is still climbing and skiing; still county cricket to watch and golf to play – even, about once a year, a brief spell on a horse. We still plan our foreign holiday as eagerly as we did in our early married days and still have unexpected adventures – though perhaps slightly less grotesque than in earlier times. Above all, we have each other which means that sorrows shared are halved and joys correspondingly doubled – I do not ask for more.

From all these bits and pieces, then, this scrap-book is composed; I hope that it will bring pleasure to those for whom it is written.

One word more – a warning or an explanation is due to those who see life through other eyes than mine. This is a happy book; it does not debunk anything or anyone – except perhaps the debunkers themselves. In spite of the complexities of the times in which we live, in spite of world problems of race and want and war which weigh upon us all; in spite of the cynics and the satirists and the destructive critics who would have us think that there is little left to believe in or to live for, I am in no way disenchanted with life. What any one individual can do to right the wrongs of mankind is infinitesimal but perhaps a positive attitude to life, a determination to infuse into daily existence something of the vision one is occasionally granted on the heights may help some others, as it continually helps me. The vision of any one person must be very limited, but without some vision, all is dark.

CONTENTS

ILLUSTRATIONS

CHAPTER 1

Author and Pilgrim

SOME years are momentous – for the world, for the country, or for oneself. World happenings can be left to the historians; in our own affairs we are the assessors. We look back, sometimes we need not look far, and we see important peaks rising above the valleys and small hills that compose most of the picture. These peaks mark occasions of events and decisions which have had an irrevocable effect upon our lives; they point the way on the next bit of the journey; they help to produce the atmosphere in which we are to live for the next few years – they are vital to life.

Such a year for us was 1961. I knew, almost on New Year's Day, that my first book was to be published in June and I could not suppress an excited thrill of anticipation almost every day of that six months. Indeed, I still hardly dared to believe that it could actually happen.

I had always wanted to write a book; ever since I left school I had slowly built up a little literary career for myself, starting with stories in women's magazines and gradually going on to articles for *The Times*, a few of the 'glossies', and talks for the BBC. I enjoyed my small successes and put out of my mind any idea of embarking on a book. When I married our busy life gave me little time for concentrated writing; I knew no publishers and certainly none knew me; it seemed a waste of time to spend perhaps a year or two labouring away on something that would probably be returned almost as soon as I had posted it.

But sometimes the seemingly impossible comes to pass. I wrote, as I quite often did, an article for the Woman's Page of *The Times*. The Woman's Page Editor, Mary Delane, was kindly disposed to me and I was lucky in acceptances, but I did not feel this particular article had much chance; it told the story of a school prize-giving as seen from the platform but it seemed to me to be unconvincing. When I showed it to my husband, Ronald remarked: 'I can't believe they'll take that'.

Neither could I – but I had typed it and written the letter – I decided to try my luck. To my surprise it was accepted and published. Within a few days a letter arrived, sent on by *The Times*, addressed to the author. It was from Philip Unwin, a director of the famous publishing house of Allen and Unwin. He wrote that he had read my article, he supposed I had probably published many books but if not his firm would be pleased to handle one for me.

We were having breakfast at the time; I dropped my knife with a resounding clatter; Ronald, who was perusing a long document from his legal secretary, looked up in alarm.

'Whatever is it now?' he demanded.

I handed over the letter in speechless amazement. Ronald cast aside the legal document and read on with an ever-widening grin suffusing his face.

'It's your chance' he announced delightedly, 'seize it with both hands. Write at once – it's marvellous. Thank goodness I'll no longer be the husband of a free-lance writer'. He had always maintained that his lot was harder than mine when my returned literary effusions plopped through the letter box—the ensuing depression spoilt his day, or so he said.

Preliminaries about a book before the contract is signed take some time; for a beginner they inevitably take longer than for an established writer. In my case they were even more prolonged owing to a lucky scoop with America. Doubledays of New York, who co-operate with Allen and Unwin, had decided to come in on my book when they heard it was likely to be autobiographical. They insisted that the fact that my husband was a bishop must be involved in the title – it was obviously a good selling point. Their suggestions, over the telephone from New York, left me gasping. *Life with My Lord the Bishop* was only one of several that I found totally unacceptable. No one actually mooted *In Bed with the Bishop* but nothing would have surprised me. However Doubledays proved to be very understanding, gave me a few days grace to ponder on the matter and were eventually delighted when Ronald came up with *Bishop's Wife – but still myself*. This urgent matter being successfully settled the contract was signed and I set out on the task of producing approximately 75,000 words, plus pictures, by a given date. As I laboured away it seemed impossible that it could ever be ready in time. Like all writers I went through periods of anguish and exhilaration; there were days when the wheels dragged and I just pushed myself along; there were others when the words dripped off my pen and I sang as I worked.

But now, at last, by the beginning of 1961 typescript and photos had been safely delivered to Mr Unwin; I could sit back and wait for the proofs and discuss plans for the jacket and end papers – it was a delicious feeling. Meanwhile, of course, life had to go on. Writing is only a spare time hobby for me; it has to be fitted in where and when I can manage it; I have never allowed it to cause me to neglect my husband, my home, my work in the diocese, my friends at home and abroad or any of the affairs I am involved in. June and publication day were a long way ahead; there was a six months' calendar of events to be worked through before that time came.

We led off with a joyous event; on January 18th a dear friend of ours, Miss Edith Baring-Gould, celebrated her ninetieth birthday. Miss Baring-Gould was widely known and had become a legend in many walks of life; she was a descendant of the famous hymn-writer, a life-long pillar of the Church Missionary Society, a tireless traveller, an intrepid climber and a fanatical devotee of Zermatt and the Riffelalp. She knew everybody; she was interested in everything; she had the news-sense of the journalist and the enthusiasm of the teenager. Almost any event could be made dramatic if she thought that was how it ought to be. She became seventy during the last war but she remained in London for the duration and journeyed daily from St John's Wood to Fleet Street to fill in the gaps left at CMS by the departure of younger staff to their war jobs. In only one aspect of her life had time stood still – she must have stopped buying clothes in 1899 at the latest; if not, she must have kept the patterns and had them copied. To the end of her days she travelled, climbed and sat on committees dressed always in her favourite fashions of the naughty nineties. But this made no difference to her many admirers and the countless hundreds who loved her. Indeed her younger friends, like myself, were rather proud of her unique appearance. E.B.G. as we called her, took us back to our grandmothers' days, the only difference being that instead of reclining in a bath chair her activities were very much akin to our own.

E.B.G.'s ninetieth birthday party was a roaring success. It was held in the sitting-room of her flat; portraits of her parents and Victorian church dignitaries smiled down upon us; the walls were almost papered with pictures of the Matterhorn; every corner of the room held some memento of her world travels. It was a period piece and yet most of her guests were young enough to be her grandchildren and were thrilled to be there. Her young second cousin Priscilla Lethbridge had concocted an iced birthday cake modelled on the Matterhorn; there was a telegram and a bouquet of dried alpine flowers from Zermatt; cards from every corner of the world decorated bookshelves and brackets. E.B.G. held court in her arm chair and in a breezy speech described the seventy-five summers she had spent at the Riffelalp. Priscilla cut the cake; Ronald dispensed the sherry and when the time came for us to depart E.B.G. asked him to pronounce the blessing. It was typical of her whole outlook on life that the one who had presided over the drinks should also give the blessing. Everyone had enjoyed themselves enormously and no one more than our ninety-year-old hostess.

Early on the morning of Thursday, February 16th we opened *The Times* and read that the Riffelalp Hotel had been burnt down on the previous night. Could it be true; it seemed impossible; surely that historic spot sacred to the British for more than seventy years could not disappear in a night? Instantly we thought of E.B.G. – if we were shocked, what about her? How would she, at her age, face the destruction of something that enshrined almost everything that was dearest to her. The speech she had made at her birthday party had become the funeral oration of the Riffelalp. As soon as possible I hurried off to see her; she sat in her usual chair; her welcome was as affectionate as always but there was a great change since her party just a month before. For the first time the dramatic had proved too dramatic; she had lost her zest for life; even her resilience could not cope with this. We talked for an hour about the dear, destroyed hotel and then I tried to interest her in other things. We were very soon to leave for our first trip to the Holy Land – would she give us any hints about that? And I had heard that my book would be out in June – she was to have a signed presentation copy. She cheered up quite a lot but when I left her I knew instinctively that we should not have E.B.G. for very much longer. She had lost the will to live; if the Riffelalp had gone perhaps it was time for her to go too. I went home and wrote an article about the Riffelalp in which I mentioned Miss Baring-Gould. I felt that if she was soon to have an obituary notice she would certainly like to read it. *The Times* printed the article on the court page and I like to think that E.B.G. was able to bask in the pleasure of that little bit of publicity for the three remaining months of her life.

I suppose the first visit to the Holy Land is a milestone in any-one's life – certainly it was in ours. In 1961 travel to Jordan and Israel for ordinary folk was only just getting into its stride; today, of course, tourists of all types and all ages set off in their thousands and how good it is that so many should have this experience. For us it was a real adventure; ours was the pioneer diocesan party and the whole enterprise was something of an experiment. It was an experiment that came off; thirty-six of us travelled, lived and ex-plored together for fourteen days. There were adventures of all kinds. We had our share of minor material and physical misfor-tunes but from the moment of take-off at Gatwick Airport there was never a discordant note. Perhaps the fact that the journey was a pilgrimage to holy places was a factor; perhaps we were particu-larly lucky in those who joined the party; whatever the reason it was an amazingly happy trip.

As is so often the case in this country we took off in blinding rain – the worst sort of April weather. The plane was unpres-surized; we could not fly over the Alps; instead we touched down at Marseilles; the subtle warmth of the Mediterranean wrapped us round and our spirits rose as quickly as the temperature. There were stops at Naples, Athens, Nicosia and then we sped away east-wards until flat-roofed houses appeared below us and the moun-tains of the Lebanon rose up on either side. We touched down briefly at Damascus; immediately Europe was forgotten – it might have belonged to another hemisphere, so utterly different was the land in which we found ourselves. This was the Middle East with all its kaleidoscope of noise and dirt; of donkeys and deserts; of mosques and minarets; of camels and Arabs with their *keffiyeh*; while into the midst of it all was projected the civilization of the West in the form of vast American cars and jazzed-up advertisements.

One more hop in our plane brought us to Amman; there the coach was waiting to take us to Jordan Jerusalem and in spite of the staccato nature of the journey most of us slept fitfully as we drove through the Jordan valley. Darkness came suddenly and seemed to rouse us from our slumbers; we sat up to find myriad lights crowning the hills ahead; shafts of moonlight glittered on castellated walls and smooth curved domes; this was the Holy City, this was Jerusalem and, for the time being, Journey's End. As we drove slowly up the hill to the city gates – to the Dung Gate to be precise – I was glad that we had arrived at dusk. I knew I could never forget that first distant vision of the city seen dimly through the veil of night; Jerusalem withheld her real self until we were better able to see and to understand but I felt vividly aware of her spiritual presence as we were admitted within the ancient walls and made our way to the little Hotel Petra guarding the top of David Street like a miniature Crusader Castle.

Month after month, year after year, the tourists pour into Jerusalem; the basic itinerary for most of us is the same but we each have our individual reactions and our own special memories. Nationality, Church allegiance and even temperament play a part in this. I remember the noise and bustle of the Via Dolorosa when I had thought of something secluded and sacred, and how, having survived the first shock of the unexpected, I found that the sheer ordinariness of it made it all the more impressive. I think of the vast courtyards of the Temple area dominated by the sparkling dome of the Mosque of Omar and the view across to the Mount of Olives which, in spite of the hideous hotel and the multitude of churches scattered about it, still tells its own unspoiled story of Bible times. I can never forget the brown habited Franciscan brothers working silently among the olive trees in peaceful Gethsemane, nor the deep purple windows of the Church of All Nations built beside it.

The Palm Sunday Path – how much that meant when we trod it for the first time and how much it still means when I return to it in memory at the beginning of each Holy Week. The coach took us to the top of the Mount of Olives; then we were free to find our own way back to the Hotel Petra. We wandered down the stony bridle path; little brown donkeys trotted by; we passed an occasional woman bearing a water pot on her head; and always before us lay the Holy City – so little altered in 2,000 years. We crossed the Brook Kedron and made our way up the hill under the shadow of the massive city walls; we walked through the gate into the noise of the midday crowds; it seemed as if only the palm branches were missing.

The Convent of the Sisters of Sion is one of my most precious memories. The Sisters who look after it are full of kindness; we were allowed to go up on the roof for what must be the most spectacular of all the views of Jerusalem; I could have stayed there for hours just looking and listening. Down in the crypt is one of the most hallowed spots in the city – the Pavement. This consists of the stones of the courtyard of the Praetorium, the only stones on which scholars are agreed that Our Lord actually walked. We have been back several times since then but our first memory is our most perfect. The Sister Superior was a Scot and a Roman Catholic; at the Pavement she turned to Ronald as leader of the party and asked quite simply – 'Bishop, will you say a prayer for us here?'

I had only one disappointment in Jordan Jerusalem; I must be the most obtuse pilgrim who has ever visited the Holy City but I just cannot take the Church of the Holy Sepulchre. For most people it is the heart of the Christian faith; I had hoped that it would be the same for me. So far, and in spite of four visits, this has not been so. The noise, the milling crowds, the fact that the shrines are divided between at least six different churches seems to dispel any sense of the tragedy of the lonely hill of Calvary or the triumph of the empty tomb. The gap between childhood pictures of 'the green hill far away', and the heavy ornate church was just too great for me to bridge. Perhaps one day I shall think and feel differently.

From the old city of Jerusalem we had, of course, to do all our Jordan sightseeing; after we had crossed into Israel there could be no return. Bethlehem was all that I had hoped for; as we approached it up the hill we passed a little party – a young woman in a blue robe riding on a donkey, a baby in her arms, her Arab husband walking beside them; the most perfect picture of the Holy Family one could wish to see. The Church of the

Nativity, with many-coloured lights decorating the nave and the crypt with the star marking the traditional place of Christ's birth, seemed tremendously real to me. No doubt the actual sites are only legendary and hallowed by time; but *somewhere* in the vicinity it all happened and that is quite good enough for me.

The afternoon that we spent visiting Bethany, the Inn of the Good Samaritan, the Caves of Qumran and the Dead Sea was truly breathtaking. I loved Bethany; it seemed the most natural thing in the world that Our Lord should have come out to this sheltered, peaceful spot to relax and have supper with his friends. Nor was there the slightest difficulty in believing that someone fell among thieves on the Jerusalem-Jericho road; I felt secretly that it could easily happen to us! The wild, arid desert, inhabited only by Bedouin tribes and fierce wild animals was quite awe-inspiring even when viewed from the comparative safety of our rather rickety coach.

We could hardly wait for the Caves of Qumran; the discomfort of the stony track over which we slithered and bumped to get there mattered not at all. For the theologians and historians amongst us – which did not include me – this was one of the thrills of the pilgrimage and even the ignoramuses sensed the timelessness of those small caves. For Ronald and me the occasion was epoch-making. The guide stooped to pick up a tiny coin in the sand.

'You had better have this,' he said to Ronald. 'We're always getting them.'

As it happened he had unearthed a treasure. After we had sent it to several museums it was proved that we are the proud possessors of the oldest coin so far discovered at Qumran.

From the caves we drove back to the Dead Sea – a most beautiful spot in spite of its uninviting name. The mountains of Moab were turning pink in the setting sun; the water reflected the last blue patches of the evening sky. It was still terribly hot and we were sticky and dirty. Within a few minutes the whole party had donned swim suits and plunged into the tepid water. I am a poor enough swimmer but in all that salt my prowess was prodigious. One simply could not sink; indeed it was almost impossible to swim; the best bet was to float in lazy fashion and enjoy the luxury of a lovely, luke-warm bath. Cooled and refreshed we gathered on the miniature Lido to enjoy our supper sandwiches and watch the

few scattered lights coming out on the steep Jericho road winding
its way up through the wicked-looking wilderness.

The time had come to leave Jordan and all of us were sad; we
loved the Arabs and, in spite of the unhappy divisions, Jordan,
Jerusalem and the whole countryside seemed to proclaim the
Bible and the foundations of our faith. And we had such fun too,
from the very moment of our arrival. As we entered the city for the
first time our coach had got wedged in the Dung Gate and caused
a sensation of no small dimensions. When we arrived at the Hotel
Petra, on a boiling hot night, the proprietor had proudly showed
us the oil heater warming our room! His son conducted us to the
little bathroom they had kindly given us because we were leaders
of the party; a bath was the very thing I was longing for; when we
turned on the taps only mud gushed out. But we *had* to be grateful; they had tried so hard and they asked so pathetically 'Do you
like it – will you come back?' In spite of everything we *did* like it,
more and more, and we think of the little Petra with nothing but
affection.

Shopping in the *Souk* was a continuous thrill. You made your
way among donkeys and camels laden with produce; Arabs
squatted on the pavements smoking their hookah pipes; almost
every dark cavernous shop seemed to sell everything from fur
coats to camel meat. The most inviting were those showing the
lovely Damascus brocades and the souvenir shops with their olive
wood boxes and jewelled Jerusalem crosses. I had made up my
mind to buy Ronald an amethyst Jerusalem cross to wear for
evening occasions; the wherewithal to buy it was to come from the
proceeds of my so far unpublished book. He nobly advanced the
cash until I had enough to repay and the cross we chose is a never-
ending source of pleasure.

There were some slightly anxious excitements occasionally. The
oldest members of our party were a charming clerical couple, both
well over eighty, who were spending the retiring present the
parish had given them to come on our trip. They were the only
ones unknown to us all but everyone loved them at once. They
were so gay and so grateful for any little offers of help. They were
also adventurous – their theme-song being 'We shall die happy if
we have seen the Holy Land'. It was this approach that caused
dear old Mr Hemmingway to hire a pair of red bathing trunks and

hurl himself into the Dead Sea. He fell flat on his face and was only rescued with difficulty by other members of the party. For a short time we were all quite worried. However, he soon pulled round, ate an enormous supper and the next morning was at the head of the queue for the coach. They were both a tonic to us all; the general verdict being that if we were as good at eighty we should think ourselves mighty fortunate.

In 1961 to cross from Jordan into Israel was an international experience. The coach deposited us at the Mandelbaum Gate; we could see our luggage piled desolately in No-man's-land. We filed through the passport control; our kind Arab guides hurriedly withdrew and we saw them no more. Clutching our passports we grabbed our luggage and almost ran into Israel; the dreary hundred yards of No-man's-land had an evil aura about it; none of us wanted to linger there.

We entered a different country and different standards prevailed. A sleek, stream-lined coach awaited us; we drove through streets lined with luxury shops; there were no *keffiyeh*, no women with water pots; we had grown accustomed to these things and for a few hours we missed them a lot.

The YMCA where we were to spend the weekend is a magnificent building with every western amenity, and in spite of our love for the Arabs and their ways, I think we all found it pleasantly relaxing. Across the road stands the King David Hotel, rendezvous of the British for very many years. It had a special interest for us. Members of the Seiler family from Zermatt had been in charge of it in the 1930s and another Swiss friend had spent his winters there as concierge. We flocked over in large numbers for coffee; it was all we could afford, the King David being beyond the price range of most pilgrims. We enjoyed it; some of us paid several visits and it was a strange experience to look out from the lovely hotel garden across to the old city we had so recently left; to hear the *muezzin* calling the faithful to prayer from the many minarets; to see our little Hotel Petra almost buried among the close-packed buildings and to know that it was impossible to return there unless we first went away at least as far as Cyprus.

The long trip from New Jerusalem to Galilee was a procession of delights. First down the famous Road of Courage to the modern capital of Tel Aviv; then for seventy miles on a road where the scent of orange blossom filled the air; where great bushes of mimosa flanked the right-hand side and the blue Mediterranean broke in frothy foam on the left.

At last we turned east and to our surprise came again upon Arab villages, donkeys and water-pots. The green grassy dome of Mount Tabor appeared on our left. We reached the top of a hill; the coach stopped; our Israeli guide motioned us to look ahead. In the distance, far far below, lay the waters of the Sea of Galilee. A great stillness fell upon the party; we sat silent, overawed until Ronald opened a little book and read a verse from Whittier's hymn

> O Sabbath rest by Galilee!
>   O calm of hills above,
> Where Jesus knelt to share with thee
>   The silence of eternity,
>   Interpreted by love.

Nothing else was necessary; he closed the book; the coach went on its way; the pilgrims slowly returned to reality; there could never be another 'first time' with the Sea of Galilee.

It seemed as if we should never stop descending; we passed the sign which says 'sea level'; we slid down another 700 feet before we reached Tiberias. The Scottish Hospice was to be our home here; a grey, rough-hewn building reminiscent of Scotch granite; bougainvillea spills down its walls; oleanders and hibiscus blossom in the garden that drops steeply to the road running beside the lake. At any hour of the day or night one could slip down to the shore for a dip in the cool water. Since the temperature was some-times well over 100 degrees cold showers or a swim were an im-perative 'must'.

Galilee thrilled us; it was less exciting than Jerusalem; in-finitely more peaceful and somehow more penetrating. Cities in-evitably change with the centuries; lakes and hills are more abiding and more easily teach eternal values. The thriving town-ships set on the Sea of Galilee in Bible times have disappeared; but, except at Capernaum, no ruins confronted us. Instead the unchanged hillside told the story of the Beatitudes with just one commemorative church to mark the spot; the fifth century mosaic nearer the lake reminded us of the loaves and fishes used for the

Feeding of the Five Thousand. At Capernaum we found incredibly ancient remains of a synagogue – the one which replaced the original that Our Lord knew.

But even these holy places were not quite the best that Galilee had to offer; it was the distant snows of Mount Hermon, the shadowy line of the Syrian hills across the lake, moonlight flecking the water with silver and the fishermen bringing in their boats at sunrise that made the deepest and most lasting impression on us. Nothing had changed in 2,000 years – except that the nets were nylon!

Nazareth was a surprise – a big, noisy Arab city. But in the old part we were soon involved in the typical *Souk*. Women drew water from Mary's Fountain still supplied by the ancient spring; beneath the church of St Joseph we found the cave where tradition says the Holy Family lived and here we sang the 'wondrous childhood' verses from 'Once in Royal David's City' – an experience that was strangely moving.

All too soon the pilgrimage, so long looked forward to, came to an end. We took off from the airport at Lod; flat roofs and eastern architecture faded into the mist behind us but our memories of the Holy Land would never fade. As a party of thirty-six we would always have something in common; as individuals we could never be quite the same again. The fact that we arrived to find Gatwick as we had left it – battered by interminable rainstorms – did not matter. We hardly noticed it; we could still smell the orange blossom; still hear the hoarse cries of the *muezzin* and the patter of donkey's hooves; still see the sunset painting the Syrian hills pink. It was over but it remained with us and would do so forever.

I got back to Leicester to find a letter from Philip Unwin awaiting me to say that publication day for my book was fixed for June 8th; a little party was planned to take place in Leicester on the 7th to give the book a boost with the City Library, the booksellers and press from a wide area, as well as the BBC. This was something that I had not anticipated and I was thrilled. I had also brought home with me from our pilgrimage another bit of literary luck. Among the pilgrims was John Fortune, Editor of the *Leicester Mercury*, and his wife Hilda. John had made tentative enquiries as to whether I would sometimes contribute an article to the *Mercury*. I was flattered to be asked and I knew it would satisfy one of my needs. There had been no time for free-lance work while I was labouring

2. Bim *en route* for a climb with Bernard

3. *Right:* Bernard 1965
Below: On one of our last big climbs with Bernard
Below Right: Ronald and Bim on the way to the Matterhorn Hut

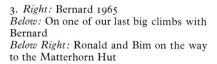

with my book; I was hoping to take this up again once the excitement of publication had died down; a regular commission was just what I wanted to get me started. Life looked rosy indeed.

With my 'publishers' party' coming off on June 7th, Ronald and I were free to plan our own celebrations for the 8th. It could hardly have worked out better. We were already invited to the Royal Army Chaplains' Garden Party at Bagshot for that day; Dick and Netta Mayston, our Provost and his wife, were going too – Dick having been an Army padre for twenty-two years before he came to us at the Cathedral.

We agreed to meet at Penn, halfway on the journey, for a festive lunch. The garden party would provide a gay afternoon and we would motor back to Leicester via London for another celebration with my Aunt in the old family home. A long trip and a bit exacting perhaps – but who cares on such an occasion?

The publishers' party was fun; all sorts of exciting people turned up; cameras flashed and the BBC made a short recording for the Midland Region; it was hard to make myself believe it was all in aid of me and my little book.

June 8th brought brilliant sunshine and a large parcel – my six author's copies of 'the book'. There was just time to sign them, present some to our household, post others to our nearest and dearest and pop one in the car to take home to London before we got ready for the day's junketings. Like all the rejoicings we have shared with Dick and Netta the lunch was a success and there was time to relax before we sped on our way to Bagshot. We went by Windsor Great Park and Ascot, one of our favourite routes, but nothing was so glorious on that day as Bagshot itself. The massed display of azaleas and rhododendrons, the smooth, fresh-smelling lawns, the military band playing under the trees, tables piled high with strawberries and cream – it was the English summer at its beautiful best. There were lots of friends to meet from our military trips to Germany and plenty of army padres – some of whom have since found their way to our diocese.

With the London visit still to come we could not stay too long; we were loath to leave but the welcome we received from the beloved old aunt, the only surviving member of the older generation I had to share the great day with me, made everything more than worth while. She hugged the book to her and said the things that the family used to say in the old days when, for instance, I got my colours at school or, less often, had some little academic success. Of course there were drinks all round and a special TV supper while we watched the recording of the wedding of the Duke and the Duchess of Kent who had been married in York Minster that day. I thought many times of my mother to whom I dedicated my book; she had taken such an interest in its beginnings and I had hoped so much she would live to see it. It was not to be but I comforted myself with the thought that perhaps she and my father, united once more, were sharing in our pleasure together.

For just a few days I lived in a whirl of excitement. This culminated in a telephone call from London asking me to give a five-minute interview on television on the Sunday evening. I was of course already committed for Sunday evening, but Ronald would have none of this. Working on the principle of first things first he packed me off on the train and promised to meet me shortly before midnight.

I had never appeared on television and had never expected to – I had no idea what would happen. Everyone was kind, and eager to put me at my ease; I drank endless cups of coffee and was whisked away to be made up – a new event for someone whose cosmetic experience was previously limited to powder compact and lipstick.

Rehearsing was cut to a minimum, which was probably a good thing; I quite enjoyed the interview but I had not the slightest idea of how well or how badly it had gone over. By the time I got in the train at St Pancras I was too tired to bother much and ate my sandwiches in a kind of daze. Ronald met me at Leicester, full of encouragement as always but somewhat startled by the eye make-up I had forgotten to remove. As we got in the car a policeman flashed his torch on me; vaguely I wondered what the crime was and which of us had committed it.

'Excuse me,' said the officer, 'haven't I just seen you on television?'

'Well, you might have done,' I stuttered.

'It was pretty good, we enjoyed it, my wife and me. Goodnight.'

That policeman and I have been buddies ever since – a useful friendship when I'm meeting Ronald with the car and the station yard is crammed to capacity.

34

Like most books, mine had a mixed reception. To begin with, there were the reviews. I was watching anxiously for every notice; my spirits soared and slumped; in fact I was thoroughly naive about the whole business. Anyone rash enough to embark on an autobiography as a first book is asking for trouble but on the whole I was very lucky – in America as well as in this country. No one raved about the book – I had never expected that they would – but for the most part the reviewers were kind and sympathetic. They admitted to enjoying what they read and one went so far as to say, 'This book should win her a host of new friends . . .' This has proved to be almost overwhelmingly correct but I fancy I may have made one or two enemies as well. Of the American reviews only two were poor and they did not prevent the book selling out fairly quickly. In this country only one was really devastating, in fact some people went so far as to say it was libellous. The reviewer just could not bear the fact that I loved my friends and seemed to enjoy life. But that review sold a lot of copies for me – 'way out' reviewers do sometimes have that effect. A year or two ago I read a very acid paragraph about Ruby Ferguson's book *Children at the Shop*. Superior remarks about the author's obviously secure and happy childhood such as 'no regrets expressed', 'no questions asked' immediately convinced me that it was just the kind of book I should enjoy: I promptly put down my name for it at the library. In fact I find that I nearly always like the books that radical reviewers reject.

My correspondence, I decided, must be answered by hand, not realizing what a task I had set myself. I had hoped to hear from close friends and relations and I was not disappointed; they turned up trumps and their letters are very precious. I was quite unprepared for the fan mail, if it can be called such. Quite two-thirds of the letters have come from people I have never met – as a result I have hundreds of miniature autobiographies! Having kindly said that they enjoyed reading about me the writers go on to say 'and now I really must tell you about myself'. It has been enormously enlightening and I am convinced quite half these people could have written a book at least as interesting as mine.

The letters come from all parts of the world, from all kinds of people and cover a variety of interests; mainly, of course, those which were pre-eminent in the book – mountains, music, travel, dogs, sport and the Church. I also have an interesting file from those of my own generation who, like me, did their war service in London. Mountain-lovers who do not climb explain apologetically that they have been with me only in spirit on the mountain tops but nevertheless dearly love the Alps. Climbers speak my own language of course and we communicate easily; some of the most challenging letters come from the parents of sons and daughters who have lost their lives among the mountains; never once have I heard from anyone who loves the hills the less because of a tragedy.

My 'doggy' correspondents are often lonely, elderly spinsters, devoted to their pets, wondering anxiously if they will be able to look after them adequately to the end; their descriptions of the passing of their close companions sometimes almost breaks my heart.

Music, having played a very important part in my life, inevitably showed up in the book. I now have quite a collection of amateur compositions sent along by readers, as well as nostalgic letters from some of my father's former pupils. And I must confess that I experienced a thoroughly adolescent thrill when I got favourable comments from Dr Gerald Knight, Sir Adrian Boult and my beloved Sir Malcolm Sargent.

Reactions from the Church as a whole were numerous but, thank goodness, usually satisfactory. Every time I opened an envelope and announced 'this is from a parson' Ronald buried his head in his hands and waited for the worst. Fortunately most of his fears were unfounded although he was pretty horrified to hear that some clerics were using bits from the book for their sermons. However, I feel I have scored a point for oecumenicity in these days of increasing unity among the churches since I have had letters from a Jewish rabbi, a Methodist minister, the sister superior of a Roman Catholic Community and an archbishop.

One completely unexpected source of correspondence has been members of the staff who taught me at school; they are long since retired of course; indeed, I could hardly believe that there were any still alive. This has brought me great happiness because, as well as writing to them, Ronald and I have been able to visit some of them and a great experience it has been. Having in the past been, more often than most, the recipient of lines for running in the corridor and detentions for more serious misdemeanours I can hardly believe my ears when unstinted praise is showered upon me. On reflection, I suppose these ladies whom, as a teenager, I had always thought to be at least well on in their fifties, were probably only about thirty at the time. Present-day headmistresses, some of whom are my climbing friends, have been most kind. Their pupils are utterly different from me and my generation but some of them have told me that they were reading certain chapters to their sixth forms; I have even had to autograph copies for one or two schools. I am sure they have no idea what childish pleasure I get out of this.

Perhaps the letters that have touched and humbled me most are those that have come from invalids, from the bereaved, from blind people and from the permanently disabled. Three blind ladies told me a friend was reading to them every week; later the book was translated into braille and they were able to have their own copies. A sick girl who has never been able to lead a normal life has knitted climbing stockings for Ronald and for me and sometimes writes as often as three times a week. I have to ration my replies but I do my best. I have a regular correspondence with a courageous travel-minded old lady living in Oxford and I have been able to put quite a few of my own friends in touch with lonely folk who have got interested in the book.

We formed a particularly rewarding friendship with a married couple down in Kent and have visited them many times. They were once gay and adventurous but the chronic ill-health of the husband brought an end to this kind of life. They taught us much by their willing and happy acceptance of their lot. Langford Duncan has gone now but Kathleen carries on pluckily and is a writer of no mean repute; she remains a permanent member of our circle of close friends.

Not all my letters were kind and friendly – how could they be? I had stuck my neck out a long way and that always produces interesting consequences. Some of those who thoroughly disliked my book took the trouble to tell me so – not so very many, really, when I come to count them up. They seem to agree that I am frivolous, or too adventurous or enjoy life too much. The best one came on a postcard from a retired major; he thought the book was the most trivial and the least interesting he had ever had the misfortune to read; he was not in the least surprised that our poor dog bit me three times – he thought I deserved it! I wrote him a polite little note saying that it was very noble of him to read to the end if it had been such a devastating experience. I nearly sent him another letter, which had come by the same post, from a nice old gentleman who announced that I would make an ideal spouse for a surprising variety of people. I thought better of it however – it might have been too much for him.

When I was writing my book it never occurred to me that it would spark off so many contacts or that I should learn so much from my own work. A new dimension has been added to my life; it has brought me untold interest and pleasure and a greatly increased sense of responsibility to the reading public. The impact of the written word is enormous, I find – even with an unimportant book like mine. Obviously one cannot afford to be careless over details such as dates and concrete facts – inevitably someone picks you up if you are – but far, far more vital is the need for integrity and absolute sincerity. Critical readers write and challenge one's statements and beliefs; I realize now that this is all part of the rough and tumble of the writer's world. Many times I have had to think carefully if I really meant and felt what I wrote; actually I hold my views so strongly and feel so intensely about so many things that I seldom have any difficulty in answering my critics – to my own satisfaction if not to theirs. I feel a much greater responsibility towards the *un*critical reader – and most people *are* uncritical. The letters I get show me that some of those who have enjoyed the book have swallowed whole everything I have said. This has given me quite a new slant on my free-lance work; I hope I have not often been guilty of saying things for effect or to be 'with-it' but it is not always easy to avoid the temptation if you are terribly keen to sell an article. I have come to feel now that it is almost criminal to fail to be true to oneself as a writer; I scrutinize every paragraph to see if I have tripped up in this way; the curious result is that I seem to sell more of my stuff now than in the past. Perhaps honesty is the best policy after all!

No one need assume that my first book was a best seller; it was not and never will be; it is not that kind of book and I am not that sort of person. It sold out in America but was not reprinted; in this country I was lucky enough to have a second edition. It is an ordinary book by an ordinary person and it is just because of this, I think, that it has brought me so many new friends.

Not far below the surface during all these happy weeks I was thinking of old Miss Baring-Gould, growing gradually weaker. After we got back from the Holy Land we went to tell her of our adventures; she was able to enjoy our visit and cap many of our stories with experiences of her own. But she knew as well as we did that the sands were running out and begged me to let her have my book as soon as it was published. This I did and her companion read it to her each afternoon; sometimes she just lay and listened, sometimes she came up with one of her shrewd remarks.

Towards the end of June, Priscilla Lethbridge telephoned to say that the doctor thought the end was not far off, could we come to say goodbye? Sadness was missing in E.B.G.'s flat that day, it was almost a happy occasion. The Victorian sitting-room, from which we used to watch the cricket at Lords before they built the new stand, was bright with the usual gay window boxes and everything in it told the story of a vigorous, adventurous life lived out in the service of others. We thought of the many parties we had had, of the missionary meetings made exciting by her interruptions with some personal anecdote; we remembered her thirst for news and her wise comments; and, above all, the fact that it was so often young people who filled her flat.

We slipped into the quiet bedroom where there was a serenity we shall never forget. She knew us quite well; she looked up at her favourite Matterhorn picture; we looked too and we knew this was the right moment to say goodbye. We kissed her and Ronald gave her his blessing; she smiled and murmured a gentle, 'Thank you'.

We went out into the summer sunshine; all was well with E.B.G., her faith told her she had nothing to fear; soon she would be with those she loved, waiting for those who were still to come. She died on the next day, Saturday, July 1st. Ronald took her simple funeral service and we laid her in the family grave in South London. All her closest friends were there; it seemed that E.B.G.'s death had given us all a greater purpose for living.

The summer was busy with all kinds of important events, inside and outside the diocese; in such an exciting year this was particularly important; it helped us to keep a proper sense of proportion about our personal affairs.

There was the consecration of Guildford Cathedral – in my opinion one of the loveliest church buildings put up in this age and worthy to take its place among the great medieval creations. For me it has a very special interest. Begun just before the war, building had to stop almost as soon as it had started. In 1944 during the six months before D-day I passed it continually when I drove loudspeaker vans down to the invasion ports; I never failed to wonder when, if ever, it would be finished. And now at last, nearly twenty years later, it stood completed, crowning the summit of Stag Hill. The outside of the cathedral did not thrill me greatly as we approached; I cannot persuade myself that red brick is the best medium for such a building. But the exquisite beauty that awaited me inside the great doors left me almost breathless. Everywhere there is white stone and a translucent brightness throwing up the blue and gold decoration of sanctuary and chancel; the great sweep of the gold brocade dorsal curtain behind the High Altar dominates the scene.

It was a thrilling service with magnificent trumpeters and a great choir; the long procession of bishops and deans made its colourful way up the nave; my heart beat faster as first Ronald and then Dick Mayston went by me; Leicester was well-represented by her Bishop and Provost. The service was not very long but perfect in every respect; as we filed out I felt that I would never tire of worshipping there.

There had been troubles and trials enough over the Deanery of Guildford in the weeks before the service; as we drove home through the lovely countryside it was easy to believe that all the bitter controversies could be redeemed by such a service in such a setting.

Back again in Leicester we had a dedication of our own to rejoice in – infinitesimal compared with Guildford but nevertheless very satisfying. For years, long before we came to Leicester, the Mission to the Deaf had carried on its work in a dreary and rather inconvenient place. In the great spate of road building which is a continuous process in our city, this building was swept away by the Ring Road. No one minded so long as it could be replaced. Fortunately it could; an excellent site and a sympathetic architect were found and it was not long before a splendid new Deaf Mission appeared, comprising a chapel, kitchen and large hall. The Deaf community was thrilled to bits and implored Ronald to find a Royal opener. Time was so short that we knew this to be next to impossible and yet for the sake of the Deaf Ronald felt he must do his best. No one could have been kinder than the Duchess of Gloucester when she was approached – if we could possibly alter the date to avoid Prince Richard's half-term she would be delighted to come. Everything was satisfactorily fixed up and our dear Deaf community, that we all admire so much, had an afternoon it will never forget.

We are proud of our Deaf Mission; it serves a wide area; busy people willingly give up their time to serve on the committees; the services we have there are some of the happiest in the diocese.

Of all the many ways that have been thought up to raise money for good causes, flower arrangements are one of the most attractive and apparently, at present, one of the most successful. In Leicester and Leicestershire many people had lent their houses to the Flower Lovers' Guild to do what they liked with for a day – the results were remarkable. Our turn came eventually; we are both much involved with the work of the Family Service Unit and the Flower Lovers offered to 'do' Bishop's Lodge in aid of their funds. We realized no one was likely to visit our house on account of its age or its architectural splendours but flower arrangers work wonders and we were most willing to hand it over. Fortunately, it was early autumn; the crimson creeper was at its best and transformed the Victorian red-brick turrets and gables; we felt nature had given us a good start. It proved to be an enjoyable affair; a marquee for luncheons and teas was erected on the lawn; the flower arrangers worked far into the night, each group taking a room for their particular display. All we had to do was to picnic in the bedroom and at 10 a.m. on the great day I began my duties as hostess. Netta Mayston came up from the Provost's House to spend the day with me and Mrs Bell was everywhere – at the beck and call of arrangers and caterers alike.

The rooms were really gorgeous; I love our home dearly and on this day I was proud of it too. People poured in from every corner of the county and from all parts of the city; dining-room, drawing-room and Ronald's study were jammed tight and a steady stream flowed upstairs to see one of the spare bedrooms and my little den. Flowers, of course, were the chief attraction but I noticed that books and pictures came in for close scrutiny and necks were nearly broken craning to see the university groups. After all, it is not every day that the Bishop can be seen in cricket flannels or hockey shorts! Personally I love having a good nose round other people's houses and I was delighted that all my visitors enjoyed themselves in ours. The Family Service Unit benefited by a goodly sum and for all of us it was a day very well spent.

As always seems to happen with us, friends of earlier years were continually popping up. Indeed, hardly a year goes by but an old friend arrives in the diocese or has some interesting appointment which causes our paths to cross again. In 1961 David Say, whom we met before the war at Holy Trinity, Marylebone, became Bishop of Rochester and John Phillips, a rugger blue in Ronald's Cambridge days, became Bishop of Portsmouth. Jimmy Good, whom we knew as Chaplain of the Guards, was due to retire from the Army; Dick Mayston, one of his oldest friends, sent him a signal to the effect that the diocese of Leicester was a good spot and Jimmy arrived as Rector of Lutterworth. He brought with him his wife Eileen and their schoolgirl daughter Diana; Tony the son was at Cambridge and the married daughter Joan not too terribly far away at Sheffield. Jimmy and Eileen, after nearly twenty-five years of happy but rather nomadic army life, were thrilled to have a real family home and took to parish life like ducks to water.

Our Cathedral, in common with most others, had been badly in need of funds for many years. Soon after we arrived in Leicester, Mervyn Armstrong, then Provost, inaugurated an appeal for £100,000. It seemed an impossible amount but everyone went to work with a will. After two years Dick Mayston succeeded Mervyn and continued the good work and by the middle of 1961 the Appeal Committee were able to announce that the fund would be completed before the end of the year. Great rejoicings were planned; Archbishop Lord Fisher, by then retired but born and bred in Leicestershire, agreed to come and preach. The day chosen was Saturday, November 11th, the day of our patron saint, St Martin. No better day could have been chosen; St Martin is a soldier saint; our Cathedral has a regimental chapel; being Remembrancetide the whole building was decorated with a wealth of scarlet poppies; and – we had a soldier Provost.

Many people laboured for many weeks to make the service the

great occasion it deserved to be; behind the scenes backroom girls like Netta and me planned the party to follow the service. Archbishop Fisher was to spend the weekend with us; Netta and Dick were to have the party in the Provost's House. Mr and Mrs Bell came down to help; Costy the golden retriever did his bit by guarding Bishop's Lodge.

When Netta and I sank down in our seats in the cathedral our heads were so full of Martha-like matters that we hardly seemed to be in the best mood for the service. We need not have worried; the first few notes on the organ put us right and as the voices of the choir rose in the opening hymn a wave of peace broke over both of us. The great procession with its glittering copes and mitres moved up the nave; clergy who had served the Cathedral years before walked in it; Mervyn Armstrong, now Bishop of Jarrow, walked with Dick; finally came Archbishop Fisher escorted by Ronald. In the crowded congregation I could see people from all walks of life in the city. Great factories, big business executives, the churches of the diocese, the many-sided people of Leicester; all had helped in their own ways to reach the target we had set ourselves – all were represented. The whole enterprise had bound cathedral and city together in a closer relationship; it was good to feel that so many cared so much.

The party was a success, Archbishop Fisher, tireless as ever, being the belle – or beau – of the ball. As Netta and I stacked endless piles of dishes for our gallant Mr and Mrs Bell and listened to the distant rumble of happy chatter still going on, we knew it had all been worth it. It was no easy task to persuade Archbishop Fisher to come home to bed, but at last we drove out of the Cathedral precincts with the bells still pealing and the flag flying in the floodlighting that, for the first time, illuminated the lofty spire. No one will forget St Martin's Day 1961, least of all those of us to whom the Cathedral means so much.

CHAPTER II

Journalist
and Transatlantic Traveller

W HEN I was at school I had many ambitions; I wanted to play cricket for England; to be the first woman to climb Mount Everest and to be a courier for a travel agency – the reason for this being the free foreign holidays I imagined it would provide. These would be part-time activities; I would, of course, need a career – as well as everything else I longed passionately to be a journalist. Obviously I spread my net too wide; none of these ambitions has been fully realized but my quest to attain them gave me my place in the school eleven; still takes me to the rewarding summits of many alpine peaks and has brought me some trivial jobs in the travel world. I have done a lot of writing ever since I left school but until 1962 I had never had a regular assignment on a newspaper. Then, suddenly, the chance came; it was not less exciting for being long delayed; hope springs eternal and it is more fun if one's desires are granted gradually – if at all. That way there is always something to look forward to.

My benefactor was John Fortune, Editor of our *Leicester Mercury*, who had asked me for a few contributions during the previous year. His plan was that I should stand in for our Woman's Page Editor, Kaye Almey, on her weekly day off and during her holidays. I was thrilled and not a little honoured; the *Leicester Mercury* is one of the few provincial daily evening papers that has survived mergers and escaped sudden death. It has a large circulation, going into almost every home in Leicester and Leicestershire and is therefore a paper of no mean reputation. I was also slightly apprehensive; Kaye Almey is a first-class reporter and much loved in city and county. Even the leading business men of the city have been heard to say that they always turned first to her column in the *Mercury*. I could not hope to emulate her prowess, nor could I attempt the wide coverage of events which she managed with such expertise. However, the Editor gave me *carte blanche* to use the column exactly as I chose and after a long talk with Kaye, who was kind and encouraging, I agreed to have a go.

It was a new experience for me in the writing world; I soon found that the job of even a stand-in journalist called for a discipline that I had never applied to my free-lance work. Hitherto I had written when I felt like it and, usually, to please myself. I chose a paper or magazine, decided on a subject, sent in the script and hoped for the best. Writing a column for the *Mercury* was a very different matter. A script of 500 words had to be delivered at the *Mercury* offices by 9.30 sharp every Saturday morning; it must, as far as possible, please and interest the vast variety of readers who paid for their paper. Everyone knew I was the Bishop's wife; this imposed special responsibilities and limitations. I had to remember that I was not writing just for our own church people, nor, indeed, necessarily for those with any religious allegiance. There seemed a lot to think of – but it was a challenge and I felt it would be fun.

It certainly *was* fun and added a new dimension to the daily round and common task. For the Saturday diary I usually produced a résumé of the highlights of our week. This always included a number of local happenings and I was able to roam farther afield when our work took us to interesting events in London, Oxford, Cambridge – even up to Durham or down to Kent and the West Country. I had kind little notes from all sorts of people who had connections with places I mentioned. Some of the letters came from distant parts – there were at least two from Ireland – which showed how wide is the circulation of the *Mercury*. Former Leicester people often take it till they die.

Of course I had my moments. There was one ghastly Friday night when the car broke down on the way back from London. Three hundred words of Saturday's article were already typed – I had saved the last 200 for our London event; this paragraph was to be written and typed when I got home. Never had a breakdown seemed more deplorable; there were we stuck out in the wilds – for heaven knew how long – and there was the *Mercury* office looming up before me like some unattainable object. We struggled home at midnight; I set the alarm clock for 5 a.m. and crawled thankfully into bed. I marched into the *Mercury* a quarter of an hour earlier than usual the next morning – just to prove to myself I had not failed them. Needless to say, I was soon sharing my woes with a sympathetic staff to whom such adventures were merely the hazards of the job.

The *Mercury* is, first and foremost, a local paper mainly concerned with the domestic happenings of Leicester and Leicestershire. I felt I needed to strike this note as early as possible in my temporary career and hit on the idea of doing a series of profiles of people whose jobs brought them into constant touch with ordinary citizens. Having selected my victims I had to cajole them into sitting for me, as it were. They were all most co-operative. I decided that married couples would widen the interest and after preliminary letters I soon received invitations to their homes. Mr and Mrs Gwilliam, at that time the stationmaster and his wife, asked me to coffee and gave me a wonderful evening; Mr Arnall, then the Lord Mayor's mace-bearer, said I must come round for 'elevenses' and it was nearly lunch-time before I said goodbye to him and his wife. I had tea with Mr and Mrs Innocent, our Provost's verger and his wife at the Cathedral. I knew them so well that I hardly thought I needed an interview, but the half had not been told me and their life story was fascinating. Finally I went to see our German friends, Pastor and Mrs Baerman who, for many, many years looked after the German Lutherans in Leicester and performed a service not widely known in the city. The profiles, when they were published, went down well with my public and I had much enjoyed the work; it was good to learn so much about such interesting people and to be able to give pleasure to so many readers. But I was lucky in the people I chose; I could not help wondering what happened to journalists in the national field who are despatched to get a story and can find no takers – life must at times be pretty desperate for them.

The dates of Kaye Almey's holidays had to be discussed and of course it turned out that her first period of leave came right in the middle of our long planned visit to America and Canada. I was determined I was not going to fall down on the job but I knew I would have to convince the sub-editor, to whom I was answerable, that the column could be done from the other side of the world. Not only a consecutive fortnight was involved; there were no less than ten Saturday nights to be covered. I sat down with pencil, paper and my diary; I worked out a scheme and timetable with mailing dates included. I then sought an interview with the sub-editor. I found him quite prepared to have an American diary running intermittently in the woman's column; mailing, especially from Florida, worried him a little, but I promised a small file of articles to hold in reserve against non-arrival of American copy. In the end the plan was agreed upon. It proved to be a testing but thoroughly rewarding adventure which gave me immense satisfaction, lots of hard work and an enormous amount of fun – but more of that anon.

We were due to leave for America immediately after Easter; the prospect of a ten weeks absence from the diocese made the early months of the year exceptionally busy, especially as some new and exciting projects had been planned. It had not been easy to promise such a long period to our American hosts, but fortunately a second Assistant-Bishop arrived just in time. Cecil Horstead, who had been Archbishop of West Africa for many years, came to join us. In spite of having spent thirty-five years in Sierra Leone, Cecil, and Olive his wife, settled down as if they had been in Leicestershire all their lives; they soon became close friends and colleagues and endeared themselves to all the diocese. It was a great relief to Ronald to know that he would not have to leave Bishop Alec Maxwell single-handed; Alec had soldiered on nobly for so long and now he would have adequate help. The diocese could be left in two pairs of capable hands.

A rather special event of this busy spring was Ronald's long-standing engagement to preach at Sandhurst. We had looked forward to this; army occasions come high on our list of pleasant experiences and this visit was no exception. We spent the weekend with the Commandant, General Gordon-Lennox and his wife, who saw to it that we had a thoroughly good time. There were so many interesting people to meet, so many thrilling things to see and none more moving than the Memorial Chapel, one of the most treasured shrines of the British Army. It is alive with the spirit of great traditions; a spirit that throbs in its present every day worship. It was a privilege to have been there and seemed to provide a special inspiration when we were about to try our wings for the first time in the great New World across the sea.

47

The parade service on the Sunday morning unfortunately took place in a blinding blizzard and Ronald somehow acquired the father and mother of all streaming colds. Bed and antibiotics were prescribed, which did not exactly help the schedule of work. However, it is an ill wind that blows nobody any good. Ronald was a fairly heavy smoker; his cold made cigarettes taste like burnt paper; he waved them away when I brought them, causing me to think that he must indeed be going downhill. After a week he rose from his couch; I pranced in, all bright and breezy, with cigarettes, holder and lighter daintily arranged on a silver salver.

'Sorry,' said Ronald, 'I think I've done with it'.

'You've *what*?' I thought he must be at death's door. 'You mean to say you can't touch a Benson and Hedges out of the nice little House of Lords packet?'

'Take them away. I haven't smoked for a week. I'm going to try to do without it.'

I was so astounded I failed to produce the congratulations he expected me to offer; nor would he, being prudence personified, make a definite pronouncement that he had finished smoking forever. But from that day to this Ronald has never touched another cigarette – in spite of the fact that, unbeknown to me, he packed his lighter, crystals and holder at the bottom of his American luggage – just in case the temptation proved too strong.

Good Friday was approaching and with it the first of the new projects for which so many people had worked so hard. It was not until we arrived in Leicester in 1954 that we realized that Good Friday is scarcely observed in the Midlands – we ignorant southerners had remained oblivious of this for the whole of our lives. It is not that there is any antipathy towards Good Friday as such; it is just a fact that for all midland cities, with the exception of Rugby, that day is, and from time immemorial, always has been, a working day. Many of those who work manage to get to church somehow, at sometime; city workers pour into the cathedral during the three hours' service to spend part of their lunch hour there; industrial chaplains arrange short services in factories; many chapels have devotional hours in the evening.

In spite of these efforts there seemed a pressing need for some combined act of witness at a time when people would be free to take part. The Leicester Council of Churches got to work; a great

48

Procession of Witness was planned for the evening of Good Friday, in which all denominations would co-operate. Our Chief Constable, Robert Mark, who had come from the North, and knew about Church processions, was approached by Ronald and agreed to close the main streets to traffic for an hour; our good friend Donald Byford made a gift of a great timber cross to be borne at the head of the procession. Enormous interest was aroused; it was the main topic of conversation among customers and shopkeepers alike in the little shopping colony in our area.

Many of us, I am sure, prayed for a fine evening; that prayer was not granted. Instead we gathered in the playground of the Alderman Newton Boys' School on a bitterly cold evening, with a high wind and occasional drizzle. It made no difference to the numbers or to the enthusiasm. In top boots, mackintoshes and scarves we formed up in our appointed positions; each church and chapel was allotted to a marker; choirs were interspersed among the marchers with the cathedral choir in the lead conducted by the organist, George Gray. The Salvation Army band headed the procession, followed by the leaders of all the different denominations.

How many times we sang our way through 'Onward Christian Soldiers' I do not know; but I do know that the crowds of sightseers gathered on the pavements gladly took hymn sheets and sang as lustily as any of us. There was a reverent hush as the eight white-robed figures, bearing the huge cross on their shoulders, passed along the route. We marched eight abreast and filled the whole width of the street. The only disturbance was the noisy approach of the Fire Brigade called out by a false alarm, possibly by some opponent of our cause, more likely by some wag with a misplaced sense of humour. No harm was done; we continued singing and ranks reformed.

At the town hall a vast crowd of ten thousand gradually filled the square; the cross was raised to its full height and floodlit. Prayers were said by a Free Church minister; there was a bible reading by a Christian of Jewish descent, a short address was given, we sang 'Abide with Me' and Ronald pronounced the blessing. Silently the great crowd melted away; it had been a gripping experience; the Christians of Leicester had given their witness in a way that could be understood by all. We were not looking for immediate results

D   49

but those who took part were conscious of a deep and abiding sense of unity.

Since that first occasion the Good Friday Procession has taken place many times – although, by common consent, not every year – and to everyone's joy the Roman Catholic community now marches with us and their representatives take part in the service. The seed sown on Good Friday evening in 1962 has brought forth abundantly.

Easter Eve brought another new venture – an unprecedented service of baptism and confirmation in the cathedral. In the early church such services were quite usual at Easter; it was remarkable how entirely suitable it all seemed in a twentieth century setting. It was moving to be taking part in a ceremony that belonged to the church seventeen hundred years ago. The cathedral was full and the whole congregation stayed on for choral evensong – always the highlight of the week for us.

We had been afraid that Easter might get a bit overshadowed by all the bustle of preparation for our departure; instead it was proving extremely happy and satisfying and when we woke up on Easter Day to find that spring had arrived with blue skies, sunshine and masses of flowers, our cup of happiness was full. The cathedral services were joyous and crowded and in my heart I felt that we should not find anything more satisfying on the other side of the Atlantic.

Every spare moment seemed to be spent packing, labelling and checking lists. Donald Byford, who must be the doyen of Cunard travellers, came on the 'phone nearly every day with useful hints of many kinds. With the Easter services over we rushed off for a couple of days to say goodbye to our families in London and Essex. At home in London, the magnolias and almond blossom were at their best – something I had feared I might miss – and my good old aunt proudly showed us envelopes already written out to our addresses in America. In Essex it was spring too, with tea in the garden with Ronald's sister and blackbirds singing in the trees overhead. And so home to Leicester, where the garden was ablaze with daffodils and tulips and one tiny gentian already in bloom; as the luggage was piled into the car home seemed so precious that, for one brief moment, I almost wished something would prevent us leaving. Our little household – Mr and Mrs Bell and Anne

Bavin our secretary, and of course, Costy the golden retriever –
gathered at the gates to see us set off with Leslie Green, our
driver, who was to take us down to Southampton. Just as all goodbyes had been said, and Costy had licked my face as clean as he
thought it ought to be for such a trip, the postman arrived.
Ronald took his packet to read on the way, leaving the less interesting-looking missives to be dealt with by Anne. There was only one
for me – a large envelope from my publishers. I opened it a little
apprehensively and immediately squealed with delight; it was the
contract for my second book *Zermatt Saga*. Enclosed with it was a
note to tell me my probable earnings on the first book, due to me
at the end of the month. 'I thought', wrote kindly Philip Unwin,
'you might like to know before you have that shopping spree in
New York!'

I could not have had a better send-off; I tucked the contract
carefully into my brief case and felt disgustingly self-satisfied. In
my handbag reposed a typewritten sheet – the first half of my
Mercury article for Saturday. By arrangement with Anne, the
remainder of the article was to be written by me as soon as we got
on board and typed by her when brought home by Leslie Green,
who had promised to deliver it at the *Mercury* office.

Neither Ronald nor I will ever forget our first sight of the *Queen
Mary* lying at anchor in Southampton Water. She was so regal, so
supremely monarch of all she surveyed. She was the first and, so
far, the only great ship in which we have sailed. For us there will
never be another like her; one wonders if her retirement is suffi-
ciently dignified.

In the long corridor that led to our cabin we met my brother
Geoffrey and his boys; to see the *Queen Mary*, and speed us on our
way, was an opportunity not to be missed, they said; certainly it
put the final stamp of happiness on our departure. Life just at that
moment was one long series of surprises; our cabin was full of
flowers and farewell telegrams from friends and relations, which I
could hardly believe were all meant for us. What had we done to
deserve so much love and attention? We read them all and put
them aside to gloat over after we sailed. Just one I stuffed in my
coat pocket – it was sent by Mr and Mrs Bell on behalf of our dear
old Costy; I longed to give him one more pat on his lovely golden
head.

The boys went off on a tour of the ship and I settled down to finish my *Mercury* article; I was almost too excited to write, but I was so happy and so touched by everyone's kindness that it was quite a relief to express it all in words. Leslie Green took it into safe custody and over tea my nephews offered all kinds of suggestions – some helpful and some otherwise – as to what I really should have written. Fortunately for me their efforts came too late; a clarion call sounded ordering all visitors ashore. As Geoffrey, John and Peter, followed by the faithful Leslie Green, filed down the gangway, we felt ourselves lucky in those who had come to send us on our way.

There is something strangely moving about the sailing of a great passenger ship; unlike the jet airliners, which are up and away in a few seconds, there is a dignity about the slow departure and time for contemplation on the part of the passengers. The gesticulating figures of my brother and his boys were lost at last and we could wave no longer. England – home – was fading away behind us; one bit of me still looked back a little wistfully, and I was glad it was months and not years before we would return. Then suddenly it was the future that mattered; the voyage and all the adventures that lay ahead became alive; I was thrilled that we were off at last.

There is a lot to learn during the first trip on an ocean-going liner but the *Queen Mary* was an ideal training ship for raw recruits. The atmosphere was so homely; within the first hour we felt as if we belonged. Probably the spirit of the crew had something to do with this; from the Captain down to the minute pageboy, who offered us peppermints and ginger after dinner every night, they all loved their ship; her reputation mattered more than anything else; nothing must be done which could bring discredit to her.

For a complete rest cure there can be nothing to beat the crossing of the Atlantic. For five days we saw no ship, no plane, no sign of land, not even a distant light; only the grey rolling ocean stretching away to limitless horizons. It would, I suppose, have been possible to eat, sleep and relax in deck chairs for the whole journey. That was not our way; nor was it the way of anyone else that I saw. There were deck games to play; the swimming pool to sample; the kennels to visit; the gym in which to work off one's surplus energy under the supervision of a cheery gentleman named Uncle Percy. There was time to read and write without interruption and there were lovely concerts to lull one into a state of blissful repose. Interspersed among these activities, as every Cunard traveller knows, there were fantastic and delicious meals such as we have never experienced before or since. According to our dining-room steward I never did justice to any of them; I was sorry to disappoint him but there is a limit to everyone's capacity.

It was an entirely new life for Ronald and me; we enjoyed every minute of it, not least the contact with the other passengers – especially the old hands who cross the Atlantic regularly; they were very helpful to the new boys. But five days of such luxury and laziness is enough; it did us lots of good; but it was time to return to the real world, to use at least something of all that the *Queen Mary* had given us in the challenging unknown weeks that lay ahead. Early one morning we passed the Ambrose Lightship and sailed into the Hudson River. Now at last we were nearing port; the famous, fabulous skyline of New York, made gently mysterious by a faint cloud of mist, met our eager eyes. It was a moment worth waiting for – as surprising as it was exciting. New York was mellow, welcoming and rather lovely; the canyon-like streets of downtown Manhattan, penetrating almost to the water-front, looked positively picturesque. Sky-scrapers, so blatantly out of place in London, seemed absolutely right in New York.

Our luggage was packed and already taken in charge by the baggage-master; only my typewriter remained in our cabin, open and ready for me to add my first impressions of the New World to the last paragraph of my *Mercury* diary. My mind was in tune with my subject; in a few moments everything was completed and the big air mail envelope stamped and sealed. That evening it would be on its way back across the Atlantic; the newspaper would have it with three days to spare. The first of my small contracts had been successfully accomplished; I was relieved and a little elated.

We were lucky travellers; not only did we have a party to bid us farewell at Southampton – there was to be someone waiting for us in New York. It was only when we had seen the weary crowd waiting endlessly for taxis that always seemed to fly past full, that we realized how fortunate we were. The piers in New York bristle with difficulties for the stranger in the States. Thoughtful Donald Byford had arranged for a member of his office staff in New York to take charge of us until we had begun to get our breath. Donald

Tennant, full of smiles, was waiting on the Cunard pier; almost before we had exchanged greetings he had hustled us and our vast pile of luggage into a waiting taxi and we were speeding across New York before introductions were properly completed. The disappearance of that taxi would have meant an hour's delay. Donald deposited us in the Hotel Pierre, made a date for dinner that night and left us to settle in.

We had only three days in New York but they were to be free from care before the work began in Florida. Three days is not long to spend in such a city but we made the most of it. By means of a coach tour we visited Greenwich Village (New York's Chelsea); Chinatown, one of the biggest Chinese settlements, where juvenile delinquency presents no problems because the children are brought up to respect their parents; and, by sad contrast; the Bowery – once a fashionable area; now the drab, uncared for haunt of chronic alcoholics. Viewed from our coach it looked an utterly hopeless, despairing problem incapable of solution; but we happened to know that day and night dedicated men and women are working tirelessly to restore at least some of these drop-outs to an established place in society.

During our visit to the United Nations we listened to part of a session of the Security Council – an unexpected slice of good luck. Memory flew back over the years to my first school-girl visit to the League of Nations building in Geneva, on which my youthful hopes were pinned and which, unbeknown to me, was already pronounced a failure. The UN still struggles on and lasting peace still eludes us; perhaps it is a quest which generation after generation must pursue, with never more than partial success, until all men are men of goodwill.

We fell into the American way of life and manner of talking within a few hours. It soon seemed perfectly natural to be sleeping on the thirty-fifth floor; we spoke of 'blocks' and 'side-walks' with the greatest of ease but we just could not bring ourselves to refer to a policeman as a 'cop' – it seemed somehow disloyal to our own British bobbies.

We window-gazed in Fifth Avenue and shopped in Maceys which announced itself in enormous letters as the largest store in the world. We dined with Donald Tennant high up in the Penthouse Club and looked out on the glittering scene that was New

York by night. On our last morning we were whisked to the top of the Empire State Building by two swift and silent elevators and looked out over the whole throbbing mass of Manhattan Island. We saw the East River, the Hudson River, Staten Island and New Jersey; we saw the Statue of Liberty and far, far beyond it a speck on the green water which they told us was the *Queen Mary* already on her way back to Southampton. I no longer felt homesick. I was completely caught up in the tremendous experience of the New World.

Surprisingly, I found myself suddenly sad as we left New York for the long journey to Florida. In our short stay we had come to feel a great affection for it; Donald Tennant had made us feel part of the place; the next stage would be another new world, another new beginning. But we were going to friends; from now on in Florida, in Michigan and in Canada our hosts would be the bishops and their wives whom we had met at the Lambeth Conference in 1958. It was they who had invited us to come; we knew already that we were wanted.

Our train rumbled on and a friendly steward with a smiling black face, topped by a huge white cap, told us we were his special charges for the trip; this was delightful and we loved him at first sight. Before midnight we came upon Washington, floodlit and very beautiful; six hours later we woke up in South Carolina to see tropical forests, hung with grey spanish moss, standing deep in dark water, and tiny townships, just a few white wooden one-storeyed houses, grouped round a cross-roads. It was hot and humid; we needed no one to tell us that we were approaching the deep south.

At Jacksonville in Florida we stepped out of the train into the arms of Hamilton West, Bishop of Florida, and his wife, Charlotte. Four years earlier we had said goodbye to them on Westminster Bridge as Big Ben was striking midnight; our arrival at Jacksonville was the fulfilment of the promise we had made that night.

Florida was gorgeous – all and more than the travel brochures proclaim it to be. It was enormously hot but the Wests' home was cool and comfortable and there we learned to live like true Americans. We took our meals in the dining-alcove of Charlotte's pretty kitchen; we soon understood that it was usual to have everything on the same plate – egg, bacon, marmalade, bread, we tipped all

55

on to one platter; it took nothing from the taste and simplified the washing up.

I was interested and glad to find that among Charlotte's friends simplicity was the keynote in dress – as in everything else. I also discovered that domestic help is even harder to come by than in England; Charlotte had a treasure, a dear coloured woman called Delia, who had been with her twenty-five years and came in three mornings a week. Most people were far less fortunate and consequently labour-saving gadgets abounded.

Church-going was popular in Florida; the churches were packed, mainly by family parties – Mum, Dad, teenagers, toddlers, and the carrycot, the lot – and very good it was to see. Most churches had to have repeat services where hymns, lessons, prayers and sermon were a replica of an earlier service. Again and again Ronald found himself preaching the same sermon at ten o'clock and at eleven-thirty. Church service was always followed by coffee, or tea, and cookies in the hall. Here the ladies of the parish, arrayed in their very best hats, took it in turn to pour tea. The significance of this ritual was lost upon me at first; I simply could not understand why it was a matter of such momentous importance that Mrs So-and-So should 'pour tea'. However Charlotte eventually put me right by explaining that this was the greatest social perquisite which could be accorded and one much sought after.

When the Wests' friends wished to entertain us they invited us not to their homes but to country clubs out on the beaches. Here, at the week-end, the entire population of Jacksonville can be seen sun-bathing. It is an unforgettable sight; miles and miles of white sand stretching away down the coast, dotted with gaily-clad family parties, and the unceasing rumble of the great Atlantic rollers breaking on the shore. Nor shall we forget the fare provided for us for lunch in the country clubs; it was delicious, but so excessive in quantity that I could eat nothing else for the rest of the day, although I had consumed less than half of what I was offered.

When Ronald's preachments and visits were finished in Jacksonville we set off with Hamilton and Charlotte for Camp Weed, the Diocesan Conference Centre on the Gulf of Mexico. Here for ten days we slept in a little log cabin, ate in the refectory, worshipped in the striking chapel and met for lectures in the hall. Everyone of all ages and sizes, and of both sexes, dressed in shorts and shirts – it was far too hot to consider anything else. Having brought only one pair of shorts with me I had to invest in another; the local general shop produced a very natty pair of pink Bermudas which gave me great joy. Ronald lectured for the first half of every morning to the clergy and their wives; after iced drinks at mid-morning we divided; I had discussions with the wives on the veranda of our cabin while Ronald and the clergy met in the hall. I loved those discussions; the American women are so oncoming and outspoken, their questions are so direct and lead to such worthwhile discussion. I was astonished and very touched at the obvious affection and admiration they had for English women; much of it stemmed from the war days – about which they wanted to talk incessantly.

We grew very close to each other during these discussions; so many problems we had in common – and so often we could find no answer. The question of race relations was raised again and again; as Christians they were agreed that racial discrimination could not be tolerated, but they felt the problem was a long, long way from solution.

Our afternoons were free after a compulsory siesta of an hour. How we spent them depended on the weather. If the breeze had not arrived by noon we knew it would not come that day; the afternoon temperature would probably be 110 degrees and swimming or sailing was the obvious answer – so long as the look-outs could assure us that there were no sharks in the vicinity. If it was cool enough we would go inland and join the Jungle Cruise in a glass-bottomed boat to see tropical fish leaping about below us and alligators snoozing on the shore on each side of us.

In the evenings after dinner Ronald lectured again in the hall; we all went – and so did the mosquitoes! Everyone was armed with a spray and your name was mud if you were careless enough to let one of the brutes in as you squeezed through the door.

Late at night in our little cabin we brewed a cup of tea, as if we were at home, and I got out my typewriter to work on my diary articles. There was so much to tell, so many wonderful things to recount, that it was a comparatively easy task. I loved sitting at my typewriter with nothing but the mosquito screens between me and the outside world. The stars glittered above our cabin; out on

57

the dark water I could see the bobbing lights of the shrimp boats. There was a magic stillness broken only by the cry of the mocking bird and the lapping of the sea. My thoughts turned towards home; there people would soon be getting up; with us it was midnight.

Back again in Jacksonville we had to pack up for the next stage of our journey. We could hardly bear to leave Hamilton and Charlotte and their lovely daughter Margaret. Just to make things harder Margaret had acquired an adorable beagle pup; he rejoiced in the name of Lord Berkeley and was thoroughly spoilt by us all. Of course he had to accompany the family to the station to see us off on the night train and we had the most affecting farewells. Our last view of the Wests as the train drew out was of a wildly waving Hamilton, Charlotte and Margaret and Lord Berkeley with a half-chewed glove – Charlotte's we thought – drooping sadly from his mouth.

It took us two days to journey from Florida, the Sunshine State, to Michigan, the Water Wonderland, and the temperature never fell below 94 degrees; mercifully the train was air-conditioned. We roared on through Georgia and Tennessee; we saw the Smoky Mountains and the Blue Ridge Mountains, but, except for Atlanta in Georgia, there never seemed to be a town or even a house. In Kentucky we came to pastures and farms and the countryside looked a little more friendly; soon we would have to change trains at Cincinnati in Ohio; we were looking forward to this after thirty-six rather monotonous hours. We shall always remember Cincinnati; the station had been baked by a blistering sun all day; even at midnight it was still like a furnace. The only air-conditioning was in the children's play room; we crept in and hoped we should be allowed to stay for twenty minutes for the price of two beakers of Coke. Fortunately our request was granted, although we would willingly have ridden on the rocking-horses if that had been the only means of legalizing our stay.

Early next morning, somewhat wilted, we arrived in Detroit. Archie Crowley, Assistant-Bishop of Michigan another friend of Lambeth days, was there to meet us. The illuminated newscasters already proclaimed the temperature to be 84 degrees at 7.30 am.

'Sorry', said Archie apologetically, 'you've struck a mighty heat-wave, but you'll feel better out at our place'.

For ten miles we followed a great six-lane highway festooned on both sides by shoddy-looking second-hand car depots. Suddenly these vulgarities vanished and we were in another world – the world of the prosperous American suburb. The Crowleys have a lovely ranch-type home in Birmingham; lawns and trees enclose it; pheasants strut on the grass; squirrels skip up and down the trees. It was bliss indeed after such a journey as we had experienced – it was refreshing just to look at it. We quickly changed into shirts and shorts and after Jean Crowley had thoroughly spoiled us with a delicious breakfast we felt fit to face the world and all the new experiences that were awaiting us in the Middle West.

Ronald's lectures took place at the Cathedral Centre in Woodward Avenue in downtown Detroit; crowds of clergy came from all parts of the diocese and quite a few came over from Canada, lying just across the Detroit River. Detroit, with a population of a million and a half, is the greatest motor city of the world. There are huge stores and banks and skyscrapers but except for our daily trips in for the lectures we did not see a lot of it; most of our commitments were in outlying districts and in America life seems to revolve round the suburbs much more than round the centre.

Ronald visited industrial missions, groups of executives and schools – including the great Cranbrook Schools for girls and boys which are the American equivalent of our public schools. I found myself involved in group dynamics, dialogues, discussions, and all kinds of things which I had not anticipated. American women are very articulate; they like to thrash out a subject and no one seemed to be tongue-tied as so often happens with us at home. I liked best the informal visits to Jean Crowley's friends; they taught me a lot about the way of life in the States that I probably could not have learned in any other way. From Jean herself I got the gen about American shopping. In the big cities one almost never shops in the centre. All the big department stores have enormous branches in the suburbs and here parking is no problem; there is always space for a thousand, and sometimes for ten thousand cars. As well as the department stores there are boutiques and the smaller chain stores and, of course, the supermarket and the drug store. Supermarket shopping is universal in the States; I hate it at home but there, like the skyscrapers, it seems just right. The drug stores took quite a bit of understanding;

they supply everything that the supermarkets do not and usually light refreshments as well. The one thing they are not is a chemist's shop, which it is just as well to remember when you run out of toothpaste or aspirins.

The heat wave continued throughout our whole visit to Detroit which meant that at the Crowley's home we lived almost entirely out of doors. Every evening when the day's work was done there was a barbecue on the lawn; friends dropped in and those evenings are precious memories. When one is cool and comfortable and coffee is served and stars prick the dark velvet canopy of the night sky, trivialities and small talk vanish and one gets down to the deeper things of life. This, more than anything else, built a bridge and a close bond between our American friends and ourselves. At that time there had been very little racial conflict in Detroit but when, a few years later, it broke out with such distressing severity, we thought back to those long quiet nights and understood more fully many of the matters that had been raised and the fears that had been expressed.

When the time came to leave Detroit for Canada we left not by train but by car – driving ourselves in our own hired chariot. This was something that had never occurred to us in our wildest dreams, but, egged on by the Crowley's and by the apparent ease with which this can be done on the American continent, we were soon telling ourselves that, with the complicated journeys and the multitude of whistle stops we would have in Canada, it would be both easier and cheaper. Both these facts turned out to be true; it also proved to be the greatest possible fun.

We kissed Archie and Jean goodbye, promising faithfully that we must all meet again, and set forth in our Ford Galaxy. We have always had a Ford at home – but never one like this! It was so wide that I could scarcely see over the wing; it also had automatic gear change and took off from traffic lights as if by magic. The trip into downtown Detroit nearly demoralized us, but, by the time we reached the Detroit River, we had both had a turn at the wheel and recovered our equilibrium. We swept over the Ambassador Bridge as if we had bought it.

Canada was more than Commonwealth – it seemed almost home. We had loved our trip through the States and looked forward to more of it before we sailed from New York but there is something about Canada that tells the British at once that they are among their own folk. It is quite indescribable but it is there.

Our first stop was at Windsor, Ontario, which included a Clergy Quiet Day for Ronald, a group discussion for us both on the shores of Lake Erie and an exciting afternoon's sailing on the Detroit River. On again to London, Ontario, and by this time the Galaxy seemed quite like a member of the family. Once more we were entertained by old friends – George and Dorothy Luxton whom we had met not only at Lambeth but also in Zermatt. George is Bishop of Huron; he had invited Ronald to preach in St Paul's Cathedral, London, Ontario, and, more exciting still, to the Red Indians at Brantford. After the service in St Paul's we were surrounded by people with Leicestershire connections; things that seemed so ordinary to us meant all the world to them; every stick and stone of the city and county had a meaning for somebody. It was grand to find that in spite of the many advantages of Canadian life England was still home – still the best place in the world.

The service at Brantford for the Mohawk Indians took place in a Chapel Royal presented to them by George III – this lovely little place is unique among the Red Indian reserves and the Mohawks are immensely proud of it. It was a special service at which George Luxton was to dedicate three stained glass windows in the presence of the Premier of Ontario. The Mohawk Chief, a direct descendent of Hiawatha, was there in all his glory. I sat immediately behind him and was able to get a close-up view of his regalia during Ronald's sermon. The service ended with the singing of the national anthem with all the Mohawk braves standing stiffly to attention – 'God save the Queen' has never seemed more moving or more meaningful.

From the Red Indian reserves we set off on our way to Niagara Falls. Relations of the Luxtons have a summer cottage on the shores of Lake Ontario. They took us there for a brief break; for twenty-four hours we swam and sunbathed and relaxed on the veranda until it was time to go to see the Falls in all their evening glory. We could not have been more fortunate – Niagara pulled out all the stops for us. We were damp with spray half a mile before we reached the Falls and puffs of water, that looked like smoke, guided us to our goal. The roar of the Falls warned us what to expect but, even so, the endless flood of green water boiling over the rocks and plunging to the depths below gave us a shock. The most memorable moment came as the sun went down and the perfect arc of a rainbow spanned the whole width of the Falls.

For the next two days we followed the St Lawrence River, spending the night in a very 'with-it' Motel where every apartment was provided with television. We never grew tired of the St Lawrence; the great ocean-going ships from Germany, Great Britain, Holland and Japan; the flat-backs, the long, low grain boats bringing their cargo from the prairies; the eager little mail-boats intercepting their bigger brothers for the giving and receiving of mail – they were all so fascinating that they slowed us up quite a bit. One picnic we ate gazing enviously at the Thousand Islands – each of which is the site of a summer cottage for some lucky Canadian.

We arrived in Montreal in the rush hour, which was the worst possible error of judgement, but several hours later we pulled up at McGill University to spend a short night with English friends there. Early next morning they took us up to Mount Royal to see the breathtaking view over the St Lawrence Seaway.

We *had* to see Quebec; it was miles off our route but how could we miss it when we might never be in those parts again? We are always glad we went; it is a beautiful and, at the same time, an extraordinary city – an outpost of France set in the British Commonwealth. At that time relations were less strained than they are at present; to the casual visitor there seemed nothing for any-one to complain about; but looking back now one can see that in these dissatisfied days, when so much of the world is going through such an adolescent phase, it is a situation where seeds of trouble can easily germinate.

From Quebec it was a hundred miles to the USA border; it was already evening, but we knew we must cover that hundred miles if we were to make St John, New Brunswick, by the next after-noon. It was an exciting road through mountainous country; we climbed up to 3,000 feet; it grew dark; tall coniferous forests closed in on us; the wind howled fitfully. Cat-like, striped racoons raced across in the headlights; great eyes glowed at us out of the darkness.

'I suppose they wouldn't be bears,' mused Ronald thoughtfully.

'Bears!' I exclaimed. 'They couldn't be; they're enormous things; what do we do if they sit down in front of the car?'

'I don't know, let's hope they don't,' and he pushed the accelerator down a little harder.

At midnight, we showed our passports to the sleepy frontier guard. He told us there was accommodation a mile farther down the road. At Moose River we came to some little log cabins; we booked the last vacant one, brewed a cup of English tea and sank into bed.

During breakfast next morning on the veranda we felt able to discuss bears more calmly. We made enquiries; yes, indeed, there were plenty of bears; in fact a bear hunt had set out early that morning. We looked at each other expressively.

'But you needn't worry about bears,' explained our informer. 'They're safe enough. It's the moose; if you meet a moose in the dark you've just about had it; they attack headlights.'

We finished our coffee rather silently; at the souvenir stall we bought a pair of moccasins each; they would remind us of the nice, friendly bears – and the moose.

St John, New Brunswick, lies on the Bay of Fundy looking across to Nova Scotia; it is very British; most of the clergy to whom Ronald lectured were men who had come out from England not so many years before. They, and especially their families, were still terribly homesick for the old country; every scrap of news we could give them was received rapturously. It is good to remember this when so many people would have us believe that the Commonwealth has lost all interest in us.

Our last weekend in Canada we spent at Fredericton with Archbishop Harry O'Neill and his wife Mardie. It was quieter than most of our week-ends had been for a long time and the cathedral where Ronald preached was a beautiful, restful little place. One fact especially endeared it to us; the organist had been trained by our own George Gray from Leicester Cathedral.

We had only four days left before the *Queen Mary* sailed from New York with us on board. We crossed from Canada into the Vacation State of Maine to spend a night in the White Mountains of New England. Our friends Robert and Miriam Underhill have a fabulous house looking on to the Presidential Range; they gave us just such an evening as we have often spent with them in Zermatt –

a real climbers' evening – and I was thrilled to have just one taste of the mountains before we left the States. The next day we drove down to Boston, where we turned in our dear old Galaxy; it was like taking leave of a close relation. We travelled from Boston to New York by the slowest train in North America, but once we were safely ensconced in the Hotel Pierre we quickly allocated the time that was left to us. My final shopping spree was of paramount importance in my view; in between dining out with Donald Tennant and packing I made a determined dash to the Lerner shop near the Empire State Building and returned triumphant with a modest haul of blouses and cotton frocks.

The *Queen Mary* was crowded to capacity with American families going on vacation in Europe – there were not many British on board. We explored our comfortable cabin and went up on deck to wait for our departure. We were leaving America; it hardly seemed possible; we felt as if we had been there for years; was it really only two months since we first sailed up the Hudson River?

Suddenly sirens screamed; the crowds on the Cunard pier cheered and waved frantically; imperceptibly the tugs began to draw us out and for the last time I stood watching the New York skyline as it faded slowly into the mist. I felt I understood it now instead of merely admiring it. The skyscrapers were not just magnificent – they were a symbol of something; a symbol of the vastness, the sheer size of America. It stretches, if not from pole to pole, at any rate from ocean to ocean. Its buildings, lakes, rivers and mountain ranges are huge; everything else has to be done on a correspondingly big scale. This is their inheritance; this is why Americans talk always in superlatives. This for them takes the place of our heritage of history and tradition, which, in its turn, accounts for our well-known British love of understatement. All our past is woven into us; they have not yet come to terms with theirs.

During the voyage home I thought a lot about America and Americans. I was glad and so grateful to have been to the States; even a short two months visit had filled in gaps in my experience of life of which I had previously been unaware. So often I had felt vaguely antagonistic towards Americans and their ideas. When we set out on our journey I had expected to find most things and people very much the same as in my own country. I discovered this to be far from the truth. Everything seemed to be strictly organized and desperately earnest. Everyone preferred to enjoy their recreation in groups – almost as if it was unsafe to go out on your own. And everyone must be *something* even if only the humblest member of the smallest committee; the lone wolf has not been heard of in the States. Talk was terribly important too – far more so than thought, it seemed to me – and theories and systems, all geared, of course, towards making the world a better place. Somehow there was little time to really relax, and none at all just to stand and stare. But I liked it; I would not have missed a minute of it. The whole experience was rewarding; to me, the New World is now a friendly place and her people a kindly, homely people.

And now we were all set for home; I could hardly wait to get there. We enjoyed the voyage; we made friends with lots of nice families; we played table tennis daily – I even won the prize for the runner-up in the competition; we passed the *Queen Elizabeth* in mid-Atlantic and were thrilled by the ritual that took place, especially as we had been invited on to the bridge by the captain.

But every day that passed was a day nearer home; when we had to anchor off the Isle of Wight to wait for the tide I could have wept; I just could not wait to set foot in England.

And what a welcome it gave us. Leslie Green met us and drove us home through fields and woods; past tiny wandering streams and thatched cottages with gardens full of roses; by grey, ancient churches; through quiet country towns; and all the time the sun shone and the birds sang. I never knew before that England was so lovely, nor her way of life so satisfying. At the gates of Bishop's Lodge, Mr and Mrs Bell and Anne were waiting as if they had stayed put since we left them; only Costy was slightly different – he wore a large label which read 'Welcome Home! We are so glad to have you back'. A perfect homecoming if ever there was one.

There was a mass of work awaiting us but we soon slipped into the routine and every day brought reunions with the people of the diocese – it was like being received back by an enormous family. It took the rest of the summer to catch up on everything but all went smoothly. Our work culminated in the great Youth Conference of the British Council of Churches which had chosen Leicester as its venue.

This was a great event and immensely worthwhile. The chief

E

organizers were Philip Race and Janet Lacey; there were over 1,000 young people involved and a remarkable spirit prevailed. When, in 1968, the same conference meeting at Edinburgh got off to such a lamentable beginning (happily reversed during the conference), I could not help thinking of those inspiring days in 1962. For us, and perhaps for the young people too, the highlight was the great Open Communion Service in our Cathedral. Ronald invited all delegates to the conference, regardless of creed or nationality, to join in the service. There were a thousand young people there and a great sense of oneness was evident among us. Ronald was criticized in some quarters, but most people were truly thankful and to this day we meet people in all parts of the world who remember that service and look back to it with gratitude. 'Leicester 1962' became a landmark in inter-church relationships. We even heard of it in East Germany in 1968.

By September life was back to normal. I was writing my Saturday articles for the *Mercury* regularly and covered the last week of Kaye Almey's holiday with a series on Switzerland. My dispatches from America had been pronounced a success by John Fortune and I was delighted to continue with my assignment. October brought me fresh adventures abroad. I was already working on my new book *Zermatt Saga* which I intended to be the story of the place and its people. I had no lack of material, indeed I had far too much, but if I was to give a true picture of the place I was convinced I ought to see it out of season. The Seiler family invited me out for a few days in mid-October and I booked a night-flight to Zürich. This was my first experience of travelling alone by air; I am not a great lover of air travel – I always think it will be my plane that develops some serious trouble, the more so on this occasion as I had to leave Ronald behind. However, I set off from Heathrow with a little glow of satisfaction that I was definitely travelling in order to write and quite enjoyed the flight until, when we arrived over Zürich, a voice told us that the airport was closed owing to fog and we were going to try Geneva. Immediately I had visions of the fuel running out or finding myself put down at Marseilles, but of course all was well and we made a perfect landing at Geneva. It was fun to be in Switzerland when it was just *Switzerland* and not overrun by tourists, better still to see Zermatt and its valley in the sole possession of its own people.

I had no idea how glorious autumn is in the Alps, nor how busy the mountain people are with their own pursuits. Everything that needs to be done on the land, to the houses or with the animals must be finished before the snows arrive in November and the great influx of visitors takes place at Christmas.

Zermatt was buzzing with activity. Roads were being repaired and chalets painted. The Monte Rosa Hotel was undergoing a great new reconstruction to the upper floors and the roof. With scaffolding erected and workmen moving in and out of the front door it looked totally unlike the familiar Monte Rosa of the summer.

I stayed at the Seilerhaus; it was strange to be almost the only visitor. On the other hand I had wonderful opportunities for talking to the people of the village; Bernard, my Guide, and his younger sister Pauly were away on holiday in Italy, but I spent a lot of time with another sister Pia and with dear old Mrs Biner, the mother of them all. They supplied me with masses of cosy, local information which I could have obtained nowhere else.

In the mornings I worked in the Alpine Museum studying the old hotel registers, ancient maps and the village archives; in the afternoon I went up to explore the lonely hills and forests in all their autumn solitude. Not many trains are running in October and the ski lift operates only once in the morning and once in the afternoon. But this was all I needed; sometimes I was the only passenger, sometimes I fell in with a family party from another district of Switzerland, out for a day's excursion. On the forest paths on the way to Riffelalp or Ried I met large toboggans, with great upturned runners, on which the men of the village were bringing down the hay from the huts on the alps to store in barns in the village. There were no cows or goats on the alps, but down in the valley and in the village I found the children giving them an airing before locking them up in their stables. Snow was lying quite thickly as far down as Riffelberg, but below that the forests were a blaze of colour. Burnished bronze bracken grew among the rocks; the larches were hung with golden lace.

The afternoons were short; sunset came early; as the evening clouds drifted down among the hills I had unexpected visions of the *Brockenspectre* when every mountain, large or small, makes a phantom of itself on the swirling mists. It was quite an eerie spectacle and I was glad to reach the friendly warmth of the hotel or the cosy *Stube* in Mme Biner's Chalet Rosa. I have never seen the mountains so tranquil as in October, nor the people so much themselves. I felt that I was seeing the village as it was seen by Whymper and the early pioneers. The days passed all too quickly; the visit had proved invaluable; I realized that my book would have been inadequate and incomplete without this picture of Zermatt that so few outsiders are privileged to see.

I was less homesick than usual when the train took me down the valley. In January I would be back again; I was invited to come and see the latest aspect of Zermatt as a winter sports centre; this would mean a few days skiing for me; my heart was already fluttering at the prospect.

In Geneva there was time to visit old friends and I arrived at the air terminal to find that all flights were delayed due to fog earlier in the day. Fog seemed to be playing a big part in this journey and the final forty-five minutes were the most unpleasant I have so far spent in a plane. Owing to air traffic congestion we had to cruise about above Heathrow for three-quarters of an hour; this seemed to me to be tempting Providence beyond all sense, and I was convinced that Staines, Windsor Castle or the Chilterns were destined to be my final resting place.

As might have been expected I was safely restored to Ronald at the airport and as we drove home to Leicester I was sure that my trip had been worth the few anxious moments which, in any case, were entirely caused by my own imaginings.

It had been a great year for travel but life at home was also becoming more and more interesting. My job as diocesan president of the Mothers' Union made increasing demands on my time; committees in Leicester, councils in London and more and more speaking in the parishes were all part of my daily lot. I found it enjoyable and infinitely worthwhile; having arrived in the MU about twenty years later than most of my contemporaries I was still amazed at the world-wide scope of its work. Also, since I rose from the ranks so quickly, and not because of any prowess on my part, I was always finding that members of committees knew much more about most things than did the President; however, I was anxious to learn and they were willing to help and I managed to keep the ship on its course without too many crises.

Ronald by this time was chairman both of the Cathedrals Commission and of the Board for Social Responsibility. Two more different bodies could hardly be imagined, but he enjoyed them both and because of that I learned a lot about the Church of England that I had never known before and also had quite a few interesting experiences on the side.

More friends had joined the episcopal ranks; Frank West as Bishop of Taunton, David Porter as Bishop of Aston. They were consecrated together and we were able to go to the service which gave us great joy. We had all been friends since our courting days; the paths of life had diverged widely and now they were running parallel again. Responsibilities seemed to be crowding in on us and all our friends; it is good to remember that once, not so terribly long ago, we were young and gay and just setting out on the paths that have led to the present.

This had been a good year, we decided, as we made our plans for Christmas – very busy, but stimulating and intensely interesting. We looked forward eagerly to the next – mercifully unaware of the sorrows that it held.

CHAPTER III

Tragedies

EVERYONE hated the great freeze – everyone except me. From Christmas until early March the whole of Europe, and Great Britain in particular, was snowbound. For decades to come people will look back and shudder and shiver when they remember the winter of 1963. But I loved it; snow does something to me; the first flurry of a few thin flakes goes straight to my head. It is a pleasure that mostly I have to enjoy in private in order not to give offence to my sorely tried friends and neighbours. But during those arctic months the moonlight caressing the silver snow fields that had once been our lawns and the spangled fir trees painted on the crimson backcloth of the wintry dawn spelt beauty in large letters to me.

I realized the drawbacks and the miseries only too well – more acutely in fact than I had done in past years. The last great snow in 1947 had caused me almost no personal inconvenience. We were at Durham then, in a college of the university; we seldom had to travel around; college life went on as usual; we skied every afternoon on Observatory Hill across the river. We put on our skis outside the college buildings and removed them only when we returned at tea-time to crumpets round the fire. The view from the hill was unforgettable; cathedral and castle glittered with frost and even the distant slag heaps, dusted with sifted snow, stood out like miniature mountains. It was the longest winter sports season I had ever had; it was gorgeous.

The delights of 1963 were more diluted; almost every evening meant a journey out into the county, or further afield. It was a case for 'bashing on regardless'; digging ourselves out in snowbound villages; slithering to an uncertain stop outside churches where congregations were wistfully waiting in the hope that the confirmation or institution would take place. Somehow we made it every time and so did the archdeacons and other clergy involved; no one had to be disappointed and usually the service started on time.

Our most lurid experience was a trip to Keele University for a debate in which Ronald had to confront a communist lecturer on the motion 'that Christianity is the greatest bar to human progress'. It was a good debate; entirely different from anything we had previously experienced. Everyone seemed to be garbed in jeans and polo necked sweaters and frequent excursions were made to the bar for mugs of beer. But the atmosphere was bracing and the speeches lively and Ronald finally managed to win for his side. He said they took pity on the older man! We left about 10 pm to find the road a sheet of ice; the first thing we met was a car advancing swiftly towards us on its roof. The occupants luckily escaped uninjured. On the borders of Staffordshire and Derbyshire the general confusion was made worse by fog; we lost our way and eventually bumped to rest in our own drive at 3 am. We were dead beat but 'the Bish had beaten the Bolshie' (to use the language of the Keele poster). It had been worth it.

As blizzard succeeded blizzard my anxieties for my poor old aunt in London became increasingly pressing; she had always loathed snow and now her nightly telephone conversations were one long lament. Whenever there was a free Saturday afternoon we skidded up the MI to spend an hour with her; it helped but it was no solution to the problem. At last, just as things were getting desperate, an understanding friend offered to go and stay with her until life was easier – an enormous load was lifted from my mind.

It was not exactly a carefree winter but I revelled in it – as unobtrusively as possible. I had little free time compared with the Durham days, but when I could take my skis out the old thrill returned; the familiar rhythm as I crunched up hill; the hiss of snow in the wake of my skis as I sped downwards with the wind in my hair and the frost on my face. It was only a prelude – before too long I should be in Zermatt for the few precious days I had been promised – but it carried me through the troubles and trials that beset us just then.

The wintry weather kept one small excitement precariously uncertain for some time, namely the Quorn Hunt Ball to which we were going in a party with Dick and Netta Mayston. It was to be at Quenby Hall; Quenby stands high and for days it was thought the roads would be impassable. At last the green light was given and we set out. Male forebodings that we might have to walk home in our long frocks did not quench our determination to enjoy ourselves. The sky was thick with stars; the hedges were cushioned with glittering snow; Quenby stood floodlit on the top of its hill, the flag flying gallantly from the tower. We could hear the subdued hum of voices mingled with music; on the untrodden snow an impudent fox noted our arrival; you could almost see a grin on his face.

Quenby lived up to its famous reputation for light and warmth and gaiety; we sipped our drinks by a blazing log fire surrounded by banks of mimosa and bougainvillia. Family portraits of heroes of Waterloo, of Flanders and Dunkirk smiled down on us from panelled walls and Sir Harold Nutting, alone now and nearly eighty, moved about among the crowds caring for the comfort of everyone as his wife had done on the last occasion when we had been there.

The assortment of guests was just right; masters of hounds from surrounding hunts; farmers and their families; members of Parliament; generals and carefree young men and maidens. There were the young and not so young; those who danced to every tune and those whose dancing days were long past – an excellent mixture where all felt at home and everyone found something to talk about.

We danced twists and the whole gamut of contemporary numbers, with some lovely old waltzes and an occasional eightsome reel. At about two o'clock, when our feet were beginning to tell us that we had been at it for some hours, a delicious aroma of bacon and eggs reached us. We made a dash for the tables and were soon regaling ourselves with sausages, eggs and bacon and wonderful, soothing hot coffee; such things had never tasted better. I glanced round at some of my sleepy neighbours; perhaps it was not a bad thing that the weather had caused the cancellation of the next day's meet. Safely snuggled up in the car we set out on the homeward journey; frost crackled under the wheels and the lights of Leicester beckoned us through a mist of fine snow. A wonderful evening we agreed as we sleepily bade each other goodbye.

'The best Hunt Ball ever,' called Dick as their car disappeared in the snow. Perhaps it was right that it was so – it was the last we ever went to together.

My long-awaited winter visit to Zermatt suddenly ceased to be a distant dream in the future and became of paramount current importance. I needed some up-to-date experience of the winter season for *Zermatt Saga*; the Seiler family and Mr Cachin of the Kurverein invited me to come to Zermatt when I liked and for as long as I liked – a generous offer and one I was delighted to accept. Clearing a space for even a short trip was no easy matter but, by careful planning months ahead, I succeeded in finding a few consecutive days when Ronald would be in London followed by a preaching engagement in Scotland and my own diary was mercifully free of diocesan and Mothers' Union engagements.

I was also free in the literary sense; my assignment for a weekly Saturday diary for the *Leicester Mercury* having come to an end in January. It had been exacting but rewarding; to work for a year for a newspaper – even in such a humble capacity as mine – gives one insights on life that could hardly be acquired in any other way. The discipline of regular production was a help to me as a writer; the knowledge that most things I saw and did carried an extra purpose with them sharpened my perception; the task of sifting relevant from irrelevant material was something from which I learnt much that I needed to learn. And it had been such fun doing something that, if done well enough, would give pleasure to a large number of people of all types.

It was a good thing for me that the request to take on the job did not come sooner than it did. In the earlier part of my career as a bishop's wife I should have been too self-conscious; too eager to justify myself as a person; too anxious about the pitfalls to which I was exposing myself. By the time John Fortune asked me to write for the *Mercury* I had secured my equilibrium and gained my second wind. We had lived through a lot in those first six years; responsibilities seemed to have devolved upon me from all sides; I was constantly having to think of other commitments and other people rather than myself. Most of the things that I felt were really *me* – love of mountains, music, dogs; my hatred of hats and similar conventions, remained unchallenged. Nobody minded that I was this kind of person; they accepted me and in doing so the diocese and all that it meant enabled me to be myself. The articles for the

Mercury helped me to become even more myself; to express my ideas publicly in a medium which I enjoyed was an immense emotional release and I was able to give of my best, such as it was.

I ceased my Saturday diaries – they were replaced by a new page of puzzles and competitions which proved to be very popular – but for another year I continued to stand in for Kaye Almey when she was on leave. We worked well together and it was good to have a little contact with the *Mercury*.

When the day came to set out for Switzerland I felt delightfully unfettered; Ronald would be busy on work he would enjoy and he would be well looked after; Bishop's Lodge and the faithful dog would be in the loving care of Mr and Mrs Bell; I had made preparations for the diocesan duties that would begin immediately I returned; all I had to do now was to make the most of every minute of my visit – I felt well capable of doing that.

It snowed, of course, all the way from Leicester to London; the train was so ice-bound that even hot coffee could not be served. Ronald gave me lunch at the House of Lords and by an extra bit of good fortune we met Lord Monckton, whose driver I had been in the war. All my old hero worship came flooding back and we had a great time recalling those tremendous days.

It was snowing all across Europe; the boat train from Victoria fought its way through a Kentish blizzard; the channel steamer crashed through ice; whenever I peeped out from my sleeper during the night it was the same story. There was a monotony about it, I suppose, but somehow I did not seem to mind – it was just how I would have wished my winter journey to be. I had to change at Berne and found myself enveloped in forty seven degrees of frost – it was almost as suffocating as extreme heat. However, when I boarded the train for Brigue the welcome tinkle of the *Speisewagen* bell greeted me; in a few minutes I was feasting on rolls, butter, cherry jam and steaming hot coffee. Soon the sun came out – I had not seen it for weeks – and in an instant the land-scape was transformed into the winter Switzerland of story books, brochures and picture postcards. It seemed too good to be true; it was all mine to enjoy to my heart's content. I wallowed in it for the rest of the journey.

At Zermatt, Bernard my guide met me just as he did in the

summer. He tucked me up in a fur rug in a horse drawn sleigh and I was whirled away up the village street to a symphony of jingling bells. Before I reached the Monte Rosa it was borne in upon me that wheels just do not exist in the village in the winter – every form of locomotion, including prams, had runners.

Although I had looked forward enormously to this visit, I had had my private misgivings. I was sure it was a necessary venture if my book was to be what I wanted it to be, but I was half afraid that my picture of Zermatt might suffer. I had seen it in spring, in summer and in autumn; always it had been lovely in its own inimitable way. Would the publicity, the prosperity, the popularity of the winter season have taken something from that mystique which one senses at all other seasons? My fears were groundless; perhaps the visitors were more sophisticated than in summer; certainly there seemed to be a few new boutiques and some rather exclusive restaurants advertized unusually *recherché* menus – but I realized that these things were extraneous. They were additions, some only temporary; all the shops and hotels that are truly Zermatt were still there and they lost nothing by comparison. And of course the Monte Rosa was unchanged; nothing ever fundamentally alters the Monte Rosa; whatever the season, it welcomes and cherishes each arriving guest.

The Matterhorn was more dominating than ever; it seemed to rise straight from the village street; it was, in fact it always is, impossible to be unaware of its presence.

I never spent a more rewarding few days. I went up on the *téléfériques* and the Gornergrat railway; as I went I discovered all our beloved summer haunts buried deep in snow; silent and deserted, waiting for spring to breathe new life into them. I sat in the sun on snow covered rocks. hidden from the crowds, and feasted my eyes on the beauty of the great mountains. I knew them all; I had climbed most of them; never had they seemed more friendly, yet never more ethereal. I loved the loneliness and the deep, deep silence; here the peace which usually one experiences only on a summit, seemed to envelope the whole scene. I was exhilarated and satisfied.

Every morning I skied; every afternoon I worked with Bernard on copy for my book; we borrowed fascinating volumes about the history of the village; I visited the people in their own homes and learned the details of their domestic life in winter. In the evenings I ate *raclette* and drank *Glühwein* with Hildi Eberhardt from the Monte Rosa and Bernard and his sister Pauly, immersing myself in the gaiety of the winter season.

Sunday was my last day; I climbed, literally, to the little English church for eight o'clock communion and slid back to breakfast. I left myself just time to pack and spent the last hour or so with Pauly going up on the ski lift to Sunegga; the forest was stiff with hoar frost as we skimmed above it; skiers sped by beneath us; and all around the great peaks stood silent.

Bernard came to see me off with yet one more book to add to my collection. We bade each other *auf Wiedersehen* happily; in seven months Ronald and I would be back. We did come back but, before we came, unforseen disaster struck both Zermatt and our life in Leicester.

The journey down the Vispthal brought unrehearsed delights; a faint mist hung over the villages, softening the outline of roofs and church spire; the peaks were clear-cut against the evening sky; one glistening silver star hung above the Matterhorn; lights came out in chalet windows as we passed. I looked down the valley; at that instant the Oberland mountains flushed deep pink in the setting sun. I watched spellbound until a turn in the line hid the view; then I sank back in my corner utterly content.

As the night express raced across Europe I tried to sort out my impressions; it was impossible; my mind was full of a medley of lovely things. I would have to wait until I could see it all in perspective. Meanwhile, there would be the joy of telling it all to Ronald; I had telephoned him at St Andrews and found him safe and well in spite of having been delayed four hours by the blizzard. He was meeting me at Victoria and then I would be able to live everything over again.

I had only been home a fortnight; work was as interesting as always, when a voice announced on the six o'clock news that there was typhoid in Zermatt; it sounded serious and, somehow, ominous.

All the world knew, and by now has probably forgotten, the tragic story of the weeks that followed. New cases occurred almost daily; by March it had become an epidemic; there were nearly 400 victims; sixty nine of them were British. As usually happens in typhoid epidemics, it proved extremely difficult to trace the original source of infection; meanwhile a scapegoat had, of course, to be found. Newspapers and radios hurled abuse at Zermatt, at the village council; at the health authorities of Canton Valais and, for some inexplicable reason, at Switzerland itself. By the end of March all visitors were ordered to leave Zermatt; all hotels and shops were closed; the Swiss army moved in and took control. The newspapers were full of harrowing tales and heart-breaking pictures of the deserted village – it was the greatest disaster that had hit Zermatt since the Matterhorn accident of 1865.

To me the whole thing seemed one long nightmare. One's first and greatest sympathy naturally was for those who were ill and for their anxious families – but sympathy did not end there. Zermatt was one of the few firm foundation stones of my life. Parents and friends had left us one by one; much of the London I loved so well had disappeared in the blitz; we had moved about from place to place, digging up our roots and trying to put them down again. Through it all, Zermatt had remained constant, inviolate – a treasure house of memories, a shrine where many of my ideals had been dedicated; a place where I was always welcome, a refuge in sorrow as in joy.

At last I could bear it no longer; not one word of defence or sympathy for the people of Zermatt in their disastrous situation had been written or said. I sat down at my typewriter and typed a letter to the *Daily Telegraph*; to my surprise it was printed. It brought down on my head vituperations such as I had never experienced before but it brought too a great chorus of gratitude, not only from Zermatt and from Switzerland, but from people all over Britain, many of whom had been in the village at the start of the epidemic; they even asked if a fund could be opened to help the people rebuild their shattered trade. Offers of help and affirmations of faith in Zermatt were innumerable; with Ronald's help I passed them all on to the right quarters.

I was quite impervious to the malicious letters I received or the insulting remarks I read. I had been able to do something to show my loyalty to Zermatt; to repay just a little of all it had given me over the years – it helped me if it helped no one else.

I would have given all I possessed to have been able to go out to the village and lend a hand. This was obviously impossible; instead we telephoned Bernard every week, thereby keeping in touch with the latest developments. Meanwhile Ronald promised that in spite of an impending trip to Canada, we would go to Zermatt for at least a few days in the summer when the village was once more declared open. This declaration did not come until June 1st, but I felt that at least there was something to hope for.

Desperately worried as I was during those weeks of early spring, I had plenty on my plate to keep my mind occupied. Commitments in the diocese must be honoured whatever the plight of Zermatt might be and knowing this helped to level up one's sense of proportion.

Most of my energies at that moment were centred on a great teenage 'Any Questions Forum'. In the Mothers' Union we had been trying for some time to think up a project that would engage the interest and sympathy of youngsters between the ages of fourteen and twenty. It is not easy for Christian organizations, with their limited financial resources, to produce entertainment that in any way measures up to the fare offered to young people on television and in the cinema. We hit on the idea of a Forum with a hand-picked panel and to our relief the idea caught on – tickets disappeared at a great pace. The panel was well-known and representative. Colonel Pen Lloyd, Chairman of the County Council, Joint Master of the Fernie and a highly popular local figure, agreed to be chairman. The rest of the cast consisted of the then governor of Leicester Prison, later that year to become the resting place of some of the great train-robbers; Kaye Lloyd, wife of the headmaster of Uppingham, well-known for her sparkling appearances on other panels; Matt Gillies, Manager of Leicester City Football and the idol of 90 per cent of Leicester's youth, whose team was already backed for the Cup Final at Wembley; and Verily Anderson, author, and mother of five children, with whom I had a special affinity. Her husband Donald, who sadly had recently died, had been CO of Ronald's Home Guard company and had often been one of my passengers in my Transport Corps days. Also Verily and I shared a Buxton ancestor, who has since brought us a lot of fun and interest.

The Forum was a sell-out before the great night arrived and the 'Coke and Crisp' bar we had provided was so heavily beseiged that I began to think that the ticket-holders must have brought hangers-on. However the more the merrier and everyone somehow managed to be comfortably seated before the fun began. We had invited questions of all kinds to be sent in beforehand; these had had to be sifted before the final selection was made but it was astonishing, and almost pathetic, to see how many of these teen-agers were concerned about home life. Fortunately it was a topic on which each member of the panel was well qualified to speak – and they spoke with one voice. We had no protests, this modern phenomenon had not taken over at that time; there was plenty of applause and no one was listened to with greater respect than the governor of the Prison. The most vociferous adulation was re-served for good old Matt Gillies who found himself left to give the last word on whether mothers should go out to work. Matt, who had a teenage daughter, was definitely on the side of the angels; he gave all kinds of reasons for and against the proposition, 'But,' he said, 'if I was a teenager I'd feel something was all wrong if Mum wasn't at home when I got in from school or work'.

The Forum broke up with everyone in great spirits and I noticed that autographs were being sought eagerly. Verily Anderson came home to spend the night with us and gave us the latest news of her vigorous and entertaining family. She autographed my copies of her books and took my one ewe lamb to read in bed. I could hardly believe that the Forum was over and all I had left to do was to write the thank-you letters. I knew there could not be any immed-iate, tangible results; I just hoped that an evening spent in that way with five such magnificent people might have some long-term effect on at least a few of the young participants.

One of the many interesting duties allotted to bishops is the preaching of the so-called Spital sermon which takes place at St Lawrence Jewry in the City of London in the presence of the Lord Mayor in April every year. Ronald's turn for this sermon was not actually due until 1970 but owing to the illness or absence of several of his brother bishops it suddenly came about that he would have to preach the sermon this very April. There was still time to collect the necessary material and mercifully it fell during the week in which he was scheduled to take prayers in the House of Lords so there were no unforeseen difficulties. He arrived home having lunched with the Lord Mayor before what proved to be a very interesting service. But this paled into insignificance when he produced from his brief case an invitation for us both to the Easter Banquet at the Mansion House and a request that we should spend the night there as guests of the Lady Mayoress. This was something quite unexpected; I had previously thought the expression 'Spital sermon' sounded quite revolting but if it brought such sequels in its train I might have to revise my ideas.

The Easter Banquet is really the diplomatic banquet given by the City of London for ambassadors and high commissioners and their ladies. It was my first involvement with the diplomatic world and I was greatly intrigued. We filed up the long staircase to be received while the pikemen in their gorgeous uniforms kept guard. Suddenly a voice came across to me; 'I want to thank you for all that you did for my country in our great trouble'. It was Dr Daeniker, the Swiss Ambassador. He and his wife were two of the very few guests we knew; they came frequently to the Alpine Club and Ladies' Alpine Club dinners and Mme Daeniker is a member of the LAC. I was excited and slightly embarrassed; I had heard from the Swiss Embassy that the Ambassador was grateful for my letter in the *Daily Telegraph* during the Zermatt typhoid epidemic but I certainly had not expected to be thanked in such illustrious surroundings.

The whole evening was memorable; it was so typically English; dignified, gracious, yet suffused with a simplicity that allowed no ostentation. It was a splendid spectacle; uniforms glittered; tiaras sparkled; the rainbow colours of the ladies' frocks were a foil to the rich reds and blues and blacks of the men. The menu, to my great relief, did not include bird in any shape or form; as we dined and talked and laughed there was a background of gay music from the minstrels' gallery. We drank from the massive gold loving cup while the orchestra played softly and mysteriously 'Drink to Me Only'.

The most unusual thing of all for us was the fact that when the members of the *Corps Diplomatique* were taking their leave of the Lord Mayor we stayed behind with our hostess and her family. We had a happy, informal half hour with them and made our way at last to our lovely room. To a fanatical Londoner like myself it was heaven to be sleeping in the middle of the City with a view on to the famous Bank Corner. Several times during the night I simply had to draw back the curtains to see the moon floodlighting the Bank and the Royal Exchange and to look down on the silent, empty streets – I had never seen them so before.

After breakfast next morning we signed our names in the Visitors' Book and said our goodbyes. Soon we were wriggling our way through the traffic, just ordinary folk again. But I never cross the Bank Corner now without a glance at the window of the room that was ours and remember that once, just for one night, I slept in the heart of the city.

Tragedy, when it comes, so often strikes swiftly and un-expectedly; perhaps that is why one seems totally unprepared for it.

The Convocation of Canterbury usually meets in May and Ronald and I set off for London as usual. I dropped off for some shopping in the West End; Ronald went on to Church House to meet Dick who had been seeing Netta off on a trip to Ireland. When I reached Church House later in the afternoon Ronald greeted me with the startling news that we must go at once to St Thomas' Hospital as Dick was arriving there from Leicester, some trouble from a past operation having flared up. We felt bewildered and anxious, but when we found Dick sitting up in bed eating a good supper our spirits revived quite a bit. Indeed, Dick seemed to take such a casual view of his condition that we had some diffi-culty in persuading him to get Netta back from Ireland. However, she came, bringing her sister with her for company, and during the rest of that week we visited Dick constantly, finding him always cheerful and convinced that he would be home within a week.

We returned to Leicester on Friday and in the evening Netta telephoned to say that she had good news. The surgeon had told her that Dick would have a small operation the next day – just an injection she understood. There was absolutely no danger involved and he would be out of hospital in a few days.

We went about our duties on Saturday quite unconcernedly, happy in the promise that all would be well with Dick. At teatime a telephone call told us that he was desperately ill – would we try to contact Netta?

The weary hours went by; late at night came the news that Dick was deeply unconscious. All through that nightmare weekend we tried, with the help of Donald Byford who was always so close to us all, to prepare the diocese and Dick's closest friends for what we

F   81

felt to be inevitable. It was almost impossible to persuade people to believe us after the hopes we had cherished. Throughout the small hours of Monday morning I lay awake, certain of the news that daylight would bring, my mind seething with sorrow and un-answered questions.

By seven o'clock we heard that it was all over; there was nothing more to be done; it only remained for Ronald to arrange Dick's funeral and for me to bring Netta back to Leicester.

On the night before the funeral a quiet little procession com-posed of Cyril Innocent, the Provost's Verger, the Precentor, the cathedral Canons, Ronald and Dick's brother and brother-in-law brought him into his beloved cathedral to rest in the chancel. On the coffin I placed a little circlet of apple blossom – one of the things he loved.

How we all got through the funeral none of us knows to this day; we only know that we were aware of an unseen presence that guided and sustained us. It was a transcendent service; impressive, yet utterly simple – rather like Dick himself. Ronald had chosen the hymns with the utmost care; the psalm was sung to a chant that Dick had composed; the lesson was read by the Colonel of the Royal Leicestershire Regiment; Jimmy Good, a friend of univer-sity and army days, gallantly preached the sermon.

The cathedral was crowded to capacity – no one was missing. For the rest of my life I shall remember the sorrow and unspoken bewilderment on the faces of the cathedral choir, the chapter and, indeed, the whole congregation – that such a thing could happen was beyond the comprehension of all of us. From the human point of view there seemed to be no redeeming feature in this death. Only the courage and dignity of Netta and the loyalty of Dick's friends shone as a light in the darkness.

For the next month I shared with Netta the harrowing task of breaking up her home; this is the inevitable lot of any clergy wife whose husband dies in office. We worked as hard and as quickly as we could; there was no point in prolonging the agony. In the midst of all this another sadness occurred; Costy, our adored golden retriever, died very peacefully on a summer Sunday morning. There was no tragedy here, his time had come; but we loved him dearly and we missed him the more because our spirits were so low.

Another casualty in Netta's home was her greatly valued daily helper Mrs Perrott. She had loved her job at the Provost's House and was convinced that she could never settle down in another. It so happened that we were badly in need of someone to help us; Mrs Perrott and I were good friends already; I asked her if she would come to us for a few weeks and see how she liked it. She came, and stayed, and the ties have grown closer as the years have passed.

The Provost's House stood empty; everything was packed and on its way to Netta's new home in Northern Ireland – she was going back to the land from whence she came, where there would be a constant background of love and companionship to help her through the coming months and years. I went with her to the airport; we said goodbye quickly, promising to meet again soon.

A chapter had closed – forever. A chapter that had opened with such promise and high hopes; that had brought so much public as well as private happiness as it unfolded; sealed now by that never-to-be-forgotten message – 'The operation was successful – but at a price'.

It was towards the end of June that Ronald tentatively suggested another dog.

'I don't think you can really live without a dog, you know,' he said one night as a neighbour passed the gate giving his spaniel its evening airing.

I shook my head. 'I don't think I could bear it; I get too fond of them; and anyway there could never be another Costy'.

'No,' he agreed, 'there couldn't – but there might be one you'd love as much. You don't look natural somehow without a dog around with you'.

We left it at that. I felt horribly ungrateful; I knew he was trying to find something to cheer me up, but all my usual enthusiasm seemed to have deserted me; it was as much as I could do to raise the energy to carry out the daily programme.

I forgot about dogs and went off to London to the MU Central Council. Ronald said he had interviews all the morning and an engagement at Whitwick in the afternoon, but he would probably manage to meet me off the tea-time train.

'Anne's making a cup of tea,' he said encouragingly as we drove up from the station through the sultry heat.

'She *is* good – I'll go and help her'. I jumped out of the car and ran indoors; Anne had performed a multitude of little extra kindnesses during the past few weeks. I heard her voice in the kitchen.

'Now just sit still and try to look your best please.'

What on earth was she talking about; I put my head round the door and caught sight of a scrap of white fur; it had two tan ears; a black saddle on its back and a stumpy tail. Two bright eyes glanced up at me and the tail gave a nervous jerk. No one could have resisted such a lovable little bundle; I seized him and hugged him. I found Ronald looking over my shoulder.

'Is he really for me? Where did you get him? How old is he'?

Anne carried the tray into the study.

'Have some tea,' she said sensibly. 'I've put an extra biscuit on for him'.

Of course I had to hear the whole story. Ronald had asked our kindly vet, Walter Carr, where he could find a quiet, reliable, wire-haired terrier puppy. A kennel at Whitwick was recommended – hence his engagement at that village. When he arrived he found this tiny little fellow sitting all by himself in a corner of the exercise yard.

'The last of the litter,' said the owner. 'Never been heard to bark yet – but a good pedigree.'

It was only a matter of minutes before the deal was clinched and our next dog was on his way to Bishop's Lodge.

We called him Martin – after Dick's cathedral – and the name met with approval all over the diocese. He must have been the smallest and most nervous puppy that ever left the kennels, but he became attached to us on that first evening. We bought him a red collar and harness and Ronald presented him with a brand new basket which he straightway started to chew. But he did something for our household; Mr and Mrs Bell, Anne, Mrs Perrott, Leslie Green – everyone loved him; it seemed as if his coming helped us all to begin the long climb back out of the depths of our despair. He could not replace Costy; he did not have to. He was a perfect successor, completely different but it was better that way. We have never loved a dog more than we love Martin.

Perhaps it was his arrival and all the fresh interest that it brought that inspired us to think of cricket again; somehow most happy things seemed to have perished, at any rate temporarily, in the sorrows of that sad summer. Cricket has always been one of our mutual joys; it means a lot to us that Leicester is a first class county and that when we have time, which is seldom, we can slip round to the county ground at Grace Road for an hour. But at this particular moment our minds turned towards Canterbury and its famous festival. We were both born in Kent and the St Lawrence ground holds treasured memories – school holidays when, unknown to each other, we were watching Frank Woolley striking the ball to the boundary. This summer, a plaque recording Woolley's service to his county was to be unveiled in the pavilion; we both had an urge to be there; we succumbed to that urge.

The Anglican Congress in Toronto was looming up in the middle of August; we were thoroughly run down; a weekend in Kent would be a real tonic, if a short one. We booked ourselves in at a motel in Hythe and drove into Canterbury on the Saturday morning. All the old magic was there as we entered the St Lawrence ground; the wide sweep of the turf; the tents grouped round the edge; the family parties with their dogs and their cars and their picnics; the friendly old-fashioned pavilion and the hordes of small boys begging autographs from famous, flanelled figures. The sun shone, the trees rustled softly and the grey towers of the cathedral brooded benignly over the roofs of the city. It was perfect; we settled down, forgetful of everything but the sweet, nostalgic pleasure of the present – we could feel it doing us good.

During the luncheon interval we perused the newspapers as we enjoyed our picnic. I had an early edition of an evening paper; the article on the sports page was on these lines –

'Tradition is out; the Canterbury Festival with its collection of tents and family parties has had its day; if the game is to continue a new era of brighter cricket must be established.'

I looked at the scene around me; it had scarcely changed since I was a teenager; the tents and the family parties were there in greater profusion than before; the ground was packed to capacity with all sorts and conditions of men, women and children; each one was enjoying every minute. I wondered where that 'with-it' reporter was at that moment; he certainly would not be watching cricket. It was only too obvious he had no love nor feeling for the game; the wish in his case was father to the thought and it had produced an idiot child.

It was a grand weekend; the cricket was absorbing; we were invited to tea in the President's tent; we went down to Dover to call on Langford and Kathleen Duncan, new-found friends my book had brought us; we attended morning service in Canterbury Cathedral with its glorious music and huge and happy congregation. We met friends from all parts of the world afterwards and had drinks with some wartime colleagues, reviving old memories.

On Monday the *pièce de résistance* was the dedication of the plaque for Frank Woolley. The great man was there himself, of course, looking as if he might still be good for a century or a hat trick. It was a homely ceremony; it could have taken place on any village green – only all the cricketing family of Kent had gathered round to honour its hero. Frank spoke briefly and movingly about the ideals and the sheer fun of the game.

'If I have given you any pleasure with my cricket, I am very pleased, because I certainly enjoyed it all,' he said.

How I wished that ignorant reporter could have heard him.

When the ceremony was over and tea was being taken, Ronald had a word with Frank Woolley with whom he had occasionally corresponded. Frank happened to notice me hovering humbly in the background.

'Is this the Bishop of Leicester's wife?' he asked. 'I want to tell you that I've read your book and enjoyed every minute of it.'

That was a bit of a change from my old habit of hanging round for autographs. When we left the St Lawrence ground I was as pleased and proud as if I had scored a century.

We were not looking forward to the Toronto Congress and we never really enjoyed it – in spite of much kindness and hospitality and the meeting of many old friends. Of course it was quite a thrill to fly the Atlantic for the first time, in a noisy old Britannia which took thirteen hours to do the trip. But we were still sick in heart and mind and we were saddened afresh by the Irish delegates, almost all of them friends of Dick's who crowded round begging for some explanation of the tragedy. We had no comfort to give them; we knew of no explanation; they went away as baffled as we were.

Nevertheless some things stand out in the memories of that fortnight and are still unforgettable. The dedication and self-sacrifice of almost every citizen of Toronto was amazing – everyone had co-operated to ensure the success of the Congress.

A leading firm of car manufacturers lent a fleet of cars for the convenience of speakers; the City Fire Brigade volunteered to drive them during their off duty periods; the churchwomen of Toronto, working in rotas, served breakfast every morning for a thousand people; boy scouts from city troops took over the onerous task of providing messengers for the whole period. It was a great Christian demonstration which many found quite inspiring.

The immense programme struck me as one great hustle, but then, hustle is a basic ingredient of life on the North American continent. The choir of the Royal School of Church Music had come out with us and sang Matins and Evensong day by day in St James's Cathedral. There was always a large congregation of Canadian city folk with a sprinkling of Congress delegates, which frequently included me. I, and a good many others, I fancy, found it absolutely essential to escape occasionally from the clamour and the dialogue, however stimulating and meaningful it might be.

Of the many generous entertainments provided for us, I recall most vividly the delightful family dinner parties given for groups of delegates in private homes; the visit to Stratford, Ontario, to see a magnificent performance of *Troilus and Cressida*; the massed ride of the Canadian Mounties at the National Exhibition; and last but not least the lunch for bishops' wives at the Hunt Club. Here we were given beautiful, hand-made silver maple leaf brooches. Mine has remained one of my really treasured possessions; I wear it so often that I am continually being stopped in the streets of London by people wanting to know if I am a Canadian.

When the time came to board the Boeing 707 for the flight home, I was not sorry. We were bound for Switzerland with a two-hour stop at Heathrow; perhaps here I would be able to regain some peace of mind; I certainly had failed to do so at the Congress. It was our first flight by jet and it was something to remember. Darkness came as we flew over Greenland and the great canopy of the night sky, lit by a million stars, gave a new and deeper meaning to the words of the psalmist – 'When I consider thy heavens'. The majesty and meaning of the universe was re-interpreted for us.

But in spite of this, at the back of my mind I was worried – worried, of all things, about our new little Martin. Mr and Mrs

Bell were taking care of him at home; I had hardly liked to leave such a tiny, frail puppy for someone else to bother about but the Bells, as always, were willing to help and we knew he could not be in better hands. But during the whole fortnight in Toronto we had received no news and this was unusual. I felt something was wrong but hoped it was due to the fact that I was in an over-wrought state of mind anyhow.

Leslie Green was coming to Heathrow to take home all the ecclesiastical impedimenta and bring us our rucksacks and holiday kit. I looked for him anxiously and saw him waving among the waiting crowds.

I had told myself that duty demanded that I should enquire about everybody else before I asked after Martin, but somehow I abandoned my good intentions.

'How's Martin, Mr Green?' the words tumbled out of my mouth before I could stop them.

'Pretty poor,' he answered gravely. 'He's had a lot of fits and there's something wrong with his hip.'

'What does the vet say?' Ronald had joined our worried little party by this time.

'He doesn't like the look of him at all,' Leslie Green replied, not mincing his words. He went on talking with Ronald while I fumbled about with cases and rucksacks. There just seemed no end to the sadness of this summer; little Martin with his pretty, puppy ways already meant a lot to me – more than I had realized prob-ably. Now it seemed as if he was doomed too; I began to wonder what disaster would overtake us next.

We did not talk much about Martin during the flight to Zürich; I felt Ronald was trying to formulate a plan of action but I was too tired and too depressed to offer any help; all I longed for was to reach Zermatt and fall asleep. But even the thought of Zermatt for the first time in my life was tinged with anxiety. I was thankful to be going there but how would they all be after the deep waters through which they had passed? And how should *I* be? In the spring I had thought only of getting there as quickly as possible to comfort and encourage all my friends in their distress. But now my own spirits had sunk so low I wondered if I should be more of a hindrance than a help. And would the beloved village seem different, would all that had happened have left some indelible mark?

'I shan't be able to stand much more,' I whispered to myself as the train threaded its way up the steep valley.

Even before it came to a standstill, I knew that my fears were without foundation. I could see houses and hotels gay with their usual window-boxes; people were laughing and talking as we drew into the station; there was sunshine everywhere.

It seemed as if the whole village had come to meet us, our friends were there in such numbers. Bernard held out his arms as I leapt out of the train; Pauly and her sisters ran towards us; even their young nephews and nieces had brought flowers. It was a tremendous homecoming – a coming home to friends who always know and understand without a word being spoken. I was ashamed of my own self-pity; they had put aside their trials and tribulations and were concerned only with the sorrows which had fallen upon us.

We walked slowly up the village street; the Matterhorn glowed gloriously in the setting sun; friends popped out of shops and offices to greet us; the little flock of piebald goats hurried past on its homeward way; by the time we reached the Monte Rosa, I was aware that the healing power of Zermatt and the mountains was already at work.

Hildi Eberhardt took us up to our room – the nicest in the hotel, with views of the Matterhorn and the village street and a little balcony all to ourselves. There were presents of chocolate and flowers awaiting us – all accompanied by loving messages and gratitude for our support during the typhoid disaster. My heart was almost too full to speak and I knew Ronald felt much the same; instinctively both of us realized that we had reached the bottom of the dark and dangerous slope we had been descending during the last few months; the climb back might be slow, but it had already begun; perhaps it would be easier than we expected.

After dinner that night we sat by the window in our peaceful little room; the Matterhorn glittered like some giant jewel in the light of the full moon; the distant murmur of the river and the slow chiming of the church clock increased rather than diminished the gentle silence of the night.

Ronald began to talk about Martin and I found myself able to discuss this difficult matter more calmly and objectively than would have been possible only a few hours earlier.

'I don't think we can let him live if he's going to suffer,' he said.
'I couldn't bear that,' I replied. 'I know we'd have to let him go.'

'But we just can't go home and put another dog to sleep,'
Ronald went on. 'We've had too much. We've got to make a new
start and do a good winter's work.'

I knew it was true; it was up to us to put the shattered fragments
together again and show that faith could rise above fate; but we
could only do this if we ourselves were revived physically, spiritually and mentally.

Between us we evolved a plan; we would telephone Mr and Mrs
Bell, find out the latest news and if it was really hopeless ask them
to get the vet to put the little chap out of his misery.

Ronald did the telephoning, I could not trust myself to do that,
but when he got through to Leicester the news was better and the
vet thought the next couple of days would show what the future
was likely to be. The Bells agreed entirely with our plan and we
arranged to telephone again before we left. As I went to sleep that
night I told myself I would not see little Martin again and then, to
my own amazement, managed to put the matter completely out of
my mind.

We had only four days to spend in Zermatt, but never have four
days made so much difference to us. There was no time to climb,
not enough even for long walks but it did not seem to matter. We
strolled up through the forest paths, rich with the hot scent of
pines; we sat among the newly-cut hay and sipped milk at the
cheesemaker's hut; we stood on the windswept Riffelberg and
drank in the great sweep of peaks from Monte Rosa to the Oberland. Best of all we spent long, long evenings talking with our
friends – above all with Bernard. Bernard had a philosophy that
always met my need; when I was a schoolgirl learning to climb;
when the war came and we left Zermatt to face we knew not what;
when Ronald became a bishop and the whole course of our lives
was changed; when my parents died – Bernard always had something worth while to say that somehow strengthened my wavering
courage. He did not fail me now; in spite of all that had happened
in Zermatt and in Leicester since we had said goodbye in January,
I knew, after we had talked with Bernard, that things were better
with us; we could take heart and build anew.

On our last night we telephoned home once more; I braced myself to hear that Martin had gone; in a few moments Ronald's broad smile told a different story. All was well; the vet had said he would survive and he would be waiting to welcome us when we arrived. I hardly knew myself; I had almost forgotten what it was like to feel gay and light-hearted and full of hope. Nothing could change the past, nor take away the bitterness, but life had a purpose and was worth living again.

We sailed down the Rhine from Basle to Rotterdam as a restful finale to our short holiday; the journey was all, and more, than we had hoped. From Rotterdam we flew to London; I could not get home quickly enough. At last, late at night, the car turned into the drive of Bishop's Lodge; there on the steps stood Mr and Mrs Bell proudly holding up for our inspection a wriggling, tail-wagging, excited little terrier, already much bigger than when we had last seen him. They thrust him into my arms and I took him upstairs for a special private reunion – there could not have been a better welcome home on that windy, wet September night.

There was a long story to tell; to this day we never forget that Martin owes his life to Mr and Mrs Bell. They had been through a grim time; after a series of fits he had rushed off to the furthest corner of the garden; they eventually found him cowering under the summerhouse smothered in mud and grit. They bathed him and dried him in front of the fire. Our vet, Walter Carr, did a grand job with injections and sedatives. For three days Martin ate nothing and never stopped shivering; when he did walk he was lame in his right hip. Everyone was in despair until one day his eyes looked a little brighter; he lapped a saucer of milk and licked Mr Bell's hand. Gradually his strength revived and Walter Carr pronounced that he could and should live.

To say that Martin was a late developer is to put it mildly; his early handicaps retarded him for a long time; he never seemed to jump about like other dogs and try as we would we could not teach him to beg. But one by one his difficulties began to disappear; by the time he was two he was leaping into the air as vigorously as any dog when a walk was suggested; when he was three he suddenly discovered that he could jump up on chairs – it goes without saying that he is now the occupant of all the best chairs in the house. He loves the car and pops in and out with the greatest alacrity; he comes everywhere with us and in his red harness and lead he has become quite a well-known personality in the diocese. One thing he never forgets – that he owes everything to the Bells. He is devoted to them and the arrival of their car when they come home from a holiday sends him into uncontrollable ecstasies of delight.

Those who are not doggy-minded will wonder how so much can be said about one rather under-sized little terrier. But others who share our feelings for dogs will understand something of what he means to us. He came to succeed our beloved old golden retriever at a time when our hearts were very sad; we almost lost him but he grew up to become a healthy, happy companion; he is an indispensable member of home and family and he bears the name of the patron saint of our cathedral. Martin is more than a pet and a companion – he is a symbol.

Very soon after our joyful return home we had to set off to London for an event of no small importance in our family – my old aunt was about to celebrate her eightieth birthday. Known as 'Auntie', not only to the family but to friends and acquaintances for miles around, she had always been a very special person to my brother Geoffrey, and to me. She was my mother's favourite sister and came to live with our parents almost as soon as we were born; we could not remember home without her and she was rather like an extra parent. Added to all this, she was the only one of our family who had succeeded in reaching the age of eighty, so obviously a celebration was called for.

Some of the arrangements we managed to keep secret – more especially the names of her guests. She was busy admiring her gaily decorated birthday cake when in marched, from various entrances, Geoffrey and four of his family; Ronald's sister Winnie and their two remaining aunts and my oldest friend Sylvia, whom Auntie remembered back in the pram-pushing days. The surprise quite shook her for a moment but she was equal to the occasion and after consuming an enormous birthday tea she interviewed each guest separately in the study while the rest of us washed up. It was quite an occasion and I was secretly thrilled that we had brought it off. Something seemed to tell me that before too long we should no longer have Auntie or the beloved family home; if that proved to be so this happy afternoon would become a treasured memory.

By the middle of September work in the diocese was in full swing and we felt ready and eager to cope with it. I had worried quite a lot about the Michaelmas Ordination; I knew Ronald would miss Dick terribly at this time and I had been trying to think of something that might help a bit. As so often happens events were guided in a quite wonderful way without any assistance from me. One of the ordination candidates was Ronald's eldest godson, David Moore, who was to be ordained deacon and go to Melton Mowbray as assistant curate – an event that was a real thrill for all of us. One evening Ronald was going through some of Dick's possessions which he had taken over from Netta; among them he found the stole which Dick wore at his own ordination and which he had valued above all others that he had. What could be better than that David should have this stole to wear on his great day? David was proud and delighted with the gift; when the ordination service took place he was appointed Gospeller; as he stood there wearing the stole, it seemed as if Dick's presence was with us in the cathedral in a very real way.

Early in the autumn I flew to Northern Ireland to see Netta – for the first time since that sad farewell in June. It was my first visit to the Mountains of Mourne and I realized at once that this was the right place for Netta – among her relations and her childhood haunts where every stick and stone held some memory of Dick. We had a great time – a thoroughly happy time. We walked and picnicked in wonderful spots like the Silent Valley and up on Slieve Donard; we went to see the fishing fleet at Kilkeel and most of Netta's many relations seemed to give parties for me. There was also time to talk – to talk about many things neither of us had felt able to speak about the during last days in Leicester. Nothing she told me brought me any comfort – I felt more bitter and baffled than before – but at least I knew everything and we realized we had to leave it as a problem forever unsolved. To my delight, Netta said that she wanted to pay a visit to Leicester as soon as possible. We got dates fixed up and the trip was an unqualified success. She has continued to come each spring and autumn; it is a joy to Ronald and me and gives pleasure to her many Leicester friends.

As 1963 drew to its close we looked back on the saddest year we had ever spent, but before it ended we were able to feel that hope was burning bright once more; life would never be quite the same again but there was very much for which to give thanks. The cathedral was in good shape again; John Hughes, one of our old Durham students who had been many years in the diocese, became Provost. No one could have taken on a more difficult and delicate task; no one could have performed it with greater sympathy and humility. With his wife Sybil, their three sons and two daughters, not to mention the dog and the Siamese cat they soon won a place in the affection of the city. We also had a new Canon Chancellor in Dudley Gundry, who immediately became part of the cathedral family – not least because he has an inexhaustible fund of funny stories.

In our own particular circle we had cause for gratitude. Our household, who had stood by us so magnificently through all the troubles, was still with us; Netta was safe and well cared for in Ireland; Martin grew livelier every day; we were both in good health and spirits again and as a kind of bonus of good cheer at Christmas we were able to drive Auntie round London to see the tree in Trafalgar Square, the Christmas lights and all the gay shops she once knew so well.

I felt convinced that she would not see them again; I was also pretty sure that some big problems lay ahead. And yet, because we had been through so much, I seemed to be less apprehensive, a little less afraid, than I might have been as I faced the unknown New Year.

CHAPTER IV

Endings and Beginnings

SOONER or later it happens to everyone – the older generation disappears; the family home is disbanded; roots laid down at birth have to be ruthlessly torn up. For some it comes comparatively early in life; for others the day is long delayed. I was among the lucky ones; I had my parents and my home for longer than most of my friends and contemporaries. The end came on my birthday when my old aunt slipped peacefully away as she sat watching the television. It was sudden but not unexpected; there was nothing tragic about it; indeed, it was a happy rather than sorrowful event, in spite of the sense of finality it brought with it.

The death of an aged aunt may not seem of much importance but it was important to me, and every detail still stands out vividly. As everyone has to go through things like this, I record my recollections.

I had been to see her a few days previously and realized she was very frail. On the morning of my birthday, a card and a record token arrived from her. Only a couple of hours later a telephone message told us that the doctor was anxious about her; there was no urgency but if I could go the next day it would be a good thing.

I longed to go at once but I was not free to do so. I had a long-standing engagement to talk to a large crowd of MU in the evening; I could not disappoint then and I knew my aunt was in good hands. She was being looked after by Margo Talbot, a clergy widow of our diocese, a selfless and devoted friend who had come to the aid of Ronald's family and mine many times when we were going through a sticky patch. Auntie adored her – I knew she would cope till I got there.

I got home from the meeting late in the evening to find Ronald trying to organize a kind of mini-celebration.

'You're having such a rotten birthday,' he explained; 'I thought we must do something. I've made a pot of tea and there's some cake and Douglas and Dorothy are coming round.'

I cheered up a lot; everything looked so comfortable and cosy and Douglas and Dorothy were just the right people for this occasion. They were very old friends who had recently come to the diocese and their daughter Anne is my god-daughter. Douglas knew my family well, so he understood the situation exactly. They arrived bringing a lovely bowl of white hyacinths; Ronald poured out tea; Douglas handed round cake; I was feeling surrounded by love and kindness when the telephone rang.

I knew what it was, Ronald hardly needed to tell me Margo's message – Auntie had died quietly as she sat in her easy chair. It could not have been better for her; in a way I felt it could hardly have been better for us. My father and my mother had both had prolonged last illnesses; Auntie had gone without pain and without any sense of fear.

When I got home to London the next morning only one thing was really troubling me – I had always promised my aunt that when anything happened to her I would see that her beloved old dog Pongo was put to sleep at once. I was sure that this was the right course; I was determined to see it through, but I did not fancy the job. Pongo had been the family pet for years; I loved him dearly. Almost the first thing Margo told me when I arrived was that a kind friend had taken on the task for me and Pongo had already followed his mistress. And Margo told me something else that brought me immense comfort. At breakfast on the day of her death Auntie had spoken of a dream she had during the night. She had arrived in some strange place but all her friends and relations were there to greet her – her parents, her brothers and sisters, my parents; all those she loved best.

'It was so wonderful,' she told Margo as she ended her story, 'I wished I need never wake up'.

I suppose psychologists and humanists could explain away that story only too easily, but I have no doubt whatever that my aunt was granted a preview, a tiny glimpse, of life beyond the grave; in telling her story she gave us a glimpse too and made death seem a gateway and a beginning.

Her funeral on a cold February day seemed almost a glad affair. The sun shone and there were snowdrops in our garden; Ronald took the service as he had done for both our parents; Geoffrey with some of his family, Sylvia, Margo and I accompanied the coffin; the church was thronged with friends of all ages who had known and loved the family – not least the children who had always been such a delight to my aunt.

As we prepared to leave the house for the funeral, I suddenly remembered the front door key – for the first time in our lives there would be nobody to let us in. I had rather dreaded the return from the crematorium to the empty house – I knew it could never again seem quite like home – but we had to be so busy getting tea and making temporary arrangements for the care of the house and garden, that there was little time for sadness. Only when we closed the door behind us and departed our several ways, Geoffrey and I with a latch-key each, did the situation stare me full in the face; there was no one to wave goodbye and there never would be again; the last chapter had been written on this era of our family history.

Breaking up a home produces some curious experiences; the wearisome checking and sorting, the endless task of going through papers, the settling of bills – in some ways it appeared almost sordid and irreverent to me. And yet it seemed at times as if I was flicking through the pages of a condensed paperback edition of my life in the family home. Documents which I scarcely knew existed, and to which I should have attached little importance if I had, took on a new significance; the announcement of my arrival into this world, christening pictures, school prospectuses, termly reports (very revealing!), arrangements for my trips abroad, the draft of our wedding invitation and a hundred other matters all carefully filed for reference. I turned them over thoughtfully; I had better preserve them; there would be nowhere else to turn for information if ever it were needed.

The family heirlooms too assumed a greater reality; the grandfather clocks both over two hundred years old, the oil paintings which had been our grandmother's, the pianos, the cabinets with their lovely china – they had been part of us ever since we could remember; we took them very much for granted. Now they were our responsibility; it was for us to decide their fate.

Dividing up our heritage was not a difficult matter for my brother and me; none of our choices overlapped; we each took away to our own homes our special favourites; the things that had meant most to us in our childhood and youth still held an honoured place in our middle-aged affections – it was evident that our respective tastes had not changed much with the passing years.

The house was sold and taken over as a hostel for students. That phase was short-lived; later it became, and has remained, a home for elderly people. I was pleased about this, it seemed an eminently suitable solution. I seldom see the house now; when I do, I feel content about the role it is fulfilling; but that does not prevent me having a nostalgic peep at the balcony and veranda which had been such a joy with each successive summer – we had eaten there and worked there and slept there under the stars. When we woke in the freshness of a summer morning we looked out over the golf course and away to the spires and towers of London; at night when we settled down to sleep the hooting of the owls rose above the muted rumble of London Transport.

It had been an ideal home for our kind of family: the sort of set-up that Dr Edmund Leach and his colleagues detest but which still, in spite of their scornful scoffings, remains, and probably will always remain, the firm foundation on which our nation, and many others, build for the future.

Just at this moment, as if to lighten the load at a time in which a certain sense of sorrow was inevitable, there appeared the second edition of *Bishop's Wife – but still myself*. I rejoiced greatly and found myself thinking that perhaps those who were gone were rejoicing with me.

After several months, our share of the old home arrived in Leicester and we had quite a time distributing it. Our great Victorian house makes an ideal setting for the new possessions; they retain their precious memories, at the same time they have taken on a new lease of life; they look to the future as well as to the past and now, after a few years, seem as permanent a part of our domain as they did in their London environment. I am grateful for the feeling of continuity which they give me; a sense of stability in an unstable world.

The end of the family meant an end to the obligation to visit, which, though always a pleasure, had prevented me from doing many other things. So it was that when the domestic upheavals had subsided I was seized with a burning desire to make a pilgrimage round our old haunts – to the scenes of my school days, to the Surrey villages where my mother's family had lived for generations, to those special spots which held a certain magic that I could hardly explain to myself and certainly not to anyone else. Ronald doubted the wisdom of this project.

'I'm afraid you'll find it just peopled with ghosts,' he said. 'You don't know what you're letting yourself in for.'

However, after a certain amount of pleading on my part he agreed for me to take the car and set off while he was busy in London.

It was a lovely late spring day; when I reached the brow of Reigate Hill and found the Weald spread out below me stretching away to the smooth outline of the South Downs, I knew it was right that I had come. This was the country in which I had spent my most impressionable years; this was where youthful ambition had soared to unattainable heights; this was where I had dreamed dreams and made friends and learned, through the stresses of adolescence, that life is sometimes lived on the mountain top and sometimes in the valley and that everyone has to come to terms with this situation. As I drifted very slowly down the hill, in order to avoid being fined for parking, I thought how lucky I had been to grow up in such a setting. In this controversial age there are those whose jealousy and animosity lead them to cast a malevolent eye on the Surrey hills and to look with favour on the Hackney Marshes as a better venue for education. I disagree – and I ought to know. As soon as I left school, my father's work caused us to live for three years within a mile of the Hackney Marshes. We were all happy there; we were surrounded by bricks and mortar; our garden comprised a few tubs on the roof; but a distant view of St Paul's Cathedral compensated for this; none of us consciously craved for a more delectable neighbourhood. But I still think I was lucky that my educational lot was cast in Surrey; everything should be done that can be done to bring loveliness into the lives of children who have to be educated in deprived areas; but those who are fortunate enough to have beauty on the doorstep should be allowed to enjoy it without shame.

I decided to take a quick peep at my old school; the school was evacuated during the war, never to return, and the buildings are now a training centre for nurses, but the sight of it brought back a host of memories. More sophisticated maidens would be learning more advanced techniques in our classrooms, cosmetics would decorate the dressing tables in the dormitories, where none were allowed, albeit a good many were concealed, in our day. I did not mind in the least that it was all so different; for me it was alive with girls in purple blazers and pleated purple gym-slips and I remembered that nearly all the days I spent there were happy days, and that I still owe a lot to those who made them so.

My next port of call was a far cry from school days – Brookwood Cemetery, where my maternal grandparents are buried. I am no grave-worshipper – my parents, by their own wish, have no graves and I am quite content for it to be so – but I had often meant to make just one visit to Brookwood. The grandparents died before my brother and I were born, but, probably because we never knew them, our childhood was made more interesting by the long and exciting tales we were told of them. To us they were always romantic, story-book figures and their last resting place seemed the nearest I could get to them.

I sped along through the well-loved places – Dorking, Shere, Abinger – with Box Hill and Ranmoor climbing steeply above them. Each one held memories of half-term picnics, of breezy bicycle rides and long days in the open air. From Guildford I found my way to Brookwood and when I saw the cemetery I realized why it is officially listed as a beauty spot worth visiting. It is basically an enormously extensive natural park. A more peaceful, contemplative place could hardly be imagined; all the grandest trees in Surrey seem to grow there. The graves lie beneath their shelter with wild flowers growing among them; it is beautifully kept, but absolutely natural and unspoiled.

I experienced quite a thrill when, with the help of a kindly sexton, I found our grave – it was as if I had discovered something I had been seeking for a very long time. I was impressed by the contemporary appearance of the gravestone – a plain pink marble slab, remarkably austere for Edwardian times. This is not surprising; both my grandparents were considered to be somewhat *avant garde* for their day. Grandfather's ancestors had been in the forefront over the abolition of slavery and he had very much followed in their footsteps. Only names and dates were inscribed on the gravestone – Henry Buxton Sheldrake, Harriet his wife,

Bernard and Harold their two sons – uncles whom I had never known.

I felt a quiet satisfaction; this little plot of ground held something of me – I lost the feeling of rootlessness that had hung over me since we finally sold the London house. Neither my mother nor any of her sisters had ever been able to explain why the grandparents had chosen to be buried at Brookwood; I should think myself that they were attracted by its peace and simplicity. I have no desire to return to that grave; it fulfilled what I asked of it. Another visit would be meaningless.

I drove up to Cobham through woods newly decked out in spring foliage. This I imagine is the so-called 'commuter belt' or even more currently the 'stockbroker belt', usually accompanied by a slight sneer. It is a mystery to me why a stockbroker should be a subject for derision any more than a stoker or a statesman or a stable-boy. The tolerant age still has its intolerances.

In Cobham I found the original home of my grandfather's Buxton cousins, built by Charles Roden Buxton, the Victorian Liberal statesman. From there I went on to Leatherhead, the Mecca of my pilgrimage. This was the home of great-grandparents a long, long way back. My grandmother's house, where my mother was born and where she lived until her marriage, which we knew when we were children, was demolished shortly before the last war. I strolled round what is now known as the Sun Mead Estate. Rows of happy homes stand on what was once the garden and the paddock; the well-kept gardens contain trees that my mother and her brothers and sisters used to climb. The children of the 1960s were climbing them with the same enthusiasm; their jeans and anoraks were more suitable for the task than the serge dresses, lace drawers and buttoned boots of my mother's generation.

The shopping colony known as Sun Mead Parade which stands, as it were, between the two entrance gates I found less attractive; it is blatantly brash and utilitarian – I suppose I had been hoping for something Olde Worlde. However, this disappointment was liquidated by the discovery that the famous old Rising Sun Inn, which had stood next door to Sun Mead, was no longer a pub (it had been one for six centuries) but an attractive restaurant. I installed myself in an ingle nook and consumed an enormous tea, which, I told myself, was just the kind of tea my grandmother would have provided had she been my hostess: homemade bread and scones with jam and cream, dainty cucumber sandwiches and thick slices of farmhouse cake.

Because of my concentration on my journey, I had forgotten to have any lunch; I tucked into my tea with zest and as I ate I thought over the events of the day and the purpose of my pilgrimage. Since the last of the older generation had gone, and, with her, the family home, I had been very conscious of the fact that I was not only custodian of my share of the material family possessions but that I was also, in some indefinable way, a trustee of the spiritual treasures – the traditions and way of life that had been handed on from generation to generation. These things are a more subtle form of legacy than pianos and pictures; they change with the changing years, they can become obsolete. 'Time makes ancient good uncouth' and ideas and views faithfully held in my grandparents' time were already untenable when I was a child; this process has speeded up considerably in my lifetime. But certain values, even some traditions, are eternal, they can never be outdated – they are not the monopoly of any one nation nor generation, still less of any particular family, but they cannot be taken away from those who have them. They are traditions which a good democracy can treasure, as well as an aristocratic society – a democracy, that is, which exerts a civilizing influence on society, which cares greatly for the individual and expects most from those who have received most. Courtesy, good manners, respect for the rights and property of others whatever their creed or class; loyalty, lack of ostentation, a sense of fair play, above all a determination to do one's duty rather than to demand one's rights – all these were bound up in the spiritual heritage I had received. Vaguely I had always been aware of it and subscribed to it; now I felt acutely responsible to protect it and to live by it. Subconsciously, no doubt, this was why I had been so eager to make my pilgrimage and brush up my background; the picture came into focus, bright and clean-cut as I meditated in my ingle nook.

'You look as if you've enjoyed yourself,' remarked Ronald as I burst light-heartedly in on his reading of the evening paper.

'I should say I have – it was perfect.'

'No ghosts?'

'No ghosts – all living people and places and ideas. I'll tell you all about it.'

'Sounds as if it might be a lengthy process,' said Ronald apprehensively.

It was, but it was fun and he understood.

This year, 1964, was certainly a year of changes and of new beginnings. We were faced with the fact that with our numerous commitments in London we must find some kind of *pied-à-terre* to take the place of my home. We toyed with the idea of a flat, but, since we wanted to be in the centre, the rent of even the most minute bed-sitter was prohibitive. I had been a member of the English-Speaking Union in Charles Street for some time; it is a mixed club so in the end Ronald decided to join this in addition to his own club. Thereafter the ESU, as it is affectionately known all over the world, became our London abode. It has become much more than that – it is a real home for us; we always get a warm welcome whatever time we arrive day or night; our room is convenient for working in if we need to; as well as the restaurant there is a snackbar that serves continental breakfast and a good *Wiener Schnitzel* for lunch or dinner. There is a patio where on summer days meals, including breakfast, can be taken out of doors; there is a second larger one where teas are served. It is a comfortable place for entertaining guests and a great rendezvous for friends, especially other bishops and their wives. It could not be more conveniently placed for Ronald's meetings in Westminster or for my shopping sprees in Oxford Street; we soon knew that we had found the answer to our needs.

I still miss my home, and even now it seems strange not to get on the Piccadilly line in the evening, but I adore London and I revel in our brief sojourns in the centre. I like seeing the cavalry going by exercising their horses in the early hours of the morning; the clip-clop of hooves invariably causes me to leap out of bed and rush to the window; it is fun to see the great tower of Westminster Cathedral, and the Royal Standard flying over Buckingham Palace as I have my bath; on winter evenings I can watch twinkling lights transform the hideous London skyscrapers into sparkling prisms.

It has become possible for me to do so many things in London now: I can spend a day working in the Reading Room of the

British Museum; I can hunt for bargain antiques in the Portobello Road and Chelsea; I scarcely ever take a tube or bus, I can walk to almost anywhere I want to go and I regularly commute across the Green Park and St James's to meet Ronald in Westminster. I have been doing this long enough now to be able to look forward to the changing seasons and see London in its many aspects. There are the spring days when the parks are ablaze with daffodils and everyone walks with a brisk, cheerful step; and there is high summer when at midday every open space is a picnic place for office workers, and gay cotton frocks make a patchwork on the lawns. There is autumn when Big Ben and the Abbey are shrouded in mist and gales send clouds of coloured leaves scurrying down the Mall; and there is mid-winter when the birds hop hopefully on the ice-bound lakes and the great Christmas tree is raised in Trafalgar Square and Regent Street and Oxford Street hang their decorations high above the heads of the hordes of shoppers.

I love it all; I never tire of this recurring pageant; each successive season brings its own special thrill; following humbly in the footsteps of Henry James and Virginia Woolf I have become a proper street haunter.

Our London visits are short, at the most three or four nights; they are spaced out at fairly regular intervals during the year and for Ronald, of course, they just mean work in a different venue. When he is kept very late for House of Lords debates it is a great boon to have a London perch within ten minutes of the House. The change freshens us up and we return to our busy Leicester programme with renewed zest and, in spite of all that London means, especially to me, a definite sense that it is grand to be home again.

We looked forward to our summer holiday more than usual after the rather restless and changeable first half of the year. It was to be Zermatt, of course, but we decided to repeat the Canterbury experiment and spend our first weekend there before we took off from Lydd for Le Touquet.

Ever since we were married the pattern had been to spend a few days with my parents at the beginning of the holiday and a little time with Ronald's family at the end. This year of course there had to be a difference; Ronald's sister would be waiting for us as usual when we came back but there was no London home to receive us at the start. At Ronald's suggestion we went via Royston instead of London and paid a surprise visit to one of my oldest and closest friends. Nancy and I have known each other for over forty years; we learnt to climb together, indeed it was her father who organized our first mountaineering holiday. She was one of my bridesmaids and Ronald proposed the toast at her wedding, so our lives have always been inextricably mixed up. However long we may be separated we always start at our next meeting exactly where we left off; this occasion was no exception. Everyone was at home, Eric her husband, their sons Tony and Michael, now undergraduates, and Janet still at school. We crashed into the middle of their lunch and it did not matter at all; Nancy and I washed up and caught up on our news; Ronald and Eric made coffee; the young folk produced deck chairs in which to sit and sip it. When we said goodbye there had been a family beginning to the holiday after all.

We explored the Moselle Valley and the Vosges on our way across Europe; when we got to Zermatt fine weather awaited us.

The *Famille Biner* were especially delighted to see us this year; for them, as for us, much had happened since our last meeting. Our dear Mrs Biner, beloved by all her family as well as by the whole village, had died, four days before my aunt, at the great age of ninety-three. She had been a constant part of the Zermatt picture since I was at school and it seemed impossible to imagine the Biner chalet without her sitting peacefully knitting on the balcony. Then in the summer Marie-Thérèse, one of Bernard's nieces, had come to stay with us; we had left her in Leicester *au pair* with a friend of ours. We had to tell all the news and hand on the many messages 'Rèse' had given us. It was good to share our joys and sorrows together.

Towards the end of the holiday Bernard and I set off for a climb on our own. His health had deteriorated a lot, he only climbed with us now; big climbs were too much for him and, like most great performers, he preferred to retire at his zenith rather than to become a shadow of his former self. He was not in the least sad or disillusioned; he was perfectly content to run his climbers' hotel, giving help and advice whenever budding mountaineers sought it, and he was never happier than sitting on his balcony watching the Matterhorn and receiving the never-ending stream of friends who came to call on him.

It was not easy to coax him up to the heights; I think he came more for my sake than his own.

'You should be doing big mountains,' he said sorrowfully, 'and I can't take you on those any more'.

'I'd rather do a small one with you,' I replied firmly – and truthfully. I had not had a proper climb for two years simply because I could not bear to go with anyone else. Bernard had taught me to climb in my teens; I had never climbed with another guide and could not imagine myself doing so.

We sat on the summit of the Stockhorn, only 12,000 feet, but high enough to be among the snows and situated in the midst of all the great Zermatt peaks. There was no difficulty in the climb, we scarcely needed the rope; when we reached the top we sat in the blazing alpine sun and talked as we had always talked when a climb was completed.

'I'm glad you made me come,' said Bernard contentedly. 'It's grand to see all this just once more.'

'You mustn't say that,' I spoke anxiously. 'We must come again another year – I don't mind about it being small and easy.'

'It gives us all we want,' he said contemplatively. 'Everything that the great peaks have always given us. But you must go on climbing for many years yet, the mountains still have a lot to offer you.'

I did not answer that one – it needed thinking out. We talked for a long time; about our early climbs, the successes and failures; about moments of sublime inspiration and those of anxiety and frozen fear. We spoke of his parents and mine and of Ronald's work, in which Bernard had always taken such a special interest. Sitting there on the Stockhorn we turned the pages of a golden book that recorded a lifetime of high adventure.

'We must go,' Bernard announced. 'Let's look at it all again before we put the rope on.'

Slowly our eyes travelled from peak to peak, each one told its own story for us. Bernard knotted the rope.

'Come on,' he called quickly, 'lead down, you can cut steps if we need them'.

We closed the book; it would be safely locked in the archives of our lives; but I knew we should never open it again together.

In October, we went to Ireland for three days to see our friend

Netta established in the home in which she was to live for the first time by herself. It is a nice little Georgian house which makes a perfect décor for all the lovely things she and Dick had collected over the years. She only moved in the day we arrived, so for a short time she did not have to be alone. Ronald christened the house and we had a series of house-warming parties. When we had to leave, Netta told us she already felt as if she had been living there for years. We admired her cheerful courage and felt that one more difficult passage had been successfully negotiated.

Inevitably this year was rather dominated by domestic matters for us, but in spite of this, or perhaps even because of it, the less personal and more spectacular happenings stand out in sharp relief.

There was a wonderful and never-to-be-forgotten occasion when Sir Malcolm Sargent came to Leicester to conduct the Symphony Orchestra in the De Montfort Hall. By a miracle we had a free evening – we can scarcely ever enjoy the luxury of a concert – and we went along to help welcome Sir Malcolm back to the scene of his early triumphs. Everyone in Leicester is proud of the fact that our city and county was the foundation stone of that magnificent musical career.

It was a great concert and for us who, over the years ever since our schooldays, had watched Sir Malcolm conduct in London, it was a particular pleasure to see him on his home ground. It came to a dramatic conclusion with a polished performance of 'The Planets' and we all sprang to our feet in spontaneous applause as the last misty, muted echoes died away. It was as if we had been drenched by a great fountain of light and loveliness.

The concert was followed by a gay supper party at which the *maestro* was, as always, the life and soul of the whole affair. He had a word for everyone and remembered immediately all those he had known in earlier years. When it was our turn to be introduced he recalled at once that Ronald had written to him when he was recuperating from TB in Switzerland; and my evening was made when he told me he had read my book and actually quoted bits from it. I went home intoxicated with joy; I had hero-worshipped Sir Malcolm ever since I was at school; I had had to wait a long time for our first meeting, but when it came it was all that could be desired.

In the summer Ronald entertained at Ripon Hall, Oxford a large group of German theologians; it was part of his job as chairman of the Lutheran and Reformed Committee of the Church of England Foreign Relations Council. Some of the theologians brought their wives with them, so I was roped in as hostess. Fortunately for me, the wives were not theologically-minded, so while our erudite husbands conferred I showed them round Oxford and took them to Blenheim Palace. This was a job after my own heart; I had spent many childhood holidays in Oxford with our paternal grandparents I had breathed in the magic of it as I grew up; it had become part of me; I enjoyed trying to make it live for my Continental guests. These Lutheran occasions are much welcomed by Ronald and me for private as well as public reasons; we get a chance to work up our German, which we are too lazy to do unless there is a definite purpose involved.

Zermatt Saga, my second book, was published during the autumn. The writing of it had been a labour of love and I minded most that it should please my Zermatt friends and my climbing companions. Fortunately it achieved these objects early in its career and I was satisfied with the notices it was given by reviewers. The most severe described me as 'a last romantic' but I rather liked that – in any case it is certainly true.

When November came, and our regular visits to London during the winter had been booked in the diary, I decided to take full advantage of the fact that, since we should now be staying in the centre, there would be a few free evenings to plan as we wished. I took myself off to Lillywhites to get enrolled in the Dry Ski School. Before the war I had had my first ski lessons in this way; they were invaluable – so much so that when we were in Durham I was taken on as an instructor in the Newcastle Ski School! I had longed to start again but for years it had been impossible; now there was a renewed chance. The likelihood of my being able to take a winter sports holiday was remote, but at least it would be good exercise and provide a taste of the world I love.

At Lillywhites I met Anni Maurer, a brilliant skier from Davos who runs the Dry Ski School from November until the end of February. One books for a course of six classes. I explained my unusual situation to Anni; I would have to fit the classes in at odd times when we were in London and the chances of my getting out to the Alps in that, or any other, winter were dim indeed. Anni understood at once; I started the course – it was first class and kept me marvellously fit. Having tasted these delights I became an addict; every year in November I book up with Anni and however dark and dreary the winter may be, however tightly packed our programme of work, I know that every few weeks I have got an hour of unalloyed bliss in store for me.

Our family Christmas festivities took on an entirely new look this year. Previously we had always spent Christmas Day at my home – although it had been only Christmas night since we came to Leicester – and Boxing Day with Ronald's family. For this particular Christmas I wanted to be really busy, without too much time to look back over the years.

'Could everyone come here,' I suggested to Ronald. 'We've plenty of room and it would make a lovely family party.'

'I'd love it,' he replied, 'if you're sure it's not going to be too much for you'.

'It's just what I'd like,' and I guessed he knew why.

It could not have worked better. Ronald's sister and two aunts came and also my friend Sylvia – to be a bit of 'family' for me. Every bed was occupied, every seat at the dining table was filled. There was lots to do; I was surprisingly happy; it was a different kind of happiness from other years but a deep one nonetheless.

For many years Bernard had telephoned to us on Christmas night; he made no exception this year and had a multitude of nice things to say about *Zermatt Saga*. He gave us all the Zermatt news and told us that he himself was much better since the summer. This was good – I had visions of more climbs after all. With his usual affectionate chuckle Bernard wished us 'Goodbye and God Bless'. It proved to be his final farewell.

The experiment of a family Christmas party in Leicester proved such a success that the arrangement has become permanent. As the years have passed the number of aunts, sadly, has been reduced to one. The vacant chair at the table has now three times been filled by our friend Arthur Eccles who looks after our garden and lives alone. He has previously been a sailor and Christmas dinner would not now be Christmas dinner without his fund of salty, seafaring stories.

After Christmas we keep up tradition with a few days in

Ronald's home where his sister dispenses hospitality as she has done for years. We sing the songs and play the games in which, in years gone by when we were a larger party, we all took such a delight – perhaps those who are gone still rejoice with us, who knows?

CHAPTER V

Depths and Heights

T HIS chapter contains rather a high proportion of deaths and funerals, but this is all part of life, especially when one has reached middle age. Everybody has to make their own adjustments to each new bereavement. Mine have certainly been no better than average, but they are my reactions and hence find their place in this narrative.

On the evening of Saturday, January 9, 1965, the BBC reported the death of Viscount Monckton of Brenchley; the announcement put out one of the brightest stars in my small personal firmament. It was not unexpected; his health had been poor for a long time. Since the New Year the regular bulletins had been increasingly serious; only I, with my unfailing optimism, had dared to hope that this might not yet be the end. Ever since 1940 Walter Monckton had been a very special person to me – someone who, in the course of only eighteen months, had made a decisive impact on my life. I am glad to have this chance of laying my own little wreath in his memory.

On that dismal day in June 1940 when France asked for an armistice I was given my first assignment as a new recruit in the Transport Corps – to drive Sir Walter Monckton, as he then was, from the Ministry of Information to 10 Downing Street. From then until October 1941 I drove him regularly; after that date we met less than half a dozen times – but each occasion was memorable.

When I had recovered from the first sadness of the short BBC announcement, and had read the obituary notices in the papers I dug out all my old log books which I have carefully preserved among my wartime treasures. As I turned the pages I was back again in those amazing, desperate days; for me the entries in the books filled in some inevitable gaps in the excellent obituary notices of Walter Monckton.

That first trip to Downing Street marked a turning point in my attitude to the war. I was worried and quite a bit frightened; the world as I knew it seemed to be falling about my ears; I had never anticipated the daily catastrophies that occurred. The newspaper placards could hardly have been more devastating as we drove down Whitehall; Sir Walter – as he remained to me in spite of his later elevation – appeared singularly unperturbed. He laughed and chatted and wanted to know all about me. I plucked up courage and daringly put a timid question.

'What do you think about it all, sir?'

'It's just about as bad as it can be now, isn't it?' came the instant reply. 'We'll have a lot to go through – we shall have to see buildings flat all over London. But don't worry – it will be all right in the end.'

It was all that needed to be said to me; my misgivings were replaced by a determination to do my tiny bit towards the victory that would certainly be ours. With the mercurial optimism of youth I looked ahead and desired above all else, if I survived, to be driving to Downing Street on the day when we would win – as it happened I was! Driving Sir Walter was always interesting; he seemed to know everyone and our trips were often entertaining occasions. At least once a week he would stride up to the car accompanied by some exciting personage. All came alike to him whether they were generals, admirals, MPs, or ambassadors. He always took the trouble to introduce his driver. He once came almost running to the car, thrust his head inside and whispered ecstatically, 'We're taking Stafford Cripps to Downing Street – you'll love him'.

Secretly I did not think this at all likely to be the case and when Sir Walter announced, 'You can have him next to you', and popped into the back of the car himself I was far from intrigued.

However, it was my job and I did my best to make my austere companion comfortable. I never confessed to my feelings – I could not bear to disappoint Sir Walter, who obviously thought the world of him. Actually since then, having met Lady Cripps and her son John, I know that my early impressions were not entirely correct.

But it was when I was driving Sir Walter alone, about London or to further destinations, that I came to know him really well and learned so much from him. We had many things in common; a fellow feeling for Kent, for cricket, for the Harrow songs, for Oxford and, alas, hay fever. However bad the news, however nerve-wracking the continual air-raid warnings and the hit-and-miss daylight raiders, we always managed to calm our ruffled feelings with conversations on these matters.

He was very thrilled at the prospect of becoming a grandfather and achieved this happy state at the height of the Blitz in 1940; for days he could talk of little else. He adored his daughter Valerie and some of my happiest memories are of driving them to have lunch together when she came up to see him.

Walter Monckton was one of the kindest men I ever met; he would take immense trouble to make life happy for those around him. I learned later that travel and holidays were anathema to him; he successfully concealed this from me; I rambled happily on, expatiating on my love of climbing and skiing and my nostalgia for Switzerland and he somehow managed to make me think that he shared my feelings. Riding of course was very dear to his heart; he was a brilliant and daring rider to hounds. I merely hacked, and only jumped if I had to, but when he heard that I was being given a day's leave which I proposed to spend cantering over Walton Heath with a school friend, his enthusiasm was so great that he nearly offered to come too.

He had infinite sympathy with those who had got themselves in a mess. I drove him one day to Holloway Prison to visit a well-known woman who was held there because of her fascist activities. He had no doubts about the justice of the situation but he nevertheless hated the fact that she had to be there. When we started the journey I regarded this lady as a deep-dyed criminal but when the trip was over even I felt a curious sympathy for her. On another occasion we went to a famous hotel to arrange the arrest of the assistant manager who had been discovered to be an exceedingly active fifth columnist.

'I'm terribly sorry for the poor chap,' said Sir Walter as we drove back to the Ministry of Information, 'he took it very well really'.

I, who had half-expected to see this gentleman escorted to my car in handcuffs, could hardly believe that anyone guilty of such enormities could be so regarded.

Walter Monckton had immense confidence in the integrity of his staff – even that of his young driver – his theory being that unless you had implicit trust in anyone it was better not to trust at all. Consequently we were all, when occasion arose, in possession of top-level secrets. For the first few months I felt almost weighed down by this responsibility; I was never tempted to divulge anything to anybody but the mere fact that I knew some of these things worried me more than it excited me. Gradually I began to carry it all more easily; in the process I learnt a lot that has stood me in very good stead as the course of my own life has unfolded.

His closest friends say that Walter Monckton was highly strung and nervy; this was a facet of his personality of which I only once had a glimpse. In June 1941 I was waiting for him outside the Dominions Office; he was much later than I had expected; when he eventually appeared he looked thoroughly haggard; all his usual buoyancy had deserted him. He sat in the car drumming his fingers on his knees and gave me a few bare facts. I knew there was nothing I could say that would help; my only contribution was to drive back to the Ministry as slowly as possible to give him time to recover his composure. For days I worried over that situation but at the back of my mind I had a feeling that he would somehow find a solution. I have always imagined that this must have been the case, for no announcement ever appeared in the press or on the radio and, in fact, the calamitous event did not occur.

One of the more unusual sidelines of my job as driver was to be presented with the front door key of the Moncktons' house in Cadogan Place and to be sent off to find and bring back papers and brief cases. This once more filled me with trepidation as to whom I should meet and how I should explain my presence but nothing ever went wrong and I began to enjoy the confidence placed in me.

If Walter Monckton's staff were determined never to let him down, I think he was equally anxious to support them. Two occasions stand out in my mind when I was the driver on duty for him. It was a boiling hot day and I had been grilling outside the War Cabinet for what seemed hours. I was streaming with hay fever, my eyes and nose and ears were itching. At last I could stand it no longer; I crept into the shade in the back of the car, loosened my

tie and my belt and was foolish enough to settle down for a snooze.
I was roused by a hearty laugh and found Sir Walter outside en-
gaging a much-bemedalled general in hilarious conversation.
Horrified I slithered into the front seat, trying to smarten myself
up as I started the engine.

'So sorry sir . . .' I began as we drove off.

'Don't worry,' came the soothing reply, 'you can't tell me anything about hay fever'.

The second occasion could have been even more disastrous had
it not been for Walter Monckton's silent support. We humble
drivers never aspired to drive the Minister – he was the only person in the whole outfit who was allowed an official chauffeur
driven car. We were great buddies with the chauffeur but that was
the nearest we got to the All Highest.

Mr Duff Cooper (later Lord Norwich) was leaving the Ministry
of Information and was being replaced by Brendan Bracken; the
car and the chauffeur were automatically bequeathed to Brendan
Bracken but for some reason, unknown to us, the transfer did not
take place on the day expected. There was an emergency call for a
driver to appear at the Savoy Hotel and bring the new Minister
and Sir Walter Monckton to the Ministry. The lot fell on me and
off I sped, rather pleased. I bowed Brendan Bracken into the back
of my little Ford and Sir Walter rode in the passenger seat. Halfway up Kingsway the car started to pull to the right and an
ominous bumping began. I glanced at Sir Walter and he glanced
at me. I knew I dare not stop; tugging furiously to keep the car on
the left and slowing down to alleviate the bumps I toiled miserably
on.

'Awful what these bomb craters have done to the roads,' observed Sir Walter smoothly, 'some of them ought to be closed to
traffic'.

'Yes, indeed,' purred the Minister deep in his papers.

Worn to a shred with anxiety I somehow bounced the equipage
through the gates of the Ministry and lurched to a standstill at the
door. Sir Walter jumped out, glanced quickly at the offside wheel,
gave me an enormous wink, and whisked the Minister within
before he could look round. I surveyed the ribbons of my ruined
tyre – just to think that the one and only time I drove the Minister
I had to have a puncture!

In the autumn of 1941 we knew that Walter Monckton was resigning as Director-General of the Ministry of Information to undertake a mission to Russia. Everyone was sad about this and no one more so than his driver – I felt I was losing a guide, philosopher and friend.

He was to take off for Russia on October 6th; on his last day with us – Friday, October 3rd – I was asked to go to Chesham Place to help Lady Monckton finish the packing and bring the cases to the MOI. I was thrilled to be the one to be given the last job and I was secretly glad for another reason. There had not been wanting those in more exalted positions than mine to drop dark hints that all was not well between Sir Walter and his wife and that he had a pretty wide circle of girl friends. I stoutly refused to believe such suggestions – my idols never have feet of clay – and when I reached the flat in Chesham Place and found Lady Monckton deeply involved in the packing, any doubts I might have had were dispelled for the moment. She triumphantly held up a sheepskin coat for my inspection; such things were almost unobtainable at that time but she had captured the last one in Harrods. We checked the lists, locked the cases and stowed them away in the car. How strange are the last mutual carings of those who have once loved, but whom time is slowly separating! When I handed the cases over to Sir Walter we said goodbye – a happy and formative chapter in my life had come to an end.

I did not see Walter Monckton again until long after the war was over. His divorce had taken place meanwhile, reminding me that those whom I had refused to believe were, after all, right. But I never lost my sense of gratitude to him nor my admiration for him and when we heard he was coming to Leicester in his capacity as chairman of the Midland Bank I was full of happy anticipation. Needless to say, the luncheon proved to be a men only affair to which Ronald was invited and not me. However, after a certain amount of correspondence, Walter Monckton and Ronald arranged that I should be on parade at some time after lunch.

The distinguished guest, according to Ronald, was in tremendous form and regaled his audience with a highly coloured account of his adventures with me in the Blitz before going on to the important business of the occasion. A telephone call from Ronald telling me to come down to the new Leicester Temperance Headquarters sent me flying off in the car with no regard to the speed limit and I arrived exactly at the time given me. The passage of time seemed to have made no difference at all to Walter Monckton – we might have been setting out from the MOI to Whitehall as we had done all those years before. He was full of stories of Valerie and her children and delighted that his son Gilbert was now married, which meant more grandchildren. I was so caught up with the past that I apparently continued to say 'Yes sir,' 'No sir,' as if I were still in uniform, to the huge delight of all the men present – mercifully I was quite unconscious of what I was doing.

A year or two later we all met again in the dining room of the House of Lords and Walter Monckton still seemed to have all his verve and *joie de vivre*. But it was the last time we saw him so. Only a year later, once more at the House of Lords, we met again by chance and his appearance shocked us both. For a long time I wished I had not seen him so terribly changed. After his death it no longer worried me – when he was gone it was easier to remember him as I had always known him.

We were grieved that we could not go to the memorial service in Southwark Cathedral but it was some consolation to learn that it was our friend Mervyn Stockwood who was to give the address – it made a small, tenuous link – and every year when his daughter Valerie puts her touching memorial notice to her father in *The Times* I think afresh for a few moments of a great man, a real friend, who taught me much for which I shall always be thankful.

The printers' ink paying tribute to Walter Monckton was hardly dry in the newspapers when disturbing bulletins began to appear about the health of Sir Winston Churchill. It took the grand old man a long time to die, but it gave the country a breathing space to adjust itself to what had long been inevitable – and yet seemed somehow impossible. To the Second War generation like myself he was almost indestructible; we could not imagine the country without him.

When arrangements were made for the funeral at St Paul's, members of the House of Lords were invited to apply for tickets; Ronald sent in his name and was rewarded with two magnificent seats under the Dome. We could hardly believe it; this was to be a great national occasion.

As always seems to happen to me when anything of outstanding importance is taking place, I found myself without a suitable hat. Black does not suit me and I invariably substitute navy blue or grey; nevertheless I was convinced that Sir Winston Churchill merited a black hat and on the day before the funeral I was scouring the West End for the requisite headgear. I succeeded in my quest and in the end my 'funeral hat' was voted a success.

It was a day to remember; as I walked with Ronald up the steps of St Paul's I was aware that I was taking part in an historic event. Inside the great cathedral we could forget the grey January day; there was light and colour and a sense of subdued pageantry. We found our seats; mine was next to Lord Boothby who kept up a most interesting commentary for the whole two hours we had to wait. It appeared that he and Sir Winston had compiled this service, down to the last detail, twelve years before. It simply could not have been true of anyone else but it was entirely in character with Sir Winston.

I glanced round the vast crowd gathered in the cathedral; the whole world was represented there; heads of state and Royal representatives marched slowly up the nave in solemn procession. I thought about Sir Winston and his tremendous sense of drama and history; I hoped so much that he could see it all and was enjoying it; nor could I suppress a wicked thought that his comments would be worth hearing! I turned the pages of my purple and white 'Order of Ceremonial'; it was 9.45 am, the procession was about to start from Westminster Hall; Sir Winston Churchill was leaving Westminster forever. My brochure told me 'The clock in the North Tower of the Palace of Westminster will strike 9.45 o'clock and will thereafter remain silent for the rest of the day'. Sir Winston would have loved that. Even Big Ben was joining in the national tribute.

Time went by; Lord Boothby announced that he was bored beyond belief with waiting so long. Why had we all had to come so early? He broke off in the middle of this diatribe to pass a few pungent comments on an assortment of politicians passing by en route to their appointed places.

I was far from bored; every minute was fraught with interest to me. A small procession of clergy moved from the south transept into the choir; among them I was delighted to notice Archbishop Lord Fisher. The Archbishop of Canterbury with the Bishop of

London went silently to the west door and returned escorting the Lord Chancellor; a little later the Dean and Chapter took the Lord Mayor and the Sheriffs to their places. And all the time there sounded in the background the muffled report of the minute guns being fired from the Tower of London as the great funeral procession wound its way through the heart of the capital.

It was a quarter to eleven; we all rose; quietly and quite unobtrusively the Queen's procession came up the nave. Her Majesty with the Duke of Edinburgh, the Prince of Wales with the Queen Mother, followed by every adult member of the Royal Family; the sovereign's tribute to the man who had saved the country in her father's reign.

And at last the great moment; to solemn, martial music the heavy coffin was borne up the nave by a bearer party from the Guards. Ahead of it walked the pall bearers, perhaps the most moving sight in the whole procession. They were all wartime comrades of Sir Winston: Sir Robert Menzies; the Earl of Avon, terribly thin and white; Earl Attlee, so old and frail, but faithful to the end; Lord Mountbatten erect and magnificent; these were only some, but they impressed me greatly as they passed. Behind the courageous figure of Lady Churchill and her son and daughters came the little group of grandchildren, gay in bright coats and white socks; a hopeful contrast to the sombre black of the older mourners.

The service lasted only half an hour; it was magnificent and expressed Sir Winston so perfectly. It was impossible to be sad. As the great congregation sang their hearts out in 'Mine Eyes have Seen the Glory of the Coming of the Lord' one was aware of a kind of rightness which governed the whole situation. Sir Winston's time had come; the nation was ready to bid its grand farewell.

As we left St Paul's we saw Sir Robert Menzies hurrying away to make his broadcast tribute to his old friend; as we parked the car in Pall Mall in preparation for lunch the roar of the RAF Fly Past told us that the river procession was on its way to Waterloo.

No one who was present in St Paul's that day can ever forget the occasion; it was a reminder of the past and an inspiration for the future.

The next day, like many other cities all over the country; we had our smaller memorial service in our own cathedral. It was a domestic occasion; our own special remembrance that it was Sir Winston Churchill who saved the homes of Britain from the hand of the invader. We had come home from St Paul's, as Ronald said in his sermon, 'to the first snowdrops in the garden, and to the scent of hyacinths in the house' – and we owed our homes to Winston.

Life moves on apace; two days after these stirring events Ronald and I set off for a conference in Holland. It was a meeting of Continental Protestant theologians and it was held at Driebergen near Utrecht. It was the beginning of February and bitter winds were sweeping across Holland; our friend Anna Roelfsema, a famous Dutch climber who shares our passion for Zermatt, met us at The Hook and took us home to Voorburg to give us a wonderful hot breakfast before we went on to Driebergen. Ronald stayed at a rather fine Conference House with the rest of the theologians; Anna had booked me in at a little hotel nearby. This gave me plenty of freedom and nearly every day I commuted the short distance to her home. From here I was able to explore The Hague and enjoy the wintry Dutch countryside; altogether I got a much more complete picture of Holland than we get in the summer when we skim swiftly across in the car on our way to and from the German *Autobahn*. I enjoyed getting to know Ronald's band of theologians, some of whom I had met before. On our last night Professor Van Unnik took us to his home in Utrecht and gave us a delightful Dutch evening before putting us on the Boat Train for The Hook. The Hook-Harwich crossing I usually find pretty trying in the summer; suffice to say that it was a thousand times worse in the winter, and the consequences were disastrous. But in spite of such an ending it was a worthwhile trip and neither of us will ever forget the impact the Churchill funeral had made on the Dutch. Sir Winston had a tremendous reputation in Holland of course; everyone we met had watched the entire television programme – their comments made us very proud.

Early in April we had a letter from Zermatt giving us excellent news of Bernard. He was active and in good health and spent hours every day in the sunshine on the balcony of the Bahnhof Hotel. Pauly told us too that Bernard had been immensely impressed by the Churchill funeral which he had seen on the television. All this was encouraging; a small climb in August seemed to be at least a possibility.

Two days later, on Friday, April 9th, I turned into the drive with a loaded shopping basket in one hand and Martin on his lead in the other. I caught sight of Ronald on top of the steps; he came down without speaking and took the shopping basket from me. As I looked at him I was sure something was wrong.

'Any news?' I asked trying to sound as casual as possible.

'Yes, there is – bad news, I'm afraid.'

'Who is it?'

'Bernard – he died this morning; Marie Thérèse and Pauly rang up half an hour ago.'

We paused in the hall and looked silently at the picture of Bernard that hangs there – we took it some years before on a glacier as we set out on the third and last day of a long expedition. It was a particularly successful photograph and had been shown in an exhibition.

We sat in the soft spring sunshine and Ronald told me what little news there was to tell. Bernard was only ill for a few hours and suffered very little. His doctor, a faithful friend since university days, had done all he could but the heart could not stand the strain; the end came swiftly and peacefully. Pauly had wanted us to know as soon as she felt equal to telling us. Ronald had promised we would contact them again in the evening.

It was impossible to imagine Zermatt without Bernard; he had always been there; he was not only a great guide and a beloved friend, in some indefinable way he was Zermatt, or at least its *genius loci*. I felt so bereft myself that I could hardly bear to think how great must be Pauly's sense of loss. For many years she and Bernard had been almost inseparable: they had embarked together on the great venture of establishing their Hotel Bahnhof as a climbers' hotel; together they had made an unqualified success of the project. But Pauly had been very much the younger sister – she leaned heavily on Bernard for all the major decisions. Now she would have to face her own future, and the future of the hotel, alone. Mercifully she had devoted sisters with husbands and children who would all help; we too, who were some of her closest friends, would have to do all we could to support her. The picture flashed through my mind so quickly; by Bernard's death the whole Zermatt scene had taken on a new dimension. It was no longer just a second home and a glorious mountain playground teeming with friends; it was all those still but now it was somewhere where we had responsibilities and our help might be needed.

It seemed strange that Bernard should die in the year that was to bring the great celebrations of the centenary of the first ascent of the Matterhorn. I knew he had been asked to be president of the committee which was to plan the programme; he had declined gently but firmly; did he know in his heart that the sands were running out, that his time would come before the great day arrived? My mind was full of these and many other thoughts as I went about my duties that day, trying to accustom myself to the fact that in this life I should never see Bernard again. I felt as if I had lost a dearly-loved elder brother; there was going to be another big gap in my life – and already there were a good many that could never be filled. Bernard and I had been very much *en rapport* since he first taught me to climb as a schoolgirl; there is often a special spiritual affinity and intimacy about friendships formed in the mountains. Perhaps it was this that was helping to keep me calmer than I should have expected to be. I seemed tremendously aware of Bernard's presence on the day of his death and during the sad and anxious days that followed.

We had many matters to think out. There was the question of the funeral – ought we to be there? Would Pauly be needing us specially just then? One glance at the diary told us that for Ronald it was utterly out of the question and for me almost as impossible. For a moment I felt rebellious: why did we have to have so many commitments, so many people depending on us, that it was impossible to break away even for an occasion as poignant as this.

Ronald realized how I was feeling.

'You are absolutely free to go if you really feel you must,' he said understandingly. 'I'll get you out of all your engagements if we decide it is best for you to go.'

That helped a lot; knowing I was free made it possible to think rationally. We studied timetables of trains and planes; we worked out every combination of travel arrangements. But with the best will in the world it would only be possible for me to arrive twenty minutes before the funeral and leave again immediately after.

I reflected on some of the advice Bernard had given me at other troublesome times, when we sat chatting on the summit of the Riffelhorn soon after Ronald became a bishop. I was expatiating on the overwhelming nature of the task that had fallen upon me and how the mountains seemed the only escape left to me.

'They are not an escape,' Bernard had said very firmly, 'they are the means by which you get the strength to do the job. You'll be all right – you've never failed on a mountain yet.'

How right he had been; since then I had always tried to put the job first and that was how it would have to be now – I could almost hear him saying so.

Having made our decision, it at once became easier to plan and to make the best arrangements we could to show our love for Bernard on this last sad occasion. There was also time to write to those climbing friends who would probably not have heard of his death; we received many grateful letters in reply. We put a brief announcement in *The Times* and Antony Rawlinson, Secretary of the Alpine Club, wrote a sensitive and satisfying obituary paragraph.

The funeral of a great guide is always a momentous, in fact a magnificent, occasion in Zermatt. Bernard's funeral was no exception, in fact the people of the village said there had been nothing like it in living memory. Pauly and Marie Thérèse sent us wonderful letters describing every detail. Anna Roelfsema was able to be present and wrote as soon as she got back to Holland. The English chaplain in residence at the time was thoughtful enough to write and to telephone to us – we felt very near to them all.

The funeral took place on a lovely spring day; climbers and skiers of all nationalities journeyed to Zermatt from Germany, France, Holland, Italy and Austria; men famous in the public life of Switzerland came from Zürich, Berne and Geneva up the steep mountain valley to pay their tribute. Guides from Chamonix, the Val Tournanche, Macugnaga and Breuil walked in the procession; six Zermatt guides carried Bernard to his grave in the village churchyard at the foot of his beloved Matterhorn. Flowers were massed around the grave, but only two arrangements placed on the coffin – one was Pauly's, the other was ours. We were touched and grateful that it was so: Bernard always loved flowers and we were glad that through something so lovely and so simple we could be near to him at the end. The funeral orations were given by two well-known Swiss, both close friends of Bernard's and through it all, as we were told by letter and by telephone, Pauly behaved with the greatest dignity and courage.

All this we heard later of course; on the day itself our thoughts were continually in Zermatt and again and again as I tried to concentrate on household chores I found Horatio's farewell to Hamlet running through my mind:

> 'Goodnight sweet prince;
> And flights of angels sing thee to thy rest.'

Antony Rawlinson wrote the obituary for the *Alpine Journal*; I was proud and pleased to be asked to do those for the *Ski Club Year Book* and the *Ladies' Alpine Club Journal*.

Only a week after these sad and memorable happenings we were due to leave for Palestine; leading a party of forty from the diocese. We telephoned Pauly to tell her where we should be and were much encouraged to find her contented and composed and ready to leave in a few weeks with her sisters for a pilgrimage to Lourdes. We set out for our trip feeling much happier than we had expected to and Ronald was able to write to Pauly from Jerusalem to tell her that he had said a prayer for Bernard as he knelt by the Holy Sepulchre.

Heraclitus, Ronald tells me, says that one can never jump into the same stream twice. There can never be a second 'first visit' to Palestine – the wonder of the first view of Jerusalem, Bethlehem and the Sea of Galilee can never quite be repeated. But something almost as rich in content takes its place. For us, to take another large group of our diocesan family for their own first experience of the Holy Land and to be able to make some small contribution ourselves was a joy and a privilege – we relived our own 'first times' in a new way when they saw the walls of Jerusalem, when they followed the Via Dolorosa and knelt in the crypt of the Church of the Nativity in Bethlehem. Once again we sang parts of 'Once in Royal David's City' in the cave of the Holy Family in Nazareth and again we looked down on the cool still waters of Galilee with the dark Syrian hills and the snows of Hermon rising beyond.

There were new experiences for us too. We visited a Bedouin Camp where the families lived in tents made of goatskin and rich Persian carpets were spread inside. We saw the Druse, those strange heretical Moslems with a secret religion, all of whom wear white head scarves. We had a picnic lunch on the shore at the honeymoon city of Naharia and bathed in the Mediterranean. We went to Acre, that superb Crusader stronghold of Richard Coeur de Lion. The blue sea laps the mighty ruined walls; there is a great mosque and a bazaar where trading takes place in a rather more cultivated atmosphere than that of Jerusalem or Nazareth. And up in the hill country above Galilee we found Safad, the original 'city set on a hill'. Mimosa, golden broom and delicious perfumes abound there; from the main street there is a dramatic view of the valleys below and as night comes on, distant little clusters of lights spring up round the shores of the Sea of Galilee.

One day we went to Hebron; nowhere have I experienced such an atmosphere of age and isolation from the contemporary scene. The streets are dark and dirty and sinister; there are potters working at their wheels; glass-makers crouch by their furnaces; blind peasants weave and spin, and over it all broods the great mosque where Abraham and his family lie buried in their gigantic tomb.

The highlight of the pilgrimage for us was undoubtedly the trip to Petra – the 'rose-red city half as old as time'. Once it was the capital of the Kingdom of Edom; then for hundreds of years it disappeared. Since its rediscovery by the Swiss historian and explorer, J. L. Burckhardt, in the early nineteenth century, the wheel has come full circle and the fame of Petra has spread throughout the world.

We left Jerusalem long before sunrise. In high-powered American cars driven by Arabs in their *keffiyeh* we sped on our way to Jericho and Amman. We turned to the right on to the great Desert Highway that leads to Aqaba; our speed increased to some phenomenal rate and as we went we saw coming across the desert a caravan that might have come straight out of the Old Testament. There were camels with the women riding in the cages between their humps; there were donkeys, dogs and black goats and a great procession of men in long white robes. They were trekking slowly from one water supply to the next. As the roar of the engine of our streamlined Dodge reverberated about me, I wondered secretly which of us had chosen the better part.

Presently we left our great Desert Highway, stretching away down to the Gulf of Aqaba; by a rocky road we came down from the high plateau on which we had been travelling to a kind of rustic rendezvous on which hordes of Bedouin tribesmen, accompanied by prancing Arab steeds, immediately converged. There were few introductions and no choice of horse: one suddenly found oneself mounted. Most of the horses had seen better days but they had lost none of their Arab vivacity; bridles were of the flimsiest design and the Bedouin who accompanied each rider brandished a flashing, scimitar-shaped knife.

In single file we set off down the dark passage until we came to the Sik, a narrow cleft in the rock through which horse and rider could only just squeeze – our swarthy attendants had to fall in behind. After about half an hour we came face to face with the rosy façade of a temple carved in the living rock; it was so sudden and unexpected that it seemed as if someone must have suddenly opened a glorious picture book in front of us. We spent several hours exploring the treasury, and the theatre and the museum; we climbed to the tops of the rocks and looked down on the city of which not a stone has been built – everything is carved from the rock.

After lunch our horses were brought again and we rode in ordered and stately procession on a long Roman pavement. Once through the Sik things became slightly less stately; our steeds decided to make for home with all possible speed and not a few of us returned cantering, some even at a full gallop – in most cases quite involuntarily.

It was a marvellous experience; we shall never forget the journey to Petra with its impressive peep into the farthest recesses of antiquity.

As we flew home from the Holy Land we were more than ever in love with it – it had taken such a hold on us that we knew even then that somehow, sometime, we should have to go back again; the members of our diocesan party, without exception, were equally captivated.

Pleasant surprises awaited both of us on our return. Ronald's commentary on the Epistles of St James and St John was published; although he has written a large number of books this was the first he had done for the Cambridge University Press and thus a special significance was attached to it. At the same time the foreign rights of my book *Zermatt Saga* had been sold to a German publishing house in Munich and the German copies would soon appear. I had been so happy that the English version of *Zermatt Saga* had been published in time for Bernard to read it; now I should be able to give the Biner family a copy in their own language to keep in their archives. When the German translation appeared, it was beautifully produced; a few illustrations were altered and there was an excellent photo of Bernard as a young guide in the days when I first knew him.

In June of this year we attended the ceremonies held in Westminster Hall to mark the 700th anniversary of Parliament. Historic events of this kind usually appeal to us but we felt it specially incumbent upon us to be present on this occasion since it was Simon de Montfort, Earl of Leicester, still venerated in our city, who was responsible for widening the representation of Parliament and who caused the King, Henry III, to summon Parliament for that purpose. A public ceremony to mark the conclusion of the work of De Montfort's Parliament was held in Westminster Hall in 1265 and it was to a similar ceremony that we were now invited 700 years later.

As I took my place in this splendid building I thought back to other visits there. The trip in the school holidays when my parents were giving us our first introduction to part of our national heritage; years later on the January evening in 1936 for the lying-in-state of King George V and, even more poignant, the same sad event only fifteen years later for the comparatively young George VI; and again, less than six months ago, the great crowd filing reverently past the coffin of Sir Winston Churchill.

The scene around me was very different from those solemn memories; the band of the Grenadier Guards was playing light-heartedly; the crowd at the moment was composed mostly of women, the wives of the 'Lords and Commons'. It being June, we were all arrayed in our gayest hats and frilliest frocks. The Lords and Commons arrived from prayers in their respective Chambers, the bishops robed, as they had been in 1265, in episcopal vestments – they did not, I noticed, carry the 'burning candles' mentioned on the earlier occasion! The Commonwealth Prime Ministers came in, followed in turn by the Speaker, the Commonwealth Speakers and the Lord Chancellor. There was an excited stir among the company as the Yeomen of the Guard took up their positions; amid a fanfare of trumpets the Royal Family were conducted to their seats and then, preceded by yet another fanfare, the Queen, looking very lovely, was escorted to the dais with the Duke of Edinburgh.

The Lord Chancellor read the address from the House of Lords; Mr Speaker read the address from the House of Commons; both were presented to Her Majesty. The Queen replied quite briefly in her inimitable and charming way; we sang the National Anthem and the royal party were conducted to the north door of the Hall. It had been a short affair, but what a chapter of history and wealth of ceremony had been packed into that half hour.

When all the official trappings had been cast aside we repaired to the Cholmondeley Room for a buffet lunch which we carried out on to the terrace. The river traffic passed up and down below us, continuous with, if different from, the traffic of centuries ago.

Exciting happenings seemed to be the order of the day in this lovely summer. On July 12th we were to leave for Zermatt to take part in the centenary celebrations of the first ascent of the Matterhorn. We had been invited (all expenses paid!) by the Swiss National Tourist Office in Zürich. Friends of Switzerland in general and mountaineers in particular from all over the world were guests of the Swiss. We were included partly as climbers and lovers of Switzerland, but more especially because Ronald was to be the officiating chaplain and because I had written *Zermatt Saga*.

We were in London the previous week for Church Assembly when I received a telephone call from the Television Authorities in Birmingham. They had heard that these centenary celebrations were to take place, they understood we were invited, they believed I had written a book about Zermatt. This was all thought to be of great interest to Midland viewers – would I come to Birmingham and give a television interview on the Friday? I consulted Ronald: I was sure he would say yes. He did so with alacrity although – as might have been expected – it could hardly have been more inconvenient. We sped down to Leicester as soon as Church Assembly was over; I changed into a frock that I hoped would be a suitable one for television and for the High Sheriff's party at which we wanted to put in an appearance near Rugby on the way back. At last we set out for Birmingham.

We arrived at the television studio to find everyone in a great state of consternation. The Open Golf Championship was running late and for the present it would not be possible to interview me. We waited and waited; fortunately we were able to watch the golf which was fascinating. At last it became obvious that we could

4. Dick Mayston 1963

Lord Monckton and Ronald

5. *Above:* At the Horseman's Service
Below: Ronald with members of the Youth Conference

wait no longer and we had to explain the situation to those concerned.

They said that at all costs they must have the interview. Could they come to Bishop's Lodge on Saturday? Reluctantly we had to say no – Ronald was preaching in Wells Cathedral and we had to make the journey there and back in the day. How about Sunday? They would willingly come if they could get all the apparatus; we closed for Sunday morning which happened to be free, but in my heart of hearts I did not expect this enterprise to come off.

On Sunday morning the rain was coming down in buckets; this was most depressing, as on that afternoon we had promised to appear mounted at the Horsemen's Service for the Pony Club at which Ronald was to preach. We had not ridden for nearly ten years (apart from the Petra jaunt) and we were a bit apprehensive as to what kind of condition we should be in to fly to Zermatt the next day. However, convinced that the television interviewers would not arrive on such a desolate morning, I changed into riding kit immediately after breakfast. I had hardly completed the operation when a ring at the bell announced the arrival of six television experts, a vast array of apparatus and a small boy who had been brought along to assuage his disappointment that Dad had to go out on Sunday morning. I flew upstairs to substitute a frock for jodphurs while Ronald helped them dismantle the drawing-room. It was all a great to-do but quite a thrill. While I was being interviewed Ronald rigged up a bar in the kitchen, not forgetting a large supply of orange squash for the excited small boy. We made great friends with all the party and I was told later that the interview, put out the next day, was a success. We could not see it, being airborne above Zürich, but I had quite an interesting little supply of fan mail later.

We ate our lunch wondering if we should be too sore to sit down for the next meal. The buttons and buttonholes of Ronald's jodphurs having refused to meet, he had decided on formal bishop's attire for his equestrian engagement. After all, why have an eighteenth-century riding outfit in the wardrobe and not wear it on the most suitable of all occasions? My jodphurs and jacket seemed too big but I managed to make the necessary adjustments; I was also equipped with a borrowed velvet cap, mine having mysteriously disappeared.

The downpour of the morning had ceased and we drove out to Market Bosworth, the village selected for the service, through shafts of watery sunshine. A colourful scene awaited us: scores of children, aged between three and sixteen, were trotting around on gleaming ponies, and a few beautifully turned out adults were also present mounted on impeccably groomed hunters. I wondered how my outfit, which dated back nearly to my school days, would compare with such elegance. However I comforted myself with the fact that none of the onlookers would care what I looked like; they had probably come to get a good giggle when I came off.

Ronald was introduced to a huge grey, seventeen hands and of enormous width on account of the succulent summer pastures he had enjoyed. With the aid of a block Ronald reached the saddle. I had a beautiful little mare who must have been mortally offended at having to carry such a clumsy creature as myself. We formed up behind the Salvation Army band and at the first salvo from the big drum our respective mounts became greatly excited. I gripped with my knees like grim death and looked furtively behind me to see if Ronald's top hat was still in position – it had got to do its duty at the Royal Garden Party in two weeks' time. This proved to be the only incident, as journalese jargon puts it; the horses soon settled down and the gay cavalcade rode slowly round the village. It was delightful: I have never felt happier on a horse and the kindly smiles and friendly waves of the villagers made me glad that we had come. Back at the village green we dismounted; only Pony Club members remained in the saddle. Ronald conducted the service from a gaily decorated farm cart – a wise precaution, as the sermon might otherwise have ended abruptly. There were prayers and hymns in which all joined lustily and Ronald preached a cheerful sermon which seemed to hold the attention of the riders if not the horses, who were more interested in an occasional nibble at tufts of fresh grass. When the service was finished the Pony Club rode past our rustic platform; this was followed by a sumptuous tea and everyone including ourselves received a scarlet and grey rosette. We were delighted with these, but even more pleasing was the request that would we please promise to come again. We were thrilled to be asked and so far we have managed to accept the invitation every other year.

The next morning we boarded a Swissair Caravelle for Zürich;

in less than an hour the great array of alpine giants was spread out before us. At Zürich smiling officials welcomed us and put us on the train for Brigue. There another welcoming party bowed us on to the mountain railway. I unravelled a medley of happy memories as we travelled up the Zermatt valley in the early evening. The excited schoolgirl who more than thirty years before had leapt from side to side of the carriage anxious to miss nothing of that first fairy-tale journey, was now arriving as a 'guest of honour' at these epoch-making celebrations. I could hardly believe it was true – in spite of all we had lived through it did not seem such a very far cry from the freshness of those first unforgettable experiences. Nor could I explain to myself why I was not tormented by tearful thoughts of Bernard. This was to be the first time in all those long years that he would not be there to meet us; I knew I should miss him terribly – Zermatt could not but be different – and yet I was certain that for me he would in some mystical sense be there 'in the next room and with the door open'. It was only for Pauly that I felt anxious as we rattled through the avalanche tunnels that now guard the last approaches to Zermatt. This was to have been such a great occasion; she would have shared in Bernard's glory as the greatest and perhaps the most beloved of all the Zermatt guides. Now she had to face it alone – I prayed hard that we would be able to help her.

How incredibly I underrated her courage and her resources of faith; she was at the station to meet us with a bouquet in her hands – a special gift for us on this great occasion. She kissed us and pointed across the street to the Hotel Bahnhof where the Union Jack hung side by side with the Swiss flag.

'For the British,' she smiled happily and we thought how delighted Bernard would have been with this imaginative touch. We walked together up the village street and halfway up her nieces Marie Thérèse and Käthy came to take us on to the Monte Rosa.

'I must go back to the Bahnhof,' explained Pauly. 'Three of Bernard's famous climbers are arriving quite soon; I must be there to welcome them.' Only the tight little squeeze she gave my hand told me the depths of her feelings.

Zermatt was *en fête* indeed: flags and banners decorated the hotels; all the greatest climbers of the world strolled up and down the narrow street; at the Monte Rosa, where the Union Jack was flying in honour of Whymper, Hildi Eberhardt gave us a royal welcome on behalf of the Famille Seiler.

The Centre Alpin gave a dinner that night at the Monte Rosa; each table was lit by candles and garlanded with alpine flowers; between courses we wandered around the lovely old dining-room greeting climbing friends from a score of countries. We went to bed early to be ready for the festivities the next day; the air was very still; moonlight silvered the snow peaks and polished the glistening rocks of the Matterhorn; muted strains of alpine songs floated up from the lighted windows of the little inns; the church clock chimed the hour; it was very, very good to be in Zermatt just then.

At eight o'clock the next morning we were all on the train en route for the Riffelberg where there was to be a great official press conference. Journalists, camera men and TV reporters were there in force; for many of them it was their first visit to the Alps and it was quite an experience to watch their spontaneous enjoyment of the glorious panorama unfolding before them. Anyone who felt energetic enough was invited to go on to the Gornergrat and bring back a stone to be placed in a memorial cairn at Riffelberg. I was bursting with energy and having collected my stone, a fairly small one, I walked down to Riffelberg to the strains of the Zermatt pipers in a party led by John Hunt.

The scene at Riffelberg was fantastic. It is a spot very precious to mountaineers; the present hotel, now one of the finest ski hotels in Europe, preserves in its exterior all the essential features of the old Riffelhaus. This was the original hotel, built by the commune of Zermatt, from which many of the pioneers started for their ascents of Monte Rosa, the Lyskamm, the Breithorn and other mountains in the area. The views are incomparable and on this day of perfect weather the scene was unforgettable. Elias Julen, an old Zermatt guide dressed in traditional costume, had driven his cows up from Riffelalp; the girls of the Zermatt choir wearing their lovely *Tracht* were ready to sing to us; the notes of an alp horn echoed across the valley; the Chief Guide had come in his Sunday best.

Grouped near the impromptu platform were the relatives of those who took part in the first ascent of the Matterhorn: the grandchildren and nephew of Charles Hudson; the nephew of Douglas Hadow, a nephew and niece of Edward Whymper, and last but not least his daughter Ethel Blandy and her daughter Nigella, both members of our Ladies' Alpine Club. The great grandson of Peter Taugwalder represented the guides. The party bearing stones for the cairn buried a tin box in which were placed the names of all those present and above it we built our cairn to remain, we hope, for all time as a memorial of a great occasion. Speeches and music then became the order of the day, with the radio and television companies of Switzerland, Great Britain and America co-operating for their countries. The most important guests were welcomed publicly and Dr Werner Kämpfen from Zürich and Constant Cachin from Zermatt then welcomed the rest of us – I was proud to hear *Zermatt Saga* mentioned in the discourse.

The entire party sat down to a mouth-watering, if slightly indigestible, meal of *raclette*, the greatest gastronomical honour that Canton Valais can offer. It was delicious but there was consternation when we could manage only two helpings: small eaters, we were told, never have less than five *raclettes*; big eaters have been known to consume twenty at one sitting! We drank our coffee sitting outside on a bench in the sun with John and Katherine Sandford. John is a parson and a member of the House of Lords. He was captain of the Parliamentary Ski Team and was present as the representative of the British Government to the Zermatt celebrations. All the mountains we loved most, from Monte Rosa to the Matterhorn and Weisshorn and away to the distant snows of the Oberland, crowded the horizon like personal friends. Some of them Ronald and I had climbed together; some I had done alone with Bernard; on some of the slopes I had skied. Below us lay Zermatt, the spiritual home of most of those present, and away down the St Niklaus valley we could pick out the tiny villages, strung out like a rope of pearls leading from the Rhône valley up to Zermatt itself. It was good to see the valley as well as the mountain heights; if we should ever get too old to climb there will always be the village and the valley, the meadows and the forests and the little grassy alps with the cowherds and the cheesemakers and the goats – all an essential and integral part of the mountain scene.

Wednesday July 14th was described as the official memorial day

– the day on which, in 1865, Whymper and his party reached the summit of the Matterhorn. Long before most of the guests were stirring in their Zermatt hotels there were parties engaged on the ascent of the mountain. One led by Chris Brasher and equipped with television cameras was tracing Whymper's route on the Hörnli Ridge; the great-grandson of Peter Taugwalder was with them. The other group was on the tremendous North Face where Ian McNaught-Davis was receiving equipment for his broadcast, dropped by helicopter. All day there were queues at the telescopes to catch a glimpse of the climbers and back at home we knew our friends and relations were glued to their television sets.

For most of us in the village the great event of the day was the open air memorial service to take place in the Festival Square – in winter the ice rink. Mass was celebrated by the priest of Zermatt; the sermon was preached by Ronald, wearing Convocation robes – a truly ecumenical venture. Every seat was taken and crowds stood six deep round the outskirts of the square. Everywhere I looked I saw friends: Arnold Lunn who was an old hero of mine and who had written the introduction to *Zermatt Saga*; John Hunt and his wife, the Sandfords, Simone Frutiger and her two little girls, the entire Biner clan from the oldest to the youngest; the old guides of Zermatt whom I had known when I was a teenager and the present giants who had been toddlers or babies in arms at that time; and a large array of our fellow members of the Alpine Club and Ladies' Alpine Club. It seemed as if the whole span of my life was unfolded here, and, indeed, far beyond it – for just visible from one spot was the Nord End of Monte Rosa climbed for the first time by my ancestors in 1861.

The service went smoothly; the congregation was still and very intent; only the domestic, daily sounds of Zermatt impinged on the silence – the occasional carillon of cowbells, the bleat of a goat, the distant clatter of horses' hooves – these enhanced rather than deflected our concentration. And over the whole scene, on this mercifully fine day, the Matterhorn reigned supreme, the flag cloud flying from the summit.

From the Festival Square we processed to the cemetery and wreaths were laid on the graves of those who perished in the Matterhorn accident. With the solemn ceremonies finished we all met once more in the garden of the Zermatterhof for cocktails;

this was a rendezvous indeed; the babel of tongues was tremendous; everyone seemed to be greeting everyone else in at least three different languages; but nothing mattered except the warm handshake that often told of reunions after years of separation.

Early in the evening the British were pledged to meet outside the Hotel Mont Cervin to go in procession to the English Church, where John Hunt was to place a wreath on the altar under which Charles Hudson lies buried. It was intended to be just a quiet, semi-private British remembrance but word had gone round and we found most of the village marching with us. When we reached the church door I found Pauly, Rèse, Käthy and Anna Roelfsema close beside me.

'Can we all sit together?' whispered Pauly. I was thrilled: these were my dearest friends, and together we took part in the moving little ceremony. The church was packed, with as many standing outside; the service had been arranged by Frank Food, the English chaplain for July. He comes from our diocese and it was a happy coincidence that he should take the service and that Ronald should preach.

When we got back to the Monte Rosa there was news that both Matterhorn climbs had been safely completed and we met with happy hearts for the Ladies' Alpine Club cocktail party at which members of the Alpine Club also appeared. It is very seldom that so many of us are in one climbing centre together. Our festivities lasted so long that we nearly missed dinner altogether.

On the next day, the Zermatt festivities were to conclude with an ascent of the Matterhorn by any who wished to take part – sufficient guides were to be provided – and the guests were then invited to Breuil, now known as Cervinia, on the Italian side of the Matterhorn. Ronald and I had been obliged to refuse this enchanting proposition as we had to leave for Leicester the next day, but I was determined not to go home without at least being *on* the Matterhorn. I got up at the crack of dawn and was wafted up to the Schwarzsee by the first *téléférique*. From there I walked up to the Matterhorn hut from which the climb begins. It is a long, slow pull of two hours up to the hut but exhilarating for those who love these things.

As I made my way up through the rocks, with fresh views breaking in on every turn in the path, I thought of the triumph and the tragedy that had produced, a hundred years later, this remarkable event in which we had all taken part. I had not much time but when I reached the hut it was possible, in just a few minutes, to recapture something of the spirit of Whymper's party as they passed the very spot on which I stood – just a hundred years ago. The Matterhorn has cast its spell over me almost all my life and at that moment I realized as never before what an irresistible challenge it must have presented to the first pioneers. How much people like me owe to those early climbers; without their example our own mountain adventures might never have been achieved and Bernard and I might never have set out from this hut to reach the summit.

As I soliloquized I saw Dr Rast striding up the path; he is a Swiss, a brilliant London surgeon and a famous climber – the very person with whom to share a drink at this memorable moment. We raised our glasses to the Matterhorn and shook hands because we were so happy to be there, and then I had to leave him and speed back to Zermatt. The weather broke as I ran gaily down the path; I had hoped to meet John Hunt's party coming up to make their climb and descent to Italy but, alas, this was the one bit of the programme that had to be abandoned on account of the weather.

Back in Zermatt I slipped round to the cemetery to find Bernard's grave. I had purposely not been before, the cemetery had been too full of interested crowds. I had gathered a bunch of autumn crocuses on the way down; flowers are really for the living but for me Bernard *was* still living and I tried to say so with my flowers. I found the grave easily; he lies beside his mother near the river, in the shadow of the great mountains. There was no stone yet – just flowers and a tiny candle lantern. It was enough for the present and the grave seemed only a half-truth, so real was Bernard's presence in his beloved village.

The next day Ronald and I left Zermatt, our rucksacks stuffed with generous gifts bestowed on us by the Swiss, while I wore proudly on my coat the badge presented to all those who have climbed the Matterhorn. We had been there only four days but they had been days packed with mountain history, with adventure, with love and kindness, with deep friendship and with undying memories. Perhaps only mountaineers could have celebrated in that way, perhaps only the Matterhorn could have evoked such an occasion – '*Le Cervin n'est pas quelque chose, c'est quelqu'un*'.

Ronald had one more Matterhorn duty to perform – on his home ground on the Sunday after we returned. Charles Hudson, who was killed in the Matterhorn disaster and was one of the most brilliant British climbers of his time, had been vicar of Skillington, the first village out of Leicestershire and in the Lincoln diocese. The present vicar had been in our diocese and was quick to seize on the opportunity to have a celebration in his parish – he is not a mountaineer, but it is not for nothing that there is a stained glass window of the Matterhorn in his church. He drew up an interesting service, invited Charles Hudson's great grand-daughter to be present and prevailed on Ronald to preach. The people of Skillington were well aware that they had suddenly come into the limelight and they came in big family parties to their little church that lovely July night. Most of them had watched the television and listened to the broadcast from Zermatt; they were thrilled to listen to someone who had been actually present at these great events. Before we left we went to have a peep at the vicarage; it is no longer used as such but it was quite moving to realize that this was the very house from which Charles Hudson set out for the great adventure – never to return.

And so the centenary celebrations came to an end; through the years I had sometimes wondered whether that first ascent would ever be commemorated, and if so, how. Never in my wildest moments had I anticipated that I should be there or that things would be done on such a magnificent scale. For nearly a week we had lived, as it were, on the summits; it had been more than satisfying. Now we must return with haste to the valleys.

We came down to earth with rather a bump, although it was a bump for which we were prepared. Our dear Mr and Mrs Bell who had served us so faithfully for over five years were retiring to their lovely old beamed cottage in a village a few miles away. We knew we were not really saying goodbye, indeed we continued to see each other frequently, but it was a parting of the ways and at that time none of us knew that it was to be only temporary. Our poor little Martin was devastated; the bottom seemed to have dropped out of his doggy world. He spent days wandering round looking for them and it was only after we had taken him for several visits to the cottage and he realized his friends were not far off that he began to eat his food and wag his tail again.

However, we were very fortunate in these days when it is so difficult to get domestic help. We still had our faithful Mrs Perrott who comes to help in the morning and who, at this time of transition, was a tower of strength and loyalty. For the first time in our lives there was a baby in our house; we engaged as caretakers John and Pat Wakelin, a nice young couple we had known for some time, and they brought with them Mark, aged five months. Mark was everybody's pet, of course, and Martin appeared to think he had some special responsibility towards him. He would sit by the pram or the carry cot for hours, only stirring to lick a minute foot or finger when it protruded from the blankets. Mark grew into one of the liveliest small boys I have ever met; he outdistanced us all if we wanted to catch him. His favourite hiding places were inside the grandfather clock or in the folds of the Bishop's copes. I never actually saw him trying on a mitre but nothing would have surprised me. We knew when John and Pat came to us that it could not be a long-term venture; before very long they would want their own little home and the family would increase. But for the moment they were having housing difficulties, so when they came to us their problem was solved as well as ours; they stayed with us for two years and we all became very fond of each other.

A joyful event of the summer season was a visit from my Czechoslovakian godson Peter Klouda. During the war his parents, Kurt and Traude, came to London as refugees from the Sudetenland. We became, and have remained, very close friends. In the middle of the war Peter was born; Ronald christened him in the Savoy Chapel and I became his godmother. When they returned to Czechoslovakia after the war we all believed that very soon we should be visiting them in their own country. Eastern European politics made this totally impossible; often it was difficult to keep contact even by post, and presents that I sent for Peter often failed to arrive. Consequently he grew up without my ever seeing him after the age of three. Then quite suddenly travel became a little easier in Czechoslovakia; Peter by this time was a student at Prague University and as such was granted permission to visit England.

We went to the station to meet Peter wondering just how we

were going to recognize each other. As it happened we did – at once. He bore no resemblance to the little toddler I had said good-bye to in 1946 but he was exactly like his parents and knew us from the photos we had sent over occasionally. It was grand to meet after twenty years and to establish once more some kind of live contact with Kurt and Traude. He had grown up in a world so different from ours but there were no barriers between us and it was a very happy visit. He left us with the assurance that as soon as his parents had permission to travel they would come at once. It was good to have seen my eldest godson; through the years I had prayed regularly for him, and when I saw him I was proud of him.

It was time for our normal August visit to Zermatt but before we could go there was another happy duty to perform. Our secretary Anne Bavin had left us to be married and she wanted Ronald to tie the knot. We had come to love Anne very much and it was a joy to see her complete happiness when Ronald married her to William.

We get a lot of pleasure from our past secretaries and their husbands and children. Jill, who was our first, brings along her schoolboy sons; Angela, who followed Anne, pops in with Caroline and William in either hand; and only a few weeks ago an overloaded estate car pulled up at our gates to decant Anne herself followed by her husband with two year old Sarah under one arm and six months old Stephen under the other. We had a great family party on the lawn and Martin mistook Stephen for a puppy – an easy mistake, since he was progressing on all fours.

Our Zermatt holiday had a special content this time, of course. By mutual consent with Pauly little had passed between us about Bernard at the centenary celebrations; we all wished to wait until we could talk quietly. Every day we visited Pauly; we went on our usual walks and picnics because she begged us to, but each evening we spent together with her or with Rèse and Käthy. We heard about Bernard's last hours and how with almost his final breath he asked the family to take care of Pauly. It was interesting to listen to his young nieces' special memories of him; the wonderful Christmas festivities he had arranged; how he was always at the window to wave a cheery greeting when they were on their way to work or school; how all their troubles could be taken to him.

And the impecunious young climbers to whom he was almost a

father sat sadly on the bench outside the Hotel Bahnhof as if they were waiting for him to return; they told us how often when they were lacking some piece of climbing equipment and had no funds to get it they would find it tucked under the rucksack flap after they had left the village.

With Pauly we discussed the future. She meant to carry on the hotel and was sure that Bernard would wish it.

'But do you think I can do it?' she pleaded. 'Can I ever make it as he would like it to be?'

We told her she could and begged her to try; without this job and its memories of Bernard life held nothing for her. We promised our support and asked her consent for British climbers to put a little memorial plaque to Bernard at the Bahnhof. She was greatly touched by this and went on to tell us her plans for Bernard's grave. As a memento Pauly gave me part of the rope that Bernard used when he took me up the Matterhorn; she could not have given me anything better. I had not been able to bring myself to climb that year but this seemed to link the past and the future in some mysterious way. It hangs in my little den above the Matterhorn certificate Bernard gave me – a symbol of past endeavours and future hopes.

When we gathered at the station to say goodbye it seemed that it would have to be an all-female party to see us off; instead Peter, Bernard's elder nephew, whom we had known since he was three, came down to join us. He has grown to be so much like Bernard had been in his twenties that my heart almost stood still. It was a happy party that said *auf Wiedersehen* that day; together we had absorbed and overcome the sadness that had befallen us; we could look trustfully to the future – it was just as Bernard would have wanted it to be.

Home again to start the winter's work, we felt full of energy and enthusiasm. We like the autumn in our diocese; it is always frighteningly busy; almost every day is packed with engagements but when one's work is happy and rewarding, it seldom seems laborious. Confirmations and institutions follow each other in quick succession; each one usually a good occasion and with its own individuality. Institutions are great times for meeting the new vicarage family and the other clergy from the deanery who come with their wives to wish the newcomers well. In one of these I had a rather unusual interest. John Smythe, son of Frank Smythe the famous mountaineer and one of my greatest heroes, came to a living in our diocese on the strength of having read my first book!

A special treat was in store for me early in November. Ronald got me a ticket for a seat in the strangers' gallery of the House of Lords for the State Opening of Parliament – and *what* a seat – I was in the middle of the gallery facing the throne and beside me were Janet Carleton (Janet Adam Smith) wife of the Headmaster of Westminster and a past President of the Ladies' Alpine Club, and Jane Fleming, wife of the Bishop of Norwich. It added much to my pleasure to have one or two buddies to talk to; all of us were there for the first time and we were entranced. It was English history at its most gracious and glorious; the great crowd of peers and peeresses below us, resplendent in their robes; the lovely, simple dignity of the throne and the moving moment when the delicate, dedicated figure of the Queen entered from the Princes' Chamber escorted by the great officers of State – it is a page of pageantry that makes me humbly and gratefully glad to be British. Ours is, after all, the mother of parliaments and in spite of everything that has happened in recent decades our country has a political maturity which is the envy of the world. Ceremony both expresses and encourages this maturity.

Afterwards when all trace of scarlet and ermine had been safely tucked away in large red sacks, everyone foregathered for a buffet luncheon and relived informally the splendour of the day.

There is usually a somewhat abrupt descent from these pinnacles of pleasure to the more mundane matters of our normal existence. On this occasion we spent the afternoon hastening up the motorway to be ready for our evening engagement. But as I heated up soup and boiled eggs and clattered through the washing up, the chores seemed a little less prosaic in the light of the day's events; in any case I was rather glad of them – they helped to keep my feet on the ground.

There was just one more historic and colourful occasion to come before the end of this particularly exciting year. Westminster Abbey was about to celebrate its 900th anniversary and the inaugural service in the Abbey on December 28th was to usher in the great year.

We bade farewell to our Christmas guests and left by train for

London on a bitterly cold morning when conditions were too bad
to risk the motorway. Outside the Abbey there was driving sleet
and a whistling wind under a dark, threatening sky. Within there
was warmth and light and loveliness. For the first time I saw the
brilliant, irridescent chandeliers of Waterford glass given by the
Guinness family; the lighted Christmas trees were still in position; the notes of the organ rose and fell softly as if it were a long
way off; above it the Abbey bell summoned us all to our seats. I
looked round for people I knew and could see no one until I
suddenly realized that I was sitting next to Gay Goodchild, the
teenage daughter of the Bishop of Kensington, and a friend of my
nephews and nieces. This was Gay's first experience of a great
Abbey occasion and we enjoyed it together, comparing notes in
whispers when we had a chance. The *Corps Diplomatique* came in
and took their seats opposite us; among them I was glad to see the
Swiss Ambassador. On the closed circuit television screens we
saw the Queen arrive with the Duke of Edinburgh, the Prince of
Wales and Princess Anne; immediately afterwards the organ
peeled out with all its strength and majesty and the long procession
came slowly through the choir. Gay looked for her father and I
looked for Ronald; we gave each other a grateful nudge when we
found that we were all in view of each other – our respective relations even managed muted smiles in our direction.

It was a good service, taking us back 900 years and yet leading
us on to the future; there could not have been a more magnificent
or more prayerful beginning to the celebrations which continued
for the whole of the next year. When the last notes of the final
organ voluntary had died away in an echoing whisper, Gay and I
joined forces to find our men folk. Clergy are notoriously difficult
to locate after big services – bishops especially so – but we ran
them to earth at last in Westminster School.

Before we left for home we paid a visit to the Abbey Bookshop
to buy copies of the commemorative book for our godchildren and
a set of Abbey sherry glasses for ourselves – we must have something to remind us of this great day. Sad to say, the glasses are
already getting fewer in number, and replacements are absolutely
impossible. It was too much to hope that they too could last for
900 years – they would probably not last 900 days.

It had been a very thrilling year, highlighted by many great occasions and some exciting travels. It had brought its sadnesses too, but who could hope or expect it to be otherwise; life would cease to be real if it was composed entirely of unalloyed happiness or unrelieved grief.

CHAPTER VI

Kaleidoscope

WHATEVER the disadvantages are in being a bishop's wife
– and every job has its quota – boredom is certainly not
one of them. It is absolutely impossible to be bored in
our kind of existence; we, and all those around us, are far too busy.
Not that I personally have ever found life boring. Ivor Novello
once said to Godfrey Winn that he was never bored when he was
young. Without suggesting any close similarity between myself
and such a world-famous, well-loved figure, we have just that in
common – I too was never bored when I was young and never have
been since. Life has always seemed satisfying; in my youth most
things were exciting, nearly everything was a treat; and the pattern
is much the same today. It is a help; things do not get clogged up,
and the wheels do not grind to a standstill.

If 1965 was a kaleidoscope of memorable national and international happenings for us, the year that followed was packed full
of domestic and diocesan events, with a scattering of wider experiences thrown in for good measure.

Our New Year festivities included a teenage party for some of
our godchildren and their brothers and sisters. It was to have been
a party to a ball in aid of the Family Service Unit but this was cancelled at the last moment; instead we arranged what one young
guest described as a 'super-duper dinner' followed by a walk up
snow-covered Beacon Hill as a midnight finale.

The next party was somewhat more adult and sophisticated –
an invitation to a New Year luncheon at the Swiss Embassy. The
Daenikers had retired from the Embassy and been succeeded by
Dr and Mme de Fischer, a charming couple, whose gatherings were
always gay and informal. Dr de Fischer had been much impressed
by the great Abbey service at the end of December; Mme had
bought copies of both my books which she asked me to autograph.

Above: Walking to help Christian Aid
Below: Bishop's Escort. Ronald and the 'ton-up boys'

7. Bim and Netta riding up mountain at Patmos

Bim enjoying the pleasures the snow

The New Year also brought suggestions about, and finally a contract for, another book to be published by Allen and Unwin. I suggested something in the way of autobiographical travel, which proved acceptable, and before many weeks had passed I was at work once more, this time on *Dear Abroad*. Philip Unwin was not much enamoured of the title but generously allowed me to keep it and quite a few people have liked it.

About this time the Board for Social Responsibility brought out a report entitled 'Fatherless by Law'; it was an attempt to bring about some kind of relationship, however slight, between the putative father and his illegitimate child and thus to ensure that the child was at least aware of his father. This blasted off a chorus of 'fors and againsts' and Ronald was invited up to Manchester for a television session on the subject with ITV. I went too, hoping to bring back some interesting titbits for our diocesan Mothers' Union. We travelled up to Manchester with Mrs Bramall, the Secretary of the Council for the Unmarried Mother and Her Child, who was to take part in the discussion. We were whisked from the centre to the suburbs and almost at once found ourselves under the intensive glare that pervades a TV studio. It proved to be a long business but very worthwhile and most informative from my point of view. The interviews were conducted by Robert Kee, one of the most courteous of interviewers, but I felt that even he was in danger of trying to put words and even sentiments into the mouths of his temporary victims. It seems to me very important that those who agree to be interviewed should refuse emphatically to be in any way slanted by the interviewer. However, we could not have met nicer people and Robert Kee travelled back with us and regaled us during dinner on the train with fascinating anecdotes from his television career. The programme attracted a large variety of viewers and Ronald received a considerable fan mail (not all of it flattering) during the next few weeks.

The cause of ecumenism, which has gathered increasing momentum as the years have gone by, was already making big strides and as a result of this it came about that Ronald went out to Mount St Bernard's Abbey in the Charnwood Forest at the invitation of the Cistercian Abbot and his monks. This was the first Roman Catholic monastery to be built in England since the Reformation.

Its foundation in 1835 caused the poet Wordsworth much concern! Ronald has seldom enjoyed a day more; the richness of the services; the common ground so obvious between our two churches; the kindness and courtesy of the monks and their genuine delight at his visit left him with rich memories that have not yet faded. They asked him to come again and bring me – an invitation I should love to accept.

The early spring brought me a very special engagement in Scotland. The time had come for the confirmation of my eldest goddaughter, Anne Michell. I had always promised myself I would be at her confirmation because I had missed her christening. Since her parents, Douglas and Dorothy, came to our diocese I have been able to see much more of Anne and I was looking forward to this occasion immensely. She was to be confirmed at school, at St Leonards at St Andrews, where she had been since she was eight. As usual it was a tight squeeze to fit it in, but by travelling up to Edinburgh on Saturday night and returning on Sunday night it proved to be possible.

I *did* enjoy that trip. Douglas and Dorothy met me off the night train at Leuchars Junction and took me off for an enormous Scotch breakfast. Then we picked up Anne who was to show me round the school. Anne, thank heaven, had none of the antipathy to school so prevalent in these days; she was thoroughly enjoying herself and was in no hurry to leave. There was a double interest in the visit to the school as Dorothy had been there herself, and we had a nice nostalgic wallow on the particular playing field where she knocked up fifty in a school cricket match and we thought of other similar achievements dear to the heart of our generation.

The confirmation service was conducted according to the rite of the Scottish Episcopal Church – slightly different from ours but equally impressive. I was so glad that the Bishop of St Andrews confirmed by name. Ronald and his assistant bishops always do this in our diocese and it somehow makes the laying on of hands more personal and complete.

Everyone was invited to tea at the school with the headmistress and as not many godparents had been able to make the journey, I felt my effort had been more than worth while. I had a round of introductions to Anne's fellow confirmees and loved being in a school atmosphere once more. So many things have changed over the years – some of them for the better; certainly Anne's confirmation was far more impressive than my own had been; and yet there is still enough left unaltered to take one back instantly to the days that were so significant in one's own life such a devastatingly long time ago.

For over a year we had been booked to attend a Lutheran conference at Bielefeld in West Germany; the date was catching up with us, but we had to find time in the midst of our preparations for two important events. One was the changing of our car, a routine matter which takes place every three or four years and seldom has much significance. This transfer had a special interest however; the car was a Ford Zephyr as usual, but we succeeded in acquiring the number plate RRW 680. The letters are Ronald's initials, the number is the date of the original founding of the diocese – a great bit of luck in our estimation! Getting this number involved buying a scrap motorcycle from the Coventry area!

The second event concerned a bell. We have a famous foundry in Loughborough, and the parish church of Hathern was having a new bell cast to add to their peal and wanted to have the Bishop's name inscribed on it. We paid a visit to the foundry and Ronald dedicated the bell in his own name. Now for all time the Bishop's bell will ring out over the fields and farms and the great motorways of North Leicestershire.

On a breezy night towards the end of March a concourse of clergy, and I, boarded the night boat at Harwich for the Hook of Holland. This was a picked team of theologians, each with a special qualification. Ronald had been asked by the Germans to be chairman of the conference, a compliment he appreciated. It had necessitated our speaking German every day at breakfast during the whole winter to increase our fluency in the language – not that our breakfast conversation ever makes any mention of theological questions, but at least it encouraged us to think a little more quickly in colloquial German.

However, no linguistic prowess was needed on the boat; nor for that matter any theological pronouncements either. All the party were old friends and the conversation, well laced with banter, was more suited to undergraduates than to pundits. When we lined up on deck at 6.30 am the next morning for disembarkation it seemed as if half the city of Leicester was invading the Hook of Holland. A large civic party was paying an official visit to Germany and it was a pleasant surprise to find our Lord Mayor and Lady Mayoress coming down the gangway with us.

The journey to Bielefeld took most of the day and it was dark before we arrived. Previously we had known Bielefeld only as one of the centres on our army tour – we had been whisked through the streets in official cars to enormous barracks. This time we were to stay at Bethel, a little township standing on a wooded hillside on the outskirts of Bielefeld.

Bethel must be unique. It was founded nearly a hundred years ago in a small farmhouse by Pastor Von Bodelschwingh as a hospital for the care of epileptics. Since then, partly because of the vision of its founder, partly because of the dedicated service of those who followed him, its work has increased to such dimensions that there are now fourteen hospitals, schools for epileptics and the educationally sub-normal, a training house for deaconesses and a theological seminary for students. It was here that we were to stay for the conference by invitation of the Lutheran Church. Our taxi turned in through big open gates and carried us up the zig zags of a steep road; the lights of Bielefeld gleamed in the depths below; the subdued roar of the great pulsating city was faintly audible above the murmuring of the trees. It made Bethel seem something special – a place apart.

We had been allotted a cosy little suite in the theological seminary and immediately were very much at home. By the end of that first evening we had met all the members of the conference, many of whom we knew already, including Klaus Kemper, who had been with us in the Durham years. The majority spoke English but some did not; we felt that our breakfast-time language labours had not been wasted.

The papers read at the conference were entirely beyond me and in any case I should have been very much *de trop* if I had put in an appearance. I did attend prayers every morning, taken sometimes in English, sometimes in German; I went to two of the discussions, which were quite an eye-opener to me, and I was also able to attend the ecumenical Communion service, which was a wholly satisfying experience. I met the theologians at meals of course – and *what* delicious German meals – but otherwise I was free to plan my own time. This suited me exactly; it snowed most of the time we were there, but our room was warm and comfortable and I managed to put in at least two hours a day on my book. I made solo excursions into Bielefeld to search for some of our old haunts and to buy chocolate Easter hares, coloured eggs and postcards in spite of the fact that the weather was more suggestive of Christmas candles.

The rest of the time I spent learning about Bethel – sometimes alone, sometimes with other members of the conference. Bethel makes a lasting impact: it is something you cannot forget – something that gives a slant to one's reactions to so many present problems. There are 7,000 inhabitants of Bethel and a remarkable spirit pervades the whole place; Bethel is their *raison d'être* – to each of them it gives a home and work and a purpose in life. There are many hundreds of workers; each family has a house which is theirs for their working life; there are regular schools for the children; there are shops, a post office, a bank – Bethel even has its own currency – and, naturally, there is a church.

We went round many of the institutions: at times this was quite terrifying – I had never come across mental suffering in such an extreme form or on such a vast scale. But all the time and everywhere we went the selfless dedication of every member of the staff and the tireless courage of the patients were uppermost in one's mind. Almost every patient at Bethel is incurable; of those who come as children only a tiny percentage live beyond the age of fourteen; those who come as adults come to spend the rest of their lives. Neither patients nor doctors expect 'results'. All that the workers seek is the love and trust of those in their charge; all that the patients look for is security and loving care.

Bethel, although in the care of the German church, is fully recognized by the state. During the war it was feared that Hitler's passion for purity of race might lead to the extermination of many of the patients in the hospitals. Relations were given the opportunity to remove them if they wished; few did so. In fact no patient was ever harmed by the Nazis and, in spite of heavy air attacks, only two stray bombs fell in the neighbourhood. No one doubted that a kindly providence watched over Bethel.

The social highlight of our visit – and we all received and accepted many kind invitations – was to a friendly little dinner party in the Schloss Sparrenburg. This is a fairy-tale castle perched fascinatingly on a hilltop. The wild March wind howled round the walls; spread out below us in all directions were the lighted cities of Westphalia. Dinner was delightful; speeches were interspersed between courses and Ronald found himself making his between the soup and the meat. My evening was made by President Thimme, a charming, gentle-voiced Lutheran who had arrived back only that day from Geneva where he was joint-chairman of some ecumenical committee. He explained to me that his co-chairman was an English woman – Freda Gwilliam. I stared at him in amazement.

'Did you say Freda Gwilliam?' I asked incredulously.

'Yes, of course,' he replied, 'do you know her?'

I did indeed. Freda and I progressed together at our school in Kent, from the kindergarten at the age of six, to the upper fourth at the age of thirteen. Many were the tennis battles that were fought out between us and above all there was the hundred yards sprint in the school sports which she *always* won with me always a near second. I left to go to school in Surrey but Freda continued accumulating one brilliant academic success after another. We have never met since those far-off days in the mid-nineteen twenties and now the missing link was supplied by none other than dear President Thimme. And then, as if to top off this extraordinary coincidence, a few weeks after we got home there was a great write-up, plus a picture, in *The Times* of none other than Freda Gwilliam in her capacity as a top civil servant in the Foreign Office!

Our stay in Bethel was not long but we were loth to leave when the time came. The conference had been a real theological and ecumenical advance; we loved the seminary, set there in a situation where Christian theology can be studied against a background of human need and Christlike service. Bethel had widened my horizon in a way that nothing else could have done.

Conferences are one of the ruling passions of this day and age. We seemed hardly to have stepped off the boat at Harwich before we found ourselves involved in an important gathering meeting under the auspices of the Board for Social Responsibility. It concerned the Church's attitude to social needs and problems in modern England. These conferences take so much time; so much hard work goes into the planning of them that, before they begin, one is tempted to ask 'Is it really worth it?' And almost without exception when it is all over one knows that it is.

This could certainly be said of this particular conference; clergy and laity were present in almost equal proportions and there were plenty of women among them. The speakers were excellent; the members were extremely vocal; some I fancy would have liked to have been even more so, and as a result other smaller conferences have evolved all over the country.

The conference was memorable to me because I found myself sitting opposite yet another ex-pupil from my school in Kent. This was Cecilia Goodenough, well-known for the magnificent work she does as missioner in the diocese of Southwark. I remembered her as a fair, immensely tall girl who always wore a white frock and red ribbons at the dancing class. By reason of her great height she was able to flourish the Indian clubs to much greater effect than a shrimp like me and I regarded her then with the greatest awe. I found myself regarding her in much the same way at this later stage in history; she is something of a prophet with outspoken views and a determination to carry them through. I asked myself if her dexterity with the Indian clubs had been a foretaste of her forthright approach to life. As I ruminated about Freda Gwilliam and then about Cecilia, I decided that the school must have been a breeding ground for those destined to be involved in good works.

Add together a lovely spring day, a magnificent, new and very modern church in a vast new housing estate, top it off with a royal visitor and you have a pretty splendid occasion. Exactly this happened to us at the end of April.

Up on Stocking Farm, one of our biggest housing estates, we had a tiny community centre which also did duty as a church. Presently we built a new vicarage and to it came a vicar, Henry Evans, brimful of vision, personality and new ideas. A site was found for a church and the foundation stone was laid. This became a church with a difference; apart from the architect and the foreman who, it was felt, must be professionals, the church was built brick by brick by the people of Stocking Farm. Never has a project aroused more interest; the whole district was involved in its own church. Plenty of hazards were met and overcome; at last the time drew near when it would be ready for consecration. Henry Evans came to see Ronald to ask if he could get a Royal visitor to be present. Ronald knew how hard the people had worked, he longed to get them what they wanted and agreed to try, but behind the scenes he knew how slim were the chances that at such relatively short notice there would be any vacant dates in Royal diaries.

However, nothing venture nothing have; Ronald wrote to Princess Margaret and told her the remarkable story of this church. Her lady-in-waiting replied that the Princess was greatly interested; if the date could be altered to one day earlier she would gladly come. I think the people of Stocking Farm would have made any date possible, so thrilled were they. Work went on to the very last vestige of daylight on the previous evening and on the great day everything was in order.

The Lord Mayor gave a lunch for Princess Margaret and then in a long motorcade we all drove up to Stocking Farm. The church stands on top of the hill and dominates the whole district; it was thrilling to see the crowds being drawn towards it as if by a magnet.

The service was a blend of ancient tradition and fresh ideas; people representing every aspect of church life in Stocking Farm took their own special parts; stirring hymns were conducted by the curate Theodore Woods (grandson of beloved Edward Woods, late Bishop of Lichfield) with such enthusiasm that his gown dropped off – to the intense amusement of the Princess. When Ronald said the age-old words of consecration and marked a cross on a stone with his staff it seemed as if the labours of long years had blossomed gloriously at last.

The church is full of colour and light with a central altar set among the people. Usually modern churches do not make much appeal to me but in this case one knows it is exactly right – a building that can speak in terms that can be understood by all those to whom it ministers.

The Princess stayed for tea and many of the people of Stocking Farm were presented to her. When the time came to say goodbye she left amid the vociferous cheers of a parish that was rightly both proud and grateful.

A few days after the Princess's visit there occurred what I considered to be a deeply distressing event. *The Times* newspaper changed its format and on Monday, May 2nd there appeared for the last time that unique front page, carrying, instead of glaring news headlines, the announcements of births, marriages and deaths and the always intriguing personal column. The next day *The Times* actually arrived with columns of news, most of it depressing, plastered over the front page; it was said to be a new look, a fresh image; to me it looked like St Paul's would look without its dome – utterly undistinguished. However, it must have been the right move for these degenerate times, for the sales of the paper have increased by leaps and bounds. I, and no doubt other like-minded sentimentalists, have got used to it, but hidden away in a drawer I have the last copy safely preserved – who knows, it may bring me a fortune one day.

Every year in mid-May, when the blossom is at its most beautiful and everything is fresh with the perfume of early summer, I arrange the flowers on the high altar in the Cathedral for Dick Mayston's anniversary. Dick's memory never fades; it is as untarnished as the flowers I arrange for him. For some time the Friends of the Cathedral had been planning a memorial to him – a provost's chair to stand in the sanctuary in place of the somewhat unworthy one that then stood there. By what seemed almost a God-given coincidence the chair was ready just at the time of the anniversary; it was planned that Ronald should dedicate it at choral Evensong – the service Dick always loved so much. Netta came over to stay with us and together we made, beside the chair, a flower arrangement that contained all his favourite blossoms. It was a beautiful little service and George Gray put on Psalm 138 to the chant Dick wrote for it. All his friends were there and the full choir to whom he was so devoted; there was no sermon, but Ronald spoke just a few words, full of meaning and remembrance for us all. There was a peace and a completeness about this little act of remembrance – so very, very different from the day of the funeral. The fires of bitterness still sometimes smoulder fiercely in our hearts but it is possible to look at the chair and believe that it represents Dick's personality and his life rather than his untimely death. Netta took back to Ireland a framed picture of the chair which John Hughes, our present Provost, had thoughtfully prepared for her.

'Butlins' is a household word to everyone and not least to the inhabitants of Leicester – Butlins Camp at Skegness is our nearest contact with the sea. When Sir Billy Butlin first opened his camps he can hardly have visualized how useful they would become to the clergy – in recent years quite a few Bishops have booked them for clergy conferences in out-of-season periods.

For some years Ronald and his diocesan staff had been planning a conference of clergy and laity; the venue was to be Butlins at Skegness and just before the high season opened scores of cars could be seen speeding eastwards out of Leicester. It was a comprehensive kind of conference; every aspect of diocesan life was represented among the delegates – church councillors, members of choirs, Sunday school teachers and youth organizations. The Lord Lieutenant and the High Sheriff came, each bringing his wife; there were industrialists from the city, farmers from the villages, bell-ringers, vergers and, of course, clergy of all ages.

The weather was appalling – ski sweaters and duffle coats were essential equipment. We were awakened every morning by a hymn sung over the tannoy; the famous Red Coats shepherded us when we got lost; our meals arrived piping hot on what appeared to be miniature cake stands. How such excellent meals were served so quickly to such vast numbers was a mystery none of us succeeded in solving.

The programme of talks and discussions was stimulating: together we really got down to brass tacks; ideas were aired; opinions were pooled; in consequence the life of the diocese was considerably strengthened.

We all came away full of admiration for the whole conception of Butlins – it provides something for which there is a genuine demand.

A bunch of sporting engagements enlivened our summer programme – if any enlivening was necessary, which is doubtful. The county cricket ground at Leicester was at last, to everyone's joy, being rehabilitated. Among other improvements was a fine and much-needed new pavilion. To Ronald's surprise and delight the club asked him to open it – an affectionate gesture which touched him very much. Cricketers and cricket lovers turned up in great numbers for the ceremony on a sunny Saturday afternoon; Ronald spoke of his life long love of cricket and his daily, devoted following of the fortunes of Leicestershire throughout each season.

He ended his speech by announcing 'And now, for once in my life, I propose to go in first'. The Captain produced the key and Ronald turned it and marched in. There were drinks all round and a great spirit of *bonhomie* and, inspired no doubt by the occasion, some sparkling cricket followed.

We had to tear ourselves away during the afternoon, after admiring the neat little plaque which commemorates the fact that Ronald opened the pavilion on June 25, 1966, in order to set off for the next event, the Henley Regatta service at which he was to be the preacher on Sunday morning. Michael Payne had left our diocese to become Rector of Henley; we missed him and Christine his wife and their lovely musical family a lot, and I was particularly looking forward to see the youngest – my godson Christopher.

We look back on this service as one of the finest we have ever attended. By tradition the Regatta service takes place on the Sunday before the Regatta begins, when all the crews have arrived and none of them are exhausted from racing.

Rowing comes high among our outdoor interests and it was great fun to meet the Isis crew who were accommodated on the top floor of the rectory. It is customary for the rector of Henley to provide house-room for crews and Michael Payne, being an Oxford man, likes to invite a crew from there. The rectory is a lovely spacious house overlooking the river and there was ample room for all of us. Like all happy family parties the great rendez-vous was the kitchen where pots of tea were continually being brewed and at any time of the day or night one might find the rector, the bishop, the cox of the boat, young Christopher or anyone else manipulating a steaming kettle.

Had tickets been sold for the service it would have been a complete sell-out; there was not one nook or cranny of the large and lovely church unoccupied. The regatta crews attended in their white flannel bags and blazers and were prominent as lesson readers and sidesmen. Ronald preached on the text, 'They do it to obtain a corruptible crown, but we an incorruptible'.

After the service Christine gave a cocktail party in the garden where there were lots of interesting people to meet, after lunch we set the car's nose for home for the last event of this momentous week-end – the Sunday School Anniversary at St Thomas's, South Wigston. It made a splendid finish; St Thomas's is a

vigorous church, reigned over at that time by Neil Robinson who
was Senior Man at St John's College, Durham in our last term.
The children and their parents had come to enjoy themselves; we
had a rousing service with many musical items from the young and
were able to meet them all before they went home. When at last
we sank down in easy chairs in the vicarage with Neil and Kathlyn
to feast on strawberries and cream we were convinced that cricket,
rowing and a sunday school anniversary are a good mixture for a
summer weekend.

Holidays were beginning to loom up on the horizon but there
was still Church Assembly to come which usually seems to wind
up the ecclesiastical summer season. On this occasion we were to
have a chance to hear the great Billy Graham who was in England
and had been specially invited to address us in Church House. Unlike a lot of my friends I had never worked up sufficient enthusiasm
to attend even one of Billy Graham's meetings; but I meant to be
present at this and hear for myself. I am pretty certain I went in a
critical frame of mind; I certainly came away full of admiration. I
am never impressed by an ever increasing crescendo of emotional
rhetoric but there was nothing like that about Billy Graham – at
that meeting at any rate. He was convincing without being in the
least overpowering and his answers to questions – some of which
were quite unfair – were first class. Some trouble-maker wanted
to know what he was going to do about Vietnam, to which his reply
was that he was as worried and confused about Vietnam as everyone else and he did not propose to add to the confusion by making
statements himself. I applauded loudly and so did most of those
present.

Just before the end of July we had a very special pleasure for
which we had waited twenty years – Kurt and Traude Klouda,
our wartime friends from Czechoslovakia, at last were given permission to come to England and visit us. As they stepped out of
the train the years slipped away: we were twenty years older; all of
us had lived through a lot since we last met, but all the joys and
sorrows and dangers of those unforgettable war years in London
came flooding back and if an air raid siren had wailed at that
moment it would have seemed the most natural thing in the world.

There was so much to hear, so much to tell. Political events had
kept us apart for so long that on both sides there were several

chapters of our lives to be spelled out and explained. The few days they could spend with us were far too short but at least contact had been made again; we could go on from there and there was a faint hope that opportunities for meeting might sometimes occur. They have done, in ways which none of us could possibly have visualized.

We can hardly believe it – being lucky enough to feel so fit that we hardly notice the passing of the years – but the time has arrived when the next generation has reached the marrying stage.

The first to provide us with a wedding was my brother Geoffrey's elder son John. John is a joy to everyone because he has followed the family tradition of music: he teaches music in a grammar school and is also an organist and choirmaster; he pursues his profession in Kent, so beloved by us all. He chose just the right bride: Janet is tall and pretty – an artist, with a flair for illustrating children's books; an excellent vocation to set beside John's music.

Ronald married them in the lovely old parish church at Horsham and there was a great gathering of the clans, especially of those whom one had scarcely seen since Geoffrey's wedding thirty years before. Despite the ravages of the years we all succeeded in recognizing each other and, notwithstanding some plain speaking about altered appearances, the general verdict was that our lot had worn pretty well.

Our summer holiday this year had two special projects. The first was a confirmation at Davos; since medical science found an answer to TB some of the sanatoriums at Davos have been taken over for the treatment of asthmatic children. A batch of these youngsters were ready for confirmation; such a service is normally taken by the Bishop of Fulham, but a new bishop was in process of being appointed; so to avoid disappointing the children Ronald was asked to pull it in during our holiday.

It was an interesting assignment from every point of view. It was grand to see these boys and girls now completely, or almost, cured and ready to return home to take their O or A levels for which they had been working in their special school at Davos. They gave us a wonderful welcome and we had a great confirmation service, followed by their first Communion, in the little English church. No parents or godparents had been able to make the journey from England. Instead the British community in

Davos turned up in force to support the candidates so no one felt lonely or left out. A generous lunch was provided which gave us an opportunity to make friends with the children before they gave us a rousing send off on our way to Zermatt.

There can be no more magnificent route across Switzerland than the journey from the Engadine to the Valais. It is one hundred and fifty miles from Davos to Visp and there are several major passes to be crossed. It was a scorching day; the sun blazed from a cloudless sky and the heat of the plain was insufferable after the clear mountain air of Davos. The road climbed steadily up the Oberalp Pass; this was new to us and we loved seeing the Romansch villages of the Grisons. The windows of almost every house, whether large or small, were protected by beautiful wrought-iron grills made bright by masses of geraniums and petunias. It was nearly thirty years since we had been in the Engadine and we had forgotten this colourful tradition which is symbolic of Grisons architecture.

We climbed all the time beside the bubbling, baby Rhine, which rises in these mountains, and near the top of the pass we came upon the great monastery at Disentis – a landmark for miles around.

Down we went again, bumping over an appalling surface until we came to Andermatt at the foot of the Furka Pass. We looked back to the great Engadine peaks and thought again of our new-found friends tucked safely away among the mountains of Davos. Suddenly the whole eastern sky turned black; blue lightning raced from peak to peak; thunder trapped among the folds of the hills, growled and then roared as it made its escape. Rain fell in transparent sheets; from the burning surface of the road there arose great clouds of steam; thick fog enveloped us; we switched on the headlights and crept on warily. Never before had we seen such a dramatic change – a bit too dramatic, we decided, as we clung precariously to our side of the road below which we were very sure there was a precipice. Road signs told us we were approaching the summit of the pass; as we reached it the sun burst through; the rain stopped as if a tap had been turned off. We got out of the car and surveyed the situation. It was a sight we shall never forget. To the west, over the Valais, the setting sun glowed softly; the great Pennine peaks glittered gold in its light; below the evening mists gently blurred the valleys – like a Victorian water-colour. Behind us in the east the storm still raged over the Engadine; dark clouds blotted out the mountains; forked lightning dived into the valleys; thunder echoed endlessly. We would not have missed it – it was one more mountain experience to add to our treasure store – but we were mighty glad we were travelling west.

Safely arrived at Visp, we parked the car and our luggage was transferred to the mountain railway. One large flat parcel we carried ourselves, not trusting it even to the careful hands of the very ancient porter who year by year looks after us at Visp. This was the plaque to be placed on the wall of the Hotel Bahnhof in memory of Bernard. For nearly a year Bernard's British friends had been sending us donations towards this plaque; it had been designed by Kenneth Tyndall, head of the Building School at the Leicester College of Art and one of our cathedral songmen. Kenneth has a great love for the mountains and he had put his best work into it. The result was admirable; the plaque is blue and is decorated with an ice-axe round which is coiled a guide's rope. Below is written in white lettering the simple message which expresses exactly what Bernard meant to his friends.

'Gratefully remembering
Bernard Biner
29th December 1900 – 9th April 1965
his British friends commemorate with this tablet
a great guide
and a good friend to all climbers.'

We hoped Pauly would like it; we were not disappointed.

The day chosen by the Biner family for the little ceremony was August 20th – the feast of St Bernard. The plaque was placed in position and covered with the Union Jack. In the late afternoon a crowd gathered at the Hotel Bahnhof. Everything was quite informal; most of us were in climbing kit because we were on our way home from the hills. All Bernard's family were there and a large assortment of his British friends; a few Swiss climbers, known to us all, came too. Peter Arengo-Jones, the British Press attaché in Berne, represented the Embassy. I looked at the crowd gathered reverently round the balcony where Bernard used to spend so many hours; most of them I had known nearly all my life. There were his cousins and other veterans who had been so dashing when I had been a schoolgirl and Bernard was a brilliant and promising young guide; there were his nieces and nephews whom we had watched grow up and there were the four little great-nieces whom he had spoilt so blatantly and who, of course, adored him.

The sun burnished the summit of the Matterhorn; the church bell tolled for vespers; a few dun-coloured cows ambled slowly by; a mother called to her child in Zermatter dialect – all sights and sounds Bernard had known and loved throughout his life. As the clock struck Ronald began his short speech and read aloud the letter sent by Antony Rawlinson on behalf of the Alpine Club. He drew back the Union Jack and said the words of dedication. For a moment we all stood in silent, thankful remembrance; then Ronald handed to Pauly the leatherbound album containing the names of the many who had subscribed for the plaque. It was so short and so simple but it expressed what we all felt. Bernard would have been pleased – and perhaps a little proud.

The next day, when our own services at the little English church were over, we went along to the village churchyard to put some flowers on Bernard's beautifully completed grave. It is a real mountaineer's grave, restrained, but full of meaning for those who understand. Beside the granite cross is carved an ice axe and rope and on the kerbstone the words, in German, from the 121st Psalm, *Ich hebe meine Augen auf zu den Bergen, von welchen mir Hilfe kommt.*

We laid our flowers beside the edelweiss Pauly's loving hands had planted. The shadow of the Matterhorn fell across the grave. It was all as it should have been – Bernard rested in peace.

On our way back to the Monte Rosa we ran into John Hunt; all mountaineers were delighted that he had been made a life peer in the birthday honours. Now he was able to tell us the date for his installation in the House of Lords, and we promised to be there or die in the attempt.

We came home to a change in our household. Leslie Green, our chauffeur-gardener whom we had inherited from Ronald's predecessor, left us after twelve happy years to train as a teacher of handicapped children. It was quite a blow to us as he had been such a permanent part of the set-up, but it seemed right that he should go to such useful work for which he had a particular gift.

A successor had to be found and we could not have been more fortunate. Another Mr Green arrived – Lawrence – an ex-police officer who fills the bill most excellently. Within a few weeks it seemed as if he had been with us for years.

A glance at the autumn diary, after we got home from our holiday, told us that among all the multitude of duties that awaited us we had at least two trips to the north. Before that there was Ronald's annual important engagement at Cromer at the end of September; during this I managed to fit in a visit to Verily Anderson at Northrepps. There had been no chance to see Verily since she had played such a noble part in our Teenage Brains Trust in 1963 but we were all agog to meet for two reasons. One was the publication of a small charming book about the Buxton family. *Family Sketch Book a Hundred Years Ago* is the work of Ellen Buxton and has been arranged by her granddaughter Ellen Creighton. The second reason was that Verily herself was working on a somewhat similar but larger book which she was to call *The Northrepps Grandchildren.* We had a wonderful family tea-party with her children, spent a long time sorting out our various relations and family names from the Buxton book and eventually ended up having drinks with the Gurneys at Northrepps Hall where we saw the famous old rocking-boat pictured in the sketch book.

Early in October I received an invitation to the Women of the Year luncheon at the Savoy. It was exciting to be asked and I decided it would be fun to go although it hardly seemed to be exactly my cup of tea. It supports the Greater London Fund for the Blind and our friend Zoë Hyde-Thomson is one of the chief protagonists. So, on the theory of 'try anything once', I wrote my acceptance.

My previous connections with the Savoy had been during the war as a driver picking up passengers; it was quite a different matter sailing in by the embankment entrance. There seemed to be millions of women seething in the foyer; I could not see a single person I knew. I felt a terribly new girl and began to wish I had never come when I suddenly spotted Zoë and that was the end of my troubles – I soon found myself linked up with people I knew and others whom I was very glad to know. I fancy we were all there to hear Mrs Harold Wilson; unfortunately she was the one speaker missing. However, we heard excellent speeches from Hermione Baddeley and Thora Hird and I caught a glimpse of Mary Quant, Mary Rand and Twiggy, so at least I could feel I had been in touch with the stage, the world of fashion and the Olympic games – not a bad haul for one lunch.

In the middle of the month we went up to Durham for Ronald to preach the Founders and Benefactors Sermon in the cathedral; this, as we remembered from our Durham days, is always the first important event of the academic year in the University (frivolously known among the students as 'Bounders and Malefactors'). It was years since we had been back; we knew there were many changes, especially in our own St John's College, but there was still a handful of people left who belonged to our time and in any case a university suffers less from change than most places.

Changes there certainly are but they have been done on the whole with great regard for the history and character of Durham; there was nothing to complain about, indeed we thought most of them were for the better.

We stayed at the deanery with John and Margaret Wild and Margaret gave a dinner party to which she had invited most of the people we still knew in Durham. As the service did not take place until the next afternoon, Mrs Wilson and Alicia, some of my closest friends since schooldays, came over from Darlington to have 'elevenses' with us. This was marvellous; we can so seldom meet now but I can never forget that when we first arrived in Durham, new and desperately homesick for London, it was Alicia and her mother who made the first few weeks bearable. We keep in touch by letter and telephone and when we do meet we begin where we last left off.

The service in the cathedral was just as it always had been in our day except that it was, if anything, bigger and grander. As I sat with Margaret Wild waiting for the procession to appear I could not suppress the memory of the ghastly occasion at an earlier service when the preacher's dentures shot out of his mouth and before we had recovered from that one, an invading bird swept down the nave and perched on the head of a don whom we had always thought exactly resembled a gargoyle.

No such diversions occurred on this afternoon; it was good to see the traditional service carried through by a new generation of dons and students, diocesan clergy and befrilled choristers with all the dignity and meaning that had characterized it for decade after decade.

The tea party which followed at the deanery was a reunion with former friends and colleagues, some of them now grown old and retired but still delighted to discuss 'the good old days'. As we climbed into our sleepers that night on the *Tynesider* – the train we used so often for term-time trips to London – we were brimming over with happy memories, now so vividly revived, of our sojourn in Durham. The north as such never has had, and I am afraid never will have, many attractions for a fanatical southerner like me; but those eight happy, busy years, perched on the rock, in the enclaves of the cathedral and university, were among the most memorable years of our married life.

Home again to the life in Leicester, which succeeded that in Durham and is equally happy and even busier, we had to find time to enjoy an event of significance only to ourselves – the publication of Ronald's paperback *What's Right with the Church of England* which occurred very appropriately on the day after the anniversary of his consecration. Sick to death of the current passion for abusing the Church, especially on the part of those within it, Ronald had at last been goaded into a small but enthusiastic and reasoned apologia in favour of it. Since I, who can seldom see two sides to any question, believe that disloyalty whether to friends or institutions is one of the most heinous crimes, I would willingly have gone round with a sandwich board proclaiming the title. Such an excess of zeal was banned by the powers that be, ie Ronald, but nevertheless the little volume had some good notices during the next few months and also a number of glad and grateful letters. Surprisingly there were very few from those who profess to depise their Church – perhaps they were too dumbfounded to put pen to paper.

Swiftly descending from the sublime to the ridiculous, my *Dear Abroad* was finished and ready to be sent to Philip Unwin about the same time, so altogether there was reason for mild satisfaction in the literary purlieus of our lives.

On November 1st we set out once more for the North, this time by car with our faithful Mr Green to drive us. This was a most special occasion – the consecration of Ian Ramsey as Bishop of

Durham. We were thrilled when the announcement was made; Ian and Margaret are old and very close friends of ours and he had been a canon theologian of Leicester for many years, making frequent visits to the cathedral. Our Provost, John Hughes, and his wife Sybil came with us to represent the Cathedral Chapter; Ian had asked Ronald to be one of his presenting bishops. Like most consecration services it was a magnificent and moving occasion and those attending from the diocese of Leicester were proud that when the Queen's mandate was read the new Bishop, who had been a professor at Oxford and had many other distinctions, was described simply and solely as 'a canon theologian of our Cathedral Church of St Martin, Leicester'. For us, of course, it was a Durham as well as a Leicester occasion and we had the pleasure of seeing all our Durham friends for the second time within a week. Before we said goodbye to Ian and Margaret we were able to arrange a luncheon party with them in the House of Lords on the day on which Ian was to be installed. That was another great day and brought to a conclusion a series of occasions which had brought much happiness and satisfaction to a large number of people.

Quite soon after all this came John Hunt's installation in the House of Lords. By a lucky coincidence we both had to be in London that day for meetings and, just to make a perfect ending, the Swiss Alpine Club dinner had been fixed for that night. I got leave of absence for an hour from the Mothers' Union Central Council, which was my chief reason for being in London, and had a good view of the ceremony from the peeresses gallery. Joy Hunt was there with some of the daughters and as I sped back to my MU meeting I ran into them and had a chance to offer my personal congratulations.

Before the year ended there came Ronald's turn to give his lecture in a series being given in the Great Hall of Lambeth Palace Library. It was an autumn course of seven lectures on Anglican approaches to Christian unity; several of his friends, among them Owen Chadwick and Sammy Greenslade, were taking part which greatly enhanced the interest. Ronald's subject was 'The Lutheran and Reformed Churches'; being chairman of this committee he had enjoyed the preparation and when the time came we both enjoyed as well the peaceful, scholarly atmosphere of that lovely old room.

Lutheran events crowded in upon us just then as the lecture was followed almost immediately by a dinner at Lambeth for the Bishop of Iceland and his wife. This was a friendly domestic affair and the Bishop's wife charmed all the guests by wearing her colourful national costume with her hair in two pretty pigtails. It added quite a Continental atmosphere to the dignity of the dining-room. Joan Ramsey and I decided it was rather a pity there was not something similar for English wives; when we said goodbye to Joan and to the Archbishop we all remembered that in another two months they would be staying with us to inaugurate the Ruby Year of the diocese of Leicester.

CHAPTER VII

Celebrations at Home and Abroad

IF one lives in a comparatively modern diocese, commemorations must of necessity have a slightly different slant from those of the ancient sees. In Leicester we think at present not in centuries but in decades. It is true that the diocese of Leicester existed for two hundred years in the dark ages; this came to an end when our Christian predecessors were somewhat precipitately driven out by the Danes. They destroyed the diocese but left a legacy of lovely names around north and east Leicestershire – Beeby, Barsby, Thurnby, Rearsby, Saxelbye to mention only a few. Ronald is in fact the twelfth Bishop of Leicester but to all intents and purposes he is only the third – the diocese and cathedral having been re-hallowed in 1927.

However, there are important milestones even in a young diocese; by common consent forty years was decided upon as an occasion worth celebrating and 1967 was designated Ruby Year. The opening event was to be a two-day visit by the Archbishop of Canterbury and Mrs Ramsey. This was billed for February, January being notorious for frightful weather and also a month that is crowded with a plethora of events extending from Sunday school parties to hunt balls.

I suppose I suffer from a certain amount of retarded development but I still enjoy these parties as much as, if not more, than those rumbustious affairs in the Christmas holidays of long ago which sent us back to school, surfeited with charades and sherry trifle and as potential propagators of infectious diseases. I still find it hard to believe, but the headmistress always assured my mother that it was the overcrowding at the Christmas parties that made the spring term such a nightmare for mumps and measles. Not that we cared: the fun and the food were well worth a swollen neck or a suspicious rash.

However, the parties we enjoy so much today seldom produce any adverse results; we can accept only a tiny percentage of the invitations we receive but January is still highlighted by a few social events. This year, being so involved with Ruby Year arrangements, we had to limit ourselves to two. One was a private dinner party in the precincts of Westminster Abbey given by one of our canons theologian, Professor Gordon Dunstan and his wife. Their delightful home in Little Cloister was a perfect setting; after dinner, muffled up to the ears in scarves and coats, we wandered round the courts and cloisters in the frosty moonlight. The Victoria Tower of the Houses of Parliament dominates this part of the precincts and Big Ben makes clocks unnecessary. We learned so much about the flora and fauna of Westminster that I collected enough material to write an article when I got home. Mercifully *The Field* accepted it, for I could ill afford the time I gave to it.

Our only other party was a military affair. Since our dearly-loved Leicestershire Regiment was disbanded Army occasions have almost, but not quite, disappeared. This was a ball in aid of SSAFA in which our Lord Lieutenant, Colonel Andy Martin, and his wife Peggy, are the moving spirits. We are immensely lucky in our Lord Lieutenant. Andy Martin has taken over the house of his uncle, the famous Sir Robert Martin loved by every man, woman and child in the city and county. It cannot have been an easy task to follow him but no better heir could have been found. When Andy became Lord Lieutenant everyone was delighted. They both labour unceasingly for Leicester and Leicestershire and every good cause, however small, has their support.

It was the first ball we had been to since 1963; we made up a party with Jimmy and Eileen Good and as Jimmy is an ex-army padre it was an excellent arrangement. We all renewed our youth like the eagle and even stayed for breakfast. We were not the last to leave – Andy and Peggy were still dancing vigorously when we decided to call it a day.

Fortified by this fun, we cleared the decks, so to speak, for Ruby Year and the visit of the Archbishop and his wife. We were looking forward to it enormously; we love them privately and admire them officially and this was to be a real state visit to the diocese. They arrived on February 21st, the exact date of the rehallowing of the Cathedral in 1927. From the very first they laid themselves out to give of their best and never spared themselves for a minute. The press naturally were eager to be in on the private as well as the public side of things. We invited them to Bishop's Lodge and all four of us, plus Martin, were photographed from every angle. The results, fortunately, were quite pleasing.

The dinner party we had arranged for that evening was kept entirely private. It was a very happy occasion; most of those we had invited had not expected to do more than shake hands with our chief guests. However, the Ramseys were very willing to be piloted from group to group while drinking their coffee and everyone present had a conversation with them. I always hope we got it across to them what enormous pleasure this informality gave.

The next morning we were all up betimes for a great Eucharist at St Philip's church at which the Archbishop celebrated. Seven fifteen on a busy weekday morning is not a normal time at which to expect a large crowd at church; events proved it could be done; people arrived by car, bus, and bicycle from near and far and we had a magnificent service attended by many hundreds.

Immediately after breakfast the Archbishop was off with Ronald on a round of engagements culminating in a luncheon for men arranged by the Far and Near Club who had changed their annual dinner into a luncheon for this year. Meanwhile Joan Ramsey and I had a more relaxed morning; we had promised ourselves a good old natter about times gone by when we were all together at Durham; when the Archbishop was a canon professor and Ronald was Principal of St John's College. We relived every minute of those days and the course of events that had led to our present situations. Neither of us had ever seen ourselves as any kind of public woman – certainly we had never desired it – but now in our different ways and out of loyalty to our husbands we seemed in some shadowy sense to have become such. So many women seem absolutely born to public careers and carry out everything with such expertise that it is quite a relief to know someone whose reactions approximate to one's own.

That evening the inauguration of Ruby Year was brought to a conclusion by festal evensong in our cathedral. The Archbishop preached an inspiring sermon to a congregation so tightly packed that it was almost impossible to feel for one's handkerchief or collection. But no one minded; the Archbishop set the tone for Ruby Year – that was all that mattered.

When our visitors left next morning our little household gathered on the steps to wave goodbye; they had endeared themselves to all of them; each one felt they had found new friends.

A big programme of events throughout the diocese was planned to begin after Easter and continue until Christmas. Each rural dean made the arrangements for his deanery and Ronald and John Hughes, as Provost of the Mother Church of the diocese, were to travel round to them all in turn. The Provost had generously undertaken the organizing of this tour. Before these strenuous months began we were to have a spring holiday – of all wonderful things, a cruise to the Eastern Mediterranean and the Holy Land.

We had never been on a cruise, in fact we had never really considered such a possibility, but our good friend Morris Perry, who had arranged our previous parties to the Holy Land, asked Ronald to lead this cruise-pilgrimage. It seemed just the thing to set us up for the busy period ahead and we said yes.

This time we had no responsibility for making up the party which numbered two hundred; but we did take with us about two dozen people from the diocese which made a pleasant nucleus of friends when we set off.

We sailed from Southampton on the *Venus* – once known as the '*Vomiting Venus*' but now fortunately fitted with stabilizers. What would have happened if this had not been so does not bear thinking about. We happened to catch a fierce spring gale while still off the Isle of Wight. I disappeared from view immediately; I understand that all but ten of the passengers took the same course; Ronald was one of the lucky ones and spent his time ministering to me. It was not until we were through the Bay and sailing gently up the Tagus to Lisbon that I surfaced again. However, from then onwards everything was pure heaven – something we shall never forget.

There is never a dull moment on a cruising liner. When we were in port there was always a shore excursion, the pleasure of which was much enhanced by the fact that there was never any packing or unpacking to be done – the ship was our home and was waiting to receive us back with all home comforts. When we were at sea there were the daily services taken by Ronald, a Methodist minister and a Roman Catholic priest. Sometimes we met separately, frequently all together. There were the lectures given before each excursion by Dick Southern, the Chichele Professor of History at Oxford, now President of St John's Oxford. These were superb and he made ancient history live for us all. There were deck games, especially table tennis which gave Ronald and me much-needed exercise every day; there were films and there was dancing and, perhaps best of all, there was time for everyone to lie in the sun, just reading and talking or thinking or even sleeping. To constant cruise passengers this may seem just what one would expect; to us it was a new and very acceptable way of life.

Lisbon was our first port and therefore rather particularly exciting. It is a peaceful place to arrive, especially after the rigours of the Bay. The great new suspension bridge and the gigantic memorial figure of Christ the King dominate the scene as the ships come into port. A motor coach took us through the tiled streets of the city and out in the cool of the evening to Cintra, Casquais and the renowned resort of Estoril where we sipped Turkish coffee under the jacaranda trees. We were charged a fabulous sum for this extravagance but it was nothing compared to the bill presented to a fellow-passenger rash enough to order a gin and tonic. He could have been excused for thinking he had bought the restaurant. Back to Lisbon through night air heavy with the perfume of oranges and lemons; the suspension bridge was brilliantly illuminated now and as the *Venus* sailed down the Tagus at midnight the statue of Christ the King glowed high above the river, reminding us of Lisbon long after the lights of the city had disappeared into the distance.

We sailed on southwards over the stretch of sea where Trafalgar was fought and won; early in the afternoon we had our first glimpse of the coast of Africa and, then at last Gibraltar, 'grand and grey' – a sight that makes the heart of every British subject beat a little faster. I had looked forward to this moment and found I had rather underestimated everything; the Rock was bigger and the Straits were wider than I had expected. That evening the setting sun lit up the snows of the Sierra Nevada, far away in Spain; when we strolled round the boat deck before turning in for the night the stars glittered with a Mediterranean brilliance. Tomorrow we should set foot in Africa – it was a thrilling thought.

The harbour area of Tunis is enormous. As we steamed slowly in we could see Cape Bon to our left. Immediately there came memories of World War II; this was where the Allies finally locked up the Axis armies and closed the African theatre of war. One gets almost schizophrenic in the Mediterranean – there is so much of ancient civilization and culture and so much of modern history all bound up in a comparatively small area.

Tunis brought to mind the Middle East: there were the bazaars and the noisy bargaining; there were veiled women and Arab men in their flowing robes. We had hardly become accustomed to this when we found ourselves in a great modern shopping centre; we might have been in the Place Vendôme or any other busy area of Paris. All notices were printed in French as well as in Arabic; it was entirely western; the Moslems had disappeared. Our coach took us to Carthage, where, scattered over the undulating environs of the bay, lay ruins of Cyprian's Christian Carthage and of its Roman predecessor, doomed to destruction by Cato's fateful watchword, *delenda est Carthago*.

From Carthage to Crete – if the atmosphere of our ship had not been so soothing and relaxing we should have been dizzy with the succession of civilizations we were caught up in. As it was there was time and leisure to arrange one's picture of Carthage in the right perspective before Dick Southern told us in his lecture, as we approached Crete, of the great Minoan civilization and the wonders of the Palace of Knossos which the excavations of Sir Arthur Evans had given to the world. We landed at the port of Heraklion and drove past the Venetian castle into the little town. Knossos lies some miles beyond; there is so much to see, so much to marvel at that I was almost surfeited – I brought away memories of huge red columns, of marble baths and of a remarkable drainage system that would probably have worked quite satisfactorily today. It is a woefully inadequate picture; one day I may be able to improve upon it. One other important discovery I made in Crete was snow-covered Mount Ida, reigning silently and majestically over the whole island; she must have provided a superb backcloth in the palmy days of Knossos; she must have seen great dynasties rise and fall; today she is just as she always was. I found Mount Ida easier to appreciate, easier to understand, than Knossos. To the Minoans it was a very natural birthplace of the gods.

For two days we sailed eastwards passing the southern coast of Cyprus and wishing all the time that we were to call there. Very soon we were to leave our ship for four days; we were to land at Beirut, visit Baalbek and Damascus, and continue to Jerusalem by car. For three days we were to stay in Jerusalem, then move north to Galilee. The *Venus* would eventually pick us up in Haifa. All this performance was because of the frontier regulations between Israel and Jordan; it seemed a lot of fuss about nothing, although those of us who had visited the Holy Land before knew only too well the tension of which we were always painfully aware at the Mandelbaum Gate. Had we but known it, tension in the Middle East had been mounting swiftly as we sailed unsuspectingly across the blue Mediterranean; far greater excitements awaited us than we could have imagined.

We packed our Jerusalem luggage overnight and at four-thirty the next morning I peeped out of our porthole; my heart stood still. Dawn was breaking over Mount Hermon; on the tawny hillside above Beirut pin points of light denoted tiny dwellings; along the water front hotels, houses and embassies had about them a translucent, opaque whiteness; in the harbour the ships of many nations were still brilliantly lighted. My first view of Beirut and the Lebanon had a romance about it that lingers with me to this day. I hear the place described as a rich and wicked city, materialistic beyond belief – a hotbed of vice. It may be so; indeed almost as soon as we landed I became aware that what I had seen from the ship was little more than a façade hiding much misery, but nothing, absolutely nothing, can take that fleeting glimpse of loveliness from me.

We went ashore in groups of forty each piloted by a leader. A fleet of shiny black cars awaited us; we were driven round the town to see the sights; as we emerged on to the Baalbek road we came upon the most appalling refugee camp I have ever seen; it seemed worse when set close beside such opulence and luxury as we had just seen in Beirut. There was nothing we could do – we had to pass by on the other side; my estimation of Beirut suffered a severe set-back.

The cars climbed up into the mountains of Lebanon; all around us were snow peaks; snow came right down to the road; skiers swung to a halt beside us. Far below, beyond the flat roofs of

Beirut, water skiers flashed across the Mediterranean in the wake
of speed boats.

I would willingly have spent the day at this spot – even the
wonders of Baalbek could not surpass this. But of course we had
to go on and at last we came to the enormous columns, and the
great arches that are all that remain of the great temples dominating the once vast city of Baalbek. It was more exciting than
Carthage or Knossos; perhaps it was the blossoming almond and
apricot trees among which it is set that seemed to have a human-
izing effect. Baalbek lived for me: it was still breathing, as if it had
never really died.

Back to the cars and away to Damascus – that was the plan of
campaign. 'Lunch in Damascus,' I whispered to Ronald contentedly. The words slipped off my tongue so easily but how much
was wrapped up in that remark. We had been to Damascus before.
Twice we had touched down at the airport, but from there one
could see only the distant outline of the city; our most vivid
memories were of swarthy, belligerent-looking Arab soldiers.
Today we were to stop for lunch and explore the street called
Straight.

We reached the Syrian frontier; the long line of cars stopped;
slowly, one by one, they began to creep across. Suddenly there was
a great commotion; everyone stopped again. We waited: half an
hour went by; an hour; another half hour. By this time we were all
suspicious and rather anxious – not to say almost suffocated by the
heat. Word went round that there was passport trouble. Presently
a group of officials with an unpleasantly Gestapo appearance progressed ruthlessly from car to car. Certain individuals were tapped
menacingly on the shoulder and commanded to alight. Our turn
came – we felt instinctively that it would! When we were all lined
up, twenty-one of us, a speech was made explaining that our passports were not in order; they carried the stamp of the Mandelbaum
Gate – an offence of the gravest magnitude. Persons who had been
in Israel must certainly not contaminate the country of Syria.

Ronald tried in vain to explain that he was the leader of the
party, that he must see them safely to Jerusalem. Not at all.
Would we please accompany the guards to the frontier post; the
cars must proceed at once to Damascus. Ronald pushed a pile of
documents into the hands of the Archdeacon of York, who seemed

to be blameless, and asked him to do the best he could. The cars roared off in a cloud of dust; we were marched sheepishly back to the post.

At that moment a diversion was caused by the appearance of a party of four hundred people led by the Bishop of Exeter.

'Hallo,' he called in an unnecessarily hearty manner, 'have you been arrested?'

'I rather think we have,' Ronald replied cautiously. 'How about yourself?'

'*You've* been in Israel before, haven't you', I remarked maliciously. 'We met you in there two years ago'.

At that moment an authoritative voice announced, 'The party from the Beeshop from Hexster please to proceed to Damascus'.

With a superior wave of the hand and an uncertain suggestion that he hoped he *might* see us again some day, Ronald's brother bishop vanished into Syria.

We sat on wooden forms in the frontier post wondering where we went from here but our immediate anxieties were soon allayed. The representative of the agency acting for Morris Perry worked miracles. He collected our passports *en bloc* from the official who refused to restore them to us; bundled us into cars which had mysteriously appeared from nowhere, and almost before we knew it we were on the way back to Beirut. We were all pretty hungry by then; it was four o'clock and breakfast on board the *Venus* had been at 6 am. None of us liked to mention the fact in our present circumstances but our rescuer remembered even this mundane detail. The cars were stopped at a restaurant-cum-souvenir shop in the little Lebanese town of Tschora; we had an excellent meal and Ronald bought me a lovely evening bag to remind me of the occasion.

We still were uncertain as to our future and when and where, if ever, we should catch up with the party again; the drive through the Lebanese mountains seemed rather less idyllic than it had on the outward journey. The kindly courier in charge of us put us down in the King's Hotel in Beirut and told us he would do his best to get us a flight to Amman – but it had to be one that flew *over* Syria; if we risked touch-down there our last state might be worse than our first.

At six thirty he rushed in calling to us to follow him. We were

driven through the rush-hour traffic of Beirut at break-neck speed
to the great international airport. There seemed to be all the in-
gredients for an Agatha Christie thriller. Searchlights wheeled
round the airport; the car brakes screeched hideously; someone
thrust our passports into our hands; no one stamped them; no one
even looked at them.

'Run, run,' implored our perspiring friend, 'we have the last
twenty-one places on the flight to Amman'.

Someone pointed towards a plane; we galloped across the concrete and arrived on board in a series of leaps. I approach any
flight with a certain trepidation. I threw discretion to the winds on
this occasion; all I desired was to find myself airborne. Once more
we saw the mountains of Lebanon, this time from above; in forty
minutes we touched down at Amman – within reach of Jerusalem
at last.

There was only one more hazard to be overcome; Ronald had
somehow to explain the discrepancy in the number of his flock;
the ticket he offered to the young Jordanian policeman mentioned
two hundred persons. The young man smilingly counted up to
twenty-one – please could the reverend say what had become of
the other one hundred and seventy-nine? The reverend did his
best; his friends had been obliged to travel by another route; cars
from Jerusalem had come to meet us at this airport; the agency had
said so. The policeman went to investigate and, to our intense surprise, found the cars waiting with their Arab drivers. With much
bowing and hand-shaking and the broadest of smiles we were
escorted out of the airport. The cars drove in close convoy up the
dark and dangerous road to Jerusalem; never had the lights of the
Holy City looked more inviting as we came up from Jericho. We
forgot the howling of the jackals and the fierce Bedouins crouching
beside their goatskin tents; our only thought was of the welcome
awaiting us in Jerusalem.

On the steps of the hotel the party has assembled to greet us;
our rooms were ready; our luggage had arrived; dinner would be
served at once in spite of the midnight hour. Astronauts from
outer space could not have been better received. As I lay at last in
my comfortable bed looking out through the open windows at the
sleeping city I thought that perhaps after all I would not have
missed the experience; it had added an unexpected spice of adven-

ture to the trip. Above the chiming of the clocks I heard once more the howl of the jackals prowling outside the city walls in search of food. I was not sorry to be safely in bed.

The sun streaming into our room roused us early next morning to a perfect day; minarets and spires pierced a cloudless sky; already the *Muezzin* were calling the faithful to prayer. All the anxieties of the previous day were forgotten; everyone was eager to explore Jerusalem. Our time was short and there was so much to be seen. The itinerary was the same as in previous years; this was our third visit but the sacred sites to which we took our party seemed to have even more meaning for us than before. Perhaps it was because almost unconciously we were aware of the tension hanging over the city; things were boiling up to a crisis, of that there could be no doubt; would Jerusalem have to endure yet another siege; would the people and places we loved so much find themselves in a dangerous situation that was not of their making? We did not know the answers; we only knew that we had never before had so strong a sense of unease in Jerusalem.

When we went to Bethlehem there was something new for us to see. We went down to the Shepherds' Fields and near them discovered a beautiful little chapel. It is very modern; very simple, almost austere – but it has three frescos on the walls that caught my imagination. The first fresco depicts the shepherds aroused by the song of the angels. With them is their dog, a big black fellow, showing his teeth but cowering among the shepherds, obviously terrified by the vision. In the second fresco the shepherds are on their way up to Bethlehem; the dog is following them but looks back, undecided whether to go or stay. In the third the shepherds are worshipping at the manger; the dog sits beside the crib, all fear vanished, utterly at peace. It was the best Christmas sermon one could have.

On the day when we left the old city of Jerusalem for New Jerusalem and Israel, our Arab guide, Hilme Dakkak, came with us to the Mandelbaum Gate to say goodbye. He had never done this before; he looked strained and anxious as we shook hands.

'Come back soon,' he whispered as the officials pushed him back over the demarcation line. His voice sounded flat and hopeless as if he did not really expect to see us again. Our party was hustled across no-man's-land in the usual unceremonious manner and the great, streamlined coaches of the Israelis were waiting to pick us up. Instinctively I knew I should never see the Mandelbaum Gate again; I could not know that the Six Days War was only three weeks away; I only knew that something catastrophic had to happen.

We love the Arabs and their timeless way of life but this does not prevent us from admiring the Israelis. They have produced a prosperous, fertile country from land that for centuries had been almost entirely barren; they have built up a disciplined, dedicated generation of young people who cannot fail to rejoice the hearts of those who meet them.

This year, all through our long coach journey from Jerusalem to Haifa we came across at intervals, groups of uniformed young Israelis, men and women, marching and drilling – always with a smile and a wave of the hand for us. It was attractive; it was also ominous; we wondered what this display of military zeal really portended. We did not know; probably they did not know either; but when the fateful Six Days War came it was not difficult for anyone who had recently been in the Holy Land to foretell the result.

It was dark when we arrived at Haifa; the coach took us up to the top of Mount Carmel 'for a special treat' the guide told us. It was indeed a treat; it must be one of the most dramatic night time views in the world. Below us, glittering like a casket of jewels, lay Haifa; farther up the coast the lights of Acre were mirrored in the water and, out at sea, were anchored trading ships, tramp steamers and great cruising liners.

The coach slipped swiftly down the steep, winding road and took us to the port where the tender was waiting to take us out to the *Venus*. What a welcome we had as we clambered up the rope ladder; the entire crew was lined up to welcome us and a special dinner was provided. We had come to think of the *Venus* as home; as we settled down again in our little cabin we recalled the extraordinary and unexpected adventures which had befallen us since we had disembarked at Beirut. For three days the ship lay in Haifa while we went ashore to visit Galilee, Nazareth and Cesarea. It was good to be in Galilee again; even there we found evidence of tension but the atmosphere was quieter, less electric than in Jerusalem.

We sailed from Haifa at five o'clock on a pearly kind of morning.

M   177

Ronald and I were up long before that to watch our departure. A pale sun peeped over the top of Mount Carmel, gilding the dome of the Bahai temple; the work of loading and unloading began briskly on the cargo ships in the harbour. Haifa came gently to life again; early morning laundry flapped on the roof tops; pedlars appeared on the water front; through a faint sea haze we could see the coast going northwards towards Tyre and Sidon. The sirens sounded on the *Venus*; almost imperceptibly we were gliding out of harbour; we were leaving the Holy Land and once more we had left a little bit of our hearts there. But it was an anxious rather than a happy farewell; we wondered vaguely what would have happened before we saw it all again; there was trouble in store for that lovely land; as it happened we were some of the last visitors to leave before the storm broke.

The *Venus* took us across the Mediterranean and northwards up the Aegean Sea. Early one morning we woke to find ourselves entering the Dardanelles; we hate to miss anything of course; we slipped on our clothes and hurried on deck. There we had a surprise; usually we and a few other enthusiasts are the only passengers who haunt the deck in the early hours. Today was different; seated on deck chairs by the ship's side, well-muffled up against the breeze, were almost all the elderly passengers belonging to our party. Suddenly we understood; they were there to see the Gallipoli peninsula and the famous memorial; they belonged to the First War generation; there were some among them who had fought there; there were others whose loved ones lay buried there; it was only history to us; to them it was part of their lives. There was a hush about the boat as we sailed through the Dardanelles and breakfast was an unusually quiet meal. I tried to translate Gallipoli into Dunkirk, Tobruk and Arnhem so that I might enter into the feelings of these older fellow-passengers. What havoc war has wrought in the lives of two generations!

Everyone was on deck as we crossed the Sea of Marmora and sailed into the Bosporus; we were approaching one of the most exciting and celebrated cities in the world – what a pity that for our generation it has to be Istanbul; Constantinople sounds infinitely more far away and glamorous.

As it happened, when we went ashore I found Istanbul disappointing and sordid as a city but seen from the sea the effect is magical. Clusters of domes and minarets cleave the sky; some rise up from the water front; some are perched on thrusting hills, dominating the whole scene. The Bosporus is crowded with a variety of shipping; liners, launches, ferry boats jostle each other like traffic in a busy street. To our left we could see the Golden Horn; ahead of us the Bosporus narrowed before opening out into the Black Sea. Part of Istanbul lies in Europe, part, across the water, in Asia. Fussy little ferry boats ply to and fro bringing businessmen, shoppers and sightseers from one continent to another – a bridge between east and west.

The *Venus* docked beside the *Nevasa*, a British school ship; her decks were alive with excited girls and boys; among them was a party from a prep school in Leicestershire – it made this cosmopolitan port seem almost homely. We stepped ashore into a seething mob of screaming street vendors; somehow we found the coaches that were to take us round the city.

The one place we were all longing to see was, of course, St Sophia. Our Turkish guide had little interest in the place and suggested that the outside was more entertaining than the inside. With one accord we all announced that we proposed to leave the coach and explore the basilica; we managed to do so before the guide could protest further and left him hurling torrents of abuse at the coach driver. Dick Southern had given us a magnificent lecture on St Sophia and as he was in our sight-seeing party we really did get some understanding of this huge, historic, treasure house – in turn Christian church, Moslem mosque, and artistic museum.

When we emerged once more we found the coach waiting for us, in spite of the threats of the guide; we were immediately whisked off to see the palace of the Sultans which he obviously considered to be the *pièce de résistance*, and were then allowed a brief look at the Blue Mosque. This I thought, secretly, was quite the most attractive building we saw – less overwhelming than St Sophia, although much less important historically. The journey back to the port was a study in traffic congestion; everything seemed to be reduced to a crawl; it made London traffic conditions look comparatively simple. Back at the port there was time for bargaining and buying at the pedlars' stalls. Every conceivable commodity was being offered; we settled for turkish delight and a pair of embroidered slippers. That night as we sailed back through the Dardanelles I lay in our clean, safe cabin and wondered why Istanbul had seemed disturbing and rather frightening; there had been something in the atmosphere that instinctively repelled me. It was not until we had been home some months that I heard that it is said to be the worst drug centre in the world.

At sea again in the North Aegean I spent the morning begging nearly every member of the crew to let me know when we were in sight of the Island of Skyros. In spite of present-day pronouncements, or more probably because of them, I remain a fervent Rupert Brooke fan; I had hoped that a call at Skyros might give me a chance to see his grave. This was not to be but a kindly young officer, who must have been heartily sick of my importuning, lent me his binoculars and for a few minutes I had a hazy view of the island. It was a glorious day, we were among the Greek islands and approaching Athens, so what better time to read poetry. I fetched my copy of Rupert Brooke's poems and for a lovely, lazy hour I soaked myself in all my favourites. Ronald, being less of a fan than I am, struck a slightly jarring note by reminding me that by this time Rupert Brooke would have been seventy; strange how one always thinks of one's heroes as still at their zenith.

Athens – is there any other name that conjures up immediately so much of culture and beauty, of history and learning, of tragedy and achievement? Something in me responds instantly to Greece and all things Greek; I love the language and the literature; the ethereal beauty and immense strength of the architecture; the limpid atmosphere which lends a luminous quality to everything one sees. There is a grace about Athens which belongs to nowhere else. Previously we had arrived there by air; to arrive by sea is a thousand times more satisfying; every minute of our leisurely entrance to the port of Piraeus was packed with pleasure.

We were driven up from the port via Phaleron Bay; there seemed to be peace and beauty on all sides and all the way. We arrived in Constitution Square to find ourselves once more in the midst of crisis and tension. Outside the Parliament House were tanks and guns and masses of police and soldiers. We enquired of our nice Greek guide what all this was about. She shrugged her shoulders and replied that she thought there was going to be a general election. She swept us off to the Acropolis and we immediately became so involved in the magnificence of our surroundings that we never gave politics another thought.

That night we dined out on our own in Athens at a little Greek restaurant and finished the day with a performance of *son et lumière* in English on the Acropolis. From our seats on Philopoppos Hill we looked across to the Parthenon, the Erectheum, the Temple of Wingless Victory; below lay the sparkling lights of Athens and the moonlit Mediterranean breaking on the coast near Piraeus; it was a night to remember.

Next day we sailed from Athens for Gibraltar; while we were still at sea the *coup* occurred in Athens and the military regime took over. One more land of light and loveliness was in the throes of political upheaval, another centre of tension was set up in the western world.

Nothing could have looked more steadfast and more noble than the great grey Rock of Gibraltar as the *Venus* came in to dock below it. We had a few hours ashore – just long enough to discover that without doubt Gibraltar was to become one of our 'places'; somewhere to which we simply had to return. But even here rumours were rife; Spain had already closed to cars the main road leading into her territory; that night new regulations were put into force regarding air space. Somehow we were not too worried; it was impossible to imagine Gib capitulating.

The *Venus* sailed out into the Atlantic and set her course for home. For hours that night I sat by our cabin porthole in my nightie watching the lights of Tangier fade into the distance and the lighthouse on Cape Esparta, the last point of Africa, flinging its beam across the water. It had been a marvellously satisfying experience, this cruise. We had seen so much and learned so much; ancient history had come alive; Phoenicians, Byzantines and Crusaders had become part of our world. We had peeped at the ruins of civilizations that were old before Palestine became the Holy Land; we had stood where our faith was born; we had followed the route that brought the gospel to the west.

And besides all this there had been the immense fun and friendship that had been provided by life on the *Venus*. We loved every bit of that ship and we loved her crew from the steady watchful figure of Captain Saetre and Vivien the delightful hostess down to our cheerful kindly Norwegian stewardess. We had found friends among the passengers too numerous to mention and the companionship of Dick and Sheila Southern has become something of more than passing value. We were bronzed and fit and bursting with health; it had been one of those gorgeous experiences that you dream of but never expect to happen.

There was a great welcome waiting for us at home and little Martin's tail nearly fell off from its furious wagging. We were ready to tackle the strenuous programme for Ruby Year with tremendous vigour. The only sadness was the memory of the troubles we had seen in the Holy Land and Athens and Gibraltar. We hoped against hope that the worst would not happen in Palestine but we had hardly settled down to work when the Six Days War broke out. We had felt it was inevitable but we had never realized how easily we might have been caught up in it all.

All through the summer we travelled about the diocese spending the long, light evenings in the sixteen different deaneries. It was rather like visiting scattered members of a big family in their own homes. Our diocese is said by some to be about the ideal size; we think it also has exactly the right variety. There is the huge industrial city of Leicester in the middle with a population of three hundred thousand. There are another three hundred thousand in the county, divided between half a dozen large country towns and more than a hundred pretty villages. The Ruby Year arrangements gave us an opportunity of meeting the people from every parish; it was quite an exacting task but again and again we remarked to each other how incredibly lucky we are in our diocesan family. There is the mining population of west Leicestershire, some of whom have spent fifty years in the pits; there are the farmers from the south and east of the county whose families have worshipped in their ancient churches for hundreds of years; there are the folk from the Vale of Belvoir who tend to feel themselves cut off from the centre and are particularly appreciative of a visitor from Leicester; and there are the country towns like Melton Mowbray and Lutterworth, with glorious churches which are the pride of the people even when they are not churchgoers. We have always felt very close to our people but when this long series of visits was over we felt the ties between us had been immensely strengthened.

In the diocesan Mothers' Union we had decided that we must celebrate Ruby Year; I was told that it was an incredible number of years since the MU had had a big social event; it was my last year as president which seemed another reason for bringing the members together. So the diocesan Council agreed to go to town on the matter and book the De Montfort Hall, the biggest hall in the city. Unbeknown to me it was also agreed to make it a farewell party for the president. The sub-committee in charge of the arrangements asked if I would leave it all to them; I was very willing to agree – I already had almost more on my plate than I could cope with.

A few weeks before the party Ronald, egged on by the MU Council, began to drop hints. *If* someone wanted to give me a really lovely present what would I choose? Of course I thought it was a leg-pull; I could think of no one who was likely to come up with such a gift. At last in desperation he demanded.

'For heaven's sake, woman, do make some suggestions or my name will be mud with the MU.'

I was so astonished I found it hard to think at all but I soon recovered from that state; there were one or two things I knew I would love to have but I had always put them out of my mind as quite impossible.

It was an absolutely lovely party and it meant more to me than most people could imagine. I had become president only because people seemed to expect it of me; I had known almost nothing about the MU but the diocese had never had a Bishop's wife to be president and I felt I had a duty to them if they wanted me so much. It had been terribly hard going at first; I had everything to learn; I was unused to public speaking and the vast number of committees which I had to attend appalled me. Gradually, however, things began to fall into place; everyone was so kind and so grateful and I was thankful to find that the whole outfit did not disintegrate under my leadership, which was what I had feared might happen. And I had enjoyed my contacts with headquarters in London when we met twice a year for Central Council. I often wished, and I still wish, that it was possible for the public to know more of what the MU really does – the far-reaching nature of its work in this country and throughout the world. How many people know, for example, how often the opinion of the MU is sought by Government departments, or the fact that when there was a suggestion that the name 'Mothers' Union' might be changed the loudest outcry came from a highly-placed official in the world of television? He happened to be a man I used to drive during the war and I should have thought he would have been the last person on earth to be impressed by the MU.

An MU diocesan president is elected for three years and can be re-elected for three terms of three years but no more. My nine years would be up in December, so I was really having my party and my present six months in advance.

Ronald and I with our two assistant bishops and their wives received the 1,500 MU guests and after refreshments I was called up to the platform to receive my lovely gifts. I could hardly believe my eyes when I saw *two* – an exotic-looking garden swing and a hostess trolley, the very last word in modern amenities. I just stood and stared; I seemed to be incapable of speech but fortunately it was not necessary for a few moments because Margaret McCandless, one of our council members, was speaking.

It was the kind of speech I never expected to hear about me – I cannot imagine how Margaret thought of so many lovely things to say. I hardly knew how to reply but I was speaking to people I loved a lot and words were somehow given to me. Nicer presents could not have been chosen; when I relax luxuriously on the swing, or when I nonchalantly produce a hot meal for a guest when seemingly I have only been in the house five minutes, I invariably think of MU and realize how during those nine years they gave me far, far more than I ever gave them.

Many times during the next six months when I was winding up my presidency I was thankful that I was not saying goodbye; I would still be there to do all I could for the MU in a minor capacity and in trying to help my successor; and the council put the finishing touch to my happiness when they elected me a life vice-president – however old and infirm I get and wherever I may be I shall still be one of them.

The Church and State Commission, of which Ronald is a member, meets sometimes in London, sometimes in other places for residential conferences. It fell to our lot this summer to entertain them at Launde Abbey, our lovely medieval retreat and conference house. I went out to the Abbey, not as a conference member, let it be said, but to help wait at table and wash up afterwards. It was the greatest fun and I thoroughly enjoyed getting to know the pundits who were working so industriously on such weighty matters. I had met most of them before as I usually take the car to meet Ronald from these meetings, but living together was far more interesting. There was Lady Ogilvie whose son, tragically, was killed on the Matterhorn. I know the grave in the Zermatt churchyard so well and was able to promise that I would find some autumn crocuses to lay on it in August. Valerie Pitt was there; I have read her writings and heard her speeches and I am always slightly envious because she read English at Oxford – which is exactly what I would have liked to have done. The Chairman, Owen Chadwick, is an old friend whom one always feels the better for meeting. He is Master of Selwyn and Regius Professor of Modern History at Cambridge; in fact, I hardly dare think how learned he really is. But if we drop in on him and his wife Ruth in Cambridge he may easily be just back from an afternoon's swimming with his little daughter André or he will call one of his mountain-minded sons to come and discuss climbing. Erudite scholarship has not in any was destroyed Owen's love of the happy, simple things of life. There were lots more exciting people around; I found that a judge, two MPs, lady professors and similar people were ready to enjoy eggs and bacon for breakfast or a deck chair on the lawn after lunch and were full of gratitude to us for producing these things. Launde Abbey sees many, many conferences from scout and guide camps to ordination retreats; probably a more celebrated group than the Church and State Commission had never gathered under its roof, but the verdict of all our visitors is the same – what a peaceful place, what a perfect setting in which to get to grips with any problem.

Conferences and discussions of all kinds take place too at St George's House at Windsor Castle. The ruling spirit here is Robin Woods, Dean of Windsor. He has generously told me to come along with Ronald any time he has to go there; having once sampled the delights of St George's I am delighted to go whenever it proves possible. The delegates to these conferences concern themselves with the widest variety of subjects, most of them far beyond my comprehension. But sometimes wives are asked to participate as when, for example, a group of high-powered industrialists had gathered, with their wives to discuss ethics and business.

If the conferences are not open to outsiders I have a great time wandering about the castle grounds and rambling in the Great Park – it is my ambition to cover the whole three miles of the Long Walk from the castle to the statue of the copper house; so far I have never achieved this but it is lovely just to be there and if one happens to be walking at the right time when the Queen is in residence one can sometimes catch a glimpse of her coming back from her morning ride.

If we are there in the spring I take the car round to Smith's Lawn and the Savill Gardens and wander among the rhododendrons; or walk farther into the park where everyone in the district seems to be exercising their dogs.

Visitors to St George's House are welcome at the services in St George's chapel; this is something I would not miss for anything; early communion or afternoon evensong in the Garter Choir are something to remember.

Robin Woods, of course, makes the whole place live in the most dramatic way and his conducted tours always end up through a private door from St George's Chapel into the deanery. During our most recent visit we were allowed to see the lovely little new hexagonal chapel in which the coffin of King George VI rests; it was only just finished and a private service of dedication was to take place within a few days. We also saw the gazebo-like lodging which Henry VIII had built for poor Katherine of Aragon after her replacement by Anne Boleyn.

Our visit to St George's House in this particular year was a kind of prelude to our summer holiday. We were, as usual, Zermatt-bound and at last the time had come for me to introduce my youngest godson to the first delights of climbing. The Payne family, from Henley, were camping down in the Rhône valley. Christopher, at the age of nine, was already a wild enthusiast for hills of any kind. His parents telephoned us at the Monte Rosa to say that the sight of the snowy mountains had gone to his head. Could they all come up and could we do something for this would-be mountaineer?

We were thrilled; we loved nothing better than introducing our friends to Zermatt; when one of the friends happens to be one's own godson, and he a potential climber, everything seems to be happening for the best in the best of all worlds.

In the village street, at one of the climbing shops, I had espied a diminutive ice-axe. I remembered my own first axe, now handed down to the five sons of one of my climbing friends, and I decided that this weapon must be Christopher's. I hid it in the ski rack at the station and when he leapt off the train, yards ahead of the rest of the family, he became its proud possessor. We went up on the ski-lift to Sunegga – Michael and Christine, Richard and Elizabeth, Christopher, Ronald and I. Christopher and I shared a chair for two; his first sight of the Matterhorn caused him to gesticulate so furiously with his ice axe that I was sure it would end up in the forest below us. We walked to Tufteren and there we spent the morning on a crop of boulders that are a paradise for practice. Christopher outshone everyone; wedging the head of his axe in every likely nook and cranny he got himself to the top before most of us had started. It was only the promise of being allowed to see the *Senn* making the great cheeses in his little hut on the alp that brought Christopher to *terra firma* and eventually to the tiny restaurant where we all imbibed pints of tea while he made friends with the *Senn*.

We saw them off in the train down the valley, the new ice-axe protruding from the window until the avalanche tunnel hid them from us; it had been a joyous kind of day and one more recruit had joined the great band of mountain-lovers. I prayed fervently that the hills would give him as much as they still give me.

As to most music-lovers the 'Proms' have always meant something very special to us. Not that we have often been able to go to hear them: the only time we treated ourselves to season tickets was in 1944, and the doodle-bug onslaught brought the concerts to an end after we had heard only two. Since then it has usually been a matter of taking pot luck on the radio whenever we happen to be at home during the 'Prom' season. But of course, until 1967 it was not just the music that attracted us; the magnetic personality of Sir Malcolm Sargent was as compelling at the 'Proms' in the 1960s as it had been at the Messiah and the Carol Concerts in our courting days. Again and again since we came to Leicester, we have driven home at top speed from an engagement out in the county in order to hear at least a part of the Choral Symphony on the last Friday night and if we could hear nothing else on the final 'Prom' night we were somehow always glued to the radio for the frenzied thrill of the last half hour and, most of all, for Malcolm Sargent's

short speech which was as thought-provoking as many a
sermon.

But this year it had all been different: through the years we had
watched Sir Malcolm valiantly defeat one illness after another; in
July 1967 for the first time he was not at the rostrum on the opening night of the 'Proms'. A few days later there was news of a
serious operation; we waited anxiously for each bulletin; good
news was a long time in coming. It did come, however, and when
we left for Switzerland early in August he was pronounced out of
danger.

When we got home in September there was no more good news,
in fact there was very little news at all – only the bleak fact that
Sir Malcolm was totally unable to be at the 'Proms'. We listened
to the Choral Symphony on Friday, September 15th, and on
Saturday the 16th we tuned in sadly for the last half hour. *Land of
Hope and Glory, Rule Britannia, Jerusalem* – it was all going on as
it always did. We were listening, not viewing, but somehow there
seemed an atmosphere of expectancy about – it was inexplicable
but it was there. Colin Davis made the traditional last night speech,
it was a great success and the applause was tremendous. Then
suddenly he electrified the whole musical world: Sir Malcolm was
in the hall and he was going to fetch him. Sir Malcolm came in,
smiling and confident, and mounted the platform. The tumult was
such that even the massive Albert Hall must have been shaken to
its foundations; the roars and whistles and squeals went on for
minutes. The BBC commentator told us what was happening;
Vivien Banfield, chosen to represent the Young Promenaders,
stepped on to the platform and gave him a bouquet and a kiss.

Sir Malcolm silenced the crowd with a wave of his arm. He
began to speak: he spoke with humour and great depth of feeling;
he spoke generously of Colin Davis. And then he told us that the
1968 'Proms' would begin on July 20th and he had been invited to
be there. There followed just one more sentence: 'I have accepted
the invitation; God willing, we will all meet again then'. Amid
roars of rejoicing the orchestra began the national anthem; involuntarily we rose and stood as if we were present. We sat down
in silence; neither of us said so but each of us knew instinctively
that we should neither see nor hear him again in this life. Did Sir
Malcolm himself know? We shall never be sure but I believe that

for that moment, perhaps *only* for that moment, he really believed that he might live to see it all once more. Three days later he knew definitely that it could not be – he was told he had inoperable cancer.

It is said that his closest friends were told that he might live six months; ordinary admirers like us had no such knowledge and when his death came a fortnight later, at midday on Tuesday, October 3rd, we were not surprised, in fact our sadness had a tinge of thanksgiving.

By a strange coincidence, on the next Sunday the Archbishop of York, Donald Coggan, came to preach the University sermon in our cathedral and stayed with us. It seemed natural that the conversation should come round to Malcolm Sargent; it was only then that we came to know that the Archbishop was a close personal friend; he had been visiting Sir Malcolm regularly during the last few weeks and in fact had a date in his diary to go on from us to see him in London.

It was comforting to be able to talk to someone who had been in close touch with him so recently. I was only just beginning to realize what a gap his death would make in my small galaxy of heroes; I had admired his courage and his gaiety for so long; he had interpreted music for me in a very special way – as a part of life, an expression of life; whenever I saw him or listened to anything he was conducting I felt inspired and lifted out of myself. There could never be anyone to take his place; life was bound to be that much poorer; I was groping for something to hang on to and some of the things the Archbishop had told us provided what I was seeking.

He also told us when the memorial service was to be. The date was a disappointment because we knew we should be abroad on an official engagement, but it was wonderful to know that Sir Malcolm himself had chosen the music for the service and that the Archbishop was to give the address.

That evening Ronald preached the Harvest Festival in one of our lovely little country churches and we had supper afterwards with our friends Paul and Zoë Hyde-Thomson. Zoë is a goddaughter of Sir Malcolm Sargent and was going the next day to his funeral at Stamford. Once more we felt strangely close to him; we spent a quiet and happy evening talking of little else but his life and his music. As we drove home through lanes lit by the harvest moon I was quite sure that it was more than a lucky chance that had given me these two experiences – experiences that produced a sense of having re-established a contact that I felt was broken. Faith can seldom be explained by logic; one just has an innate knowledge that one's needs have been met.

In the middle of October a large and interesting-looking parcel arrived for me – it proved to be nothing less than the complimentary copies of my new book *Dear Abroad* due for publication on the next day. There are few things more exciting for an amateur author than to see the result of one's labours in its final form. The proofs are interesting even if they mean more hard slog; the arrival of the jackets for perusal gives one some idea of what to expect; but the firm feel of the finished article, with the shiny jacket suitably inscribed with title and author and the end-papers carrying the blurb and blatant advertisements of one's earlier efforts, produces a very considerable sense of satisfaction and well-being. This can only too soon be obliterated by a couple of scathing reviews, but just for a little while, before anyone has had time to be rude, there is a feeling that this is part of one's very self; it may not be much perhaps, but it is something – 'a poor thing but mine own'.

At the end of the month we set out on a journey that very few people have the opportunity to make. In Wittenberg in East Germany the German Evangelical Church was about to celebrate the 450th Anniversary of the Reformation. Wittenberg, being Martin Luther's town – the *Lutherstadt* – was the natural rendez-vous and the German Church had invited representatives from all over the world to take part in the celebrations. The British Council of Churches was sending a delegation and Ronald, representing the Archbishop of Canterbury, was taking a smaller party from the Church of England.

The date had been booked for a year but no one, either here or in Germany, had dared to hope that it would really come off. The East German Government might throw a spanner in the works at any moment. Our flights were booked, masses of literature had been received; with typical German thoroughness the programme was organized to the last detail, but it was only two days before we were due to leave that we received a telegram from East Berlin to say that our visas were waiting for us at Schönefeld airport. We breathed a sigh of relief; at least I breathed a sigh of relief – I was dying to have a peep behind the Iron Curtain. Ronald was not quite so sure: more than one of his clerical friends had got detained in East Berlin on various occasions. They had always been reprieved in the end – but he did not exactly relish the idea of languishing in an East German gaol until someone decided to let him out.

We took off from Heathrow for Amsterdam on a horrible blustery morning with press photographers running round in circles taking pictures – none of which we ever saw. Our travelling companions included Owen Chadwick Paul Oestreicher, and Michael Moore from the Council of Foreign, Relations, who was to act as chaplain for Ronald when necessary. We came down at Schiphol airport in Amsterdam; many times at the end of our summer holiday we have spent a night at the motel at Schiphol and watched the planes coming in and out; we rather thought there would not be many watching us on a wet, cold late autumn day. We had two hours at Schiphol so we rang up our friends the Roelfsema's at Voorburg and gave them a great surprise.

The next flight was on a Polish plane. No one has to travel about Schiphol airport on little buses; the plane is brought to the door, as it were. In other words a mobile tunnel is attached to the assembly channel and passengers march out of the airport building and find themselves on the plane. It was a bumpy flight but mercifully planes are the only form of transport that has not, so far, made me sick. We quite enjoyed the flight; the autumn colours were brilliant below us; as we roared over the fields and villages *en route* for Berlin – a new flight for us – we thought of our bomber pilots, twenty-five years ago, making their way night after night over this same terrain on their devastating missions to Berlin.

We touched down at Schönefeld airport; the Government of the Deutsche Demokratische Republik – the DDR – is obviously not interested in producing any kind of welcome to arriving travellers. It is quite the shabbiest little airport we have ever seen and certainly the quietest: the continuous coming and going of planes from all parts of the world that one associates with a airport were missing – I had the impression that our flight was the only one scheduled for that day.

We were herded into a hall equipped with a few wooden benches fastened to the walls and immediately a smiling, gentle-faced man stepped forward to greet us. He was a Lutheran pastor, the leading *Oberkirchenrat* of the district who had come to welcome the British party. Having said how delighted he and the whole East German Church were to receive us, he went on to explain that already there was a disappointment. The government had only that day decreed that no visitors would be allowed to travel outside the immediate neighbourhood of Wittenberg. This meant that the scores of sermons that were to have been preached in all the churches of East Germany on the coming Sunday had been cancelled. It is almost impossible to explain what this meant to the German Church. For nearly a year plans had been going forward to ensure that every hard-working pastor and his faithful congregation all over the country should have the opportunity of hearing someone from outside; it would have been a breath of new life to these people who seldom see, and even less often hear, someone from another country. The pastor was at pains to explain that this was not intended as an insult to the delegates; it was a way of penalizing the Church for some imagined misdemeanour – no one knew what.

We had been booked for months to spend the Sunday at Rostock on the Baltic coast; it would have been interesting, but it meant a journey of five hundred miles, so we were not too badly disappointed. But we were desperately sick at heart for the German Church who had laboured so hard and now found their dreams turned to ashes by one dogmatic announcement.

We went through the endless routine of passports and customs and were mightily relieved to be given our visas at last. The visas of two members of our party could not be found; they were not allowed to travel with us but were taken off to Berlin while enquiries were made. Ronald gave me a meaningful 'I told you so' glance but at that minute orders were given for us to board the coach and we all rushed off as one man, lest we be left behind in this inhospitable spot.

The coach journey to Wittenberg, a distance of about eighty miles, was a surprise to us. We know West Germany very well and, with the exception of the industrial area of the Ruhr, we have always thought of it as a beautiful country with magnificent scenery, fine towns and lovely villages. East Germany seems entirely different and this particular aspect of the country cannot be laid at the doors of the regime. It is flat: there are very few towns, little industry and a scanty population; the dominant feature is miles of rather wild heathland.

Dusk was falling; the gaunt arms of the trees threw eerie shadows across the shafts of light made by our coach; we felt we were in a very strange land which it was difficult to assess. I looked at my watch; it was nearly half-past six; in Westminster Abbey the memorial service for Sir Malcolm Sargent had just begun. I thought of the light and warmth of the glorious building; of the paeans of praise that would be winging their way among the Gothic arches seeking to interpret the spirit of one who said that he loved life so much that he would love death still more. There would be no sadness there – only thanksgiving and dedication. I thought how lucky we were to live in a land where the qualities of a man like Sir Malcolm Sargent could have full rein and be publicly understood and applauded. Here in this drab country, where individual freedom was almost non-existent, there must be many who had these same qualities and could give no expression to them – people who were beating their wings against the bars of a cage and might presently become too exhausted to do anything but acquiesce.

Probably the dreary countryside and the long, bumpy journey had made me unnecessarily depressed; as we approached the old city of Wittenberg I realized that here at least was one lovely place.

We rumbled slowly down the medieval main street and drew up outside the Augusteum – the great building, once a monastery, where Martin Luther studied and taught. Immediately the street was full of life: German theological students, men and women, seized our luggage and escorted us to a hall where there was ample accommodation for us all to rest. Trays of sandwiches and coffee appeared at once; whatever may have been lacking at Schönefeld airport was more than made up for in the Augusteum. We revived at once; people from all parts of the world surged in, travel-stained and weary; all quickly rehabilitated by the warmth of the welcome that was waiting for them. We spotted friends from America, from Scandinavia, from France, and last, but by no means least, one very dear friend, Marcel Pradervand from Geneva, who had been the Swiss pastor in London during the war.

Eventually we were asked to attend at what were described as the 'official rooms'. First, it need hardly be said, passports had to be produced; from there we went on to someone who gave us a card for our accommodation; in the next room meal tickets must be collected – a different one for each meal of our stay! Then there was *Sanitatsdienst* – health service. One look at us convinced the doctor that we were in disgustingly good health and we quickly passed on to the door which said '*Geschenk*'. Here for every delegate was arranged an intriguing parcel of books, commemoration stamps, a writing compendium, picture postcards, and a magnificent 'Luther Seal'. We were touched beyond words; how could these people and their Church, so cut off from the outside world, possibly manage to be so generous? We reached the last room; an even more moving sight awaited us – there was a little envelope containing pocket money for each of us! We begged them to take it back; surely they needed it more than we did; we explained falteringly that we had come empty-handed – we had brought nothing for them. '*Das macht nichts*,' smiled the young man in charge. 'You have come – it is the best present you could bring us.'

We examined our accommodation cards more closely and discovered that we were all to be entertained at the village of Bad Schmiedeberg, about eighteen miles away, and the limit of our freedom of movement. The accommodation was the contribution of the DDR to the Reformation celebrations. The resident patients at a huge clinic for rheumatic diseases had all been sent home and we took their places. Ronald and I were given what we imagined must be a kind of side ward for two; it was warm and comfortable; there was a slightly clinical atmosphere about it but we were extremely happy there and considered ourselves to be most fortunate.

The next morning was to be set aside for exploring Wittenberg or, more accurately, for discovering all there was to discover about Martin Luther. We somehow managed to miss the local bus; instead a pastor from a nearby village gave us a lift in his car. We learned many things from him during that trip. The Church in East Germany is terribly poor, but the Church in West Germany supports them generously and in that way they keep going. He told us that his little car was a gift from the Church in a small West

German town. Life was not easy, he explained, but within restricted limits they were able to carry on and the churches were full. The one thing that everyone minded most was the almost complete lack of contact with the outside world. This was why these Luther celebrations were of such immense importance and had been looked forward to so eagerly – for the first time for years there was an influx of people from outside. In the course of the drive into Wittenberg we frequently saw large groups of Russian troops in the lanes and fields. We asked no questions but their presence made the atmosphere uncertain and rather sinister.

Arrived at the Augusteum we did ourselves well on Martin Luther. It is easy to drop back four or five hundred years there; the quiet grey buildings; the peaceful garden; the old, old trees, some of which were said to date back to Luther's time; it all made a décor against which it became easier to understand and appreciate Luther. There were at least two rooms entirely devoted to his books; there were galleries of pictures and old prints which made the local life of those days come alive most vividly. But best of all there was Luther's house: here we saw the bed where he slept, the table at which he worked, the window from which he watched the life of the place going on below. I found it fascinating. Having been taught history at school by an Irish Roman Catholic my previous picture of Martin Luther had been, to say the least of it, one-sided – some would say distorted. I enjoyed re-thinking it all and getting things in better perspective.

The afternoon we meant to give to the town of Wittenberg, having had just about as much as we could take of Luther by that time. The whole town was *en fête*; it was an enchanting scene on a late autumn afternoon. An ox was being roasted whole on the market place; gaily decorated stalls attracted eager crowds. At first we thought this must all be in honour of the Reformation – we soon discovered our mistake. By a remarkable fact of history the fiftieth anniversary of the Lenin Revolution coincided with the four-hundred-and-fiftieth anniversary of the Reformation. This suited the government of the DDR exactly; four hundred years of the Reformation and then the Lenin Revolution; what could be more natural! what a happy coincidence! All the shops and houses were decorated; nearly everyone had a picture of Luther festooned in purple ribbon and beside it one of Lenin framed in red ribbon.

Just a few households, but only very few, had dared to defy convention and showed the picture of Luther alone. It must have called for great courage; we wondered anxiously what might be the result.

We tried to sum up our idea of the population – how they differed from the people of West Germany. They looked quite well-fed; they did not look poor; their clothes were not particularly shabby. And yet in some subtle way they were different from people of other countries; they looked dowdy, old-fashioned; they might have belonged to 1912 or some such date; they so obviously had little or no idea of what was going on elsewhere.

In the evening we had promised to go to a youth conference; this was to make up for our cancelled visit to Rostock. In some ways it was more worth while. Fifteen hundred boys and girls from all over East Germany had managed to get themselves to Wittenberg and were sleeping in halls and hostels and schools. Unlike other young people in Europe they spoke no English; the youth leader of the German Church also spoke no English; she was one of the most remarkable and dedicated women I have ever met. Our German was taxed to the uttermost but we rather enjoyed trying to do our best. We were asked to tell them about ourselves. Ronald had a real bit of luck; it happened to be the anniversary of his consecration, October 28th. He told them that not only was he an '*Oktober Bube*' – his birthday is in October – but on this very day, fourteen years ago, he was consecrated Bishop of Leicester in Canterbury Cathedral. This brought down the house – they could talk of nothing else. What happened? How long did the service last? Was I there? Were there many other people there? For us it brought back most vividly that tremendous day in 1953 and we loved sharing it with them in their own language.

This youth conference took place in the hall of the *Stadtkirche*; just before we finished we learned something of the tensions which exist, even in a gathering of this kind. The pastor of the church came in and begged everyone to be very quiet as they left the building; any excitement or singing or laughing would be hailed as a demonstration by the authorities – and demonstrations are *verboten*.

The youth leader drove us back to Bad Schmiedeberg as it was on her way home. During the journey she told us of some of her difficulties. Church youth groups are not banned – but a member of a Church youth group is ineligible as a member of a State youth group. The State youth groups have every amenity provided by the State; they are made most attractive. The Church youth groups are poor and are hard put to it to compete at all with the luxuries of the State groups. In this way the State hopes gradually to reduce the number of young people attached to the churches. It is a subtle and wicked way of enticing the young. At present the youth work of the East German Church is strong but it is a constant struggle to keep it so.

On the Sunday, with no official engagements, we decided to attend the Church of Bad Schmiedeberg. As we walked through the village there seemed to be no one about at all; we feared we might find an empty church. Not a bit of it; the place was packed to the doors long before the service was due to begin. We were treated to three sermons which seemed to me a bit much, but the glorious singing of the Bach chorales more than compensated for this excess. This is the one thing, and I think the only thing, that East Germany has in common with the West – the love of Bach, and indeed of all music, transcends frontiers and even ideologies. It is the one healing factor in a country torn in two.

On Monday we had to leave Bad Schmeideberg by 7.15 am for a great service in the *Stadtkirche* of Wittenberg. There was to be a sermon and also a series of greetings brought by delegates from the countries they represented. On this day Ronald was to give the greeting from the Archbishop of Canterbury on behalf of the British delegation. It was written out in German, which had been vetted by an expert, and Ronald had practised it assiduously. In the *Stadtkirche* we met the pastor in charge of the proceedings; Ronald asked him when he would want him to speak. The pastor looked down his list and shook his head.

'No,' he said, 'it is not arranged'.

'Well I'm afraid it will have to be,' replied Ronald, 'I can't come all this way without giving the Archbishop's greeting'.

'*Ja, natürlich,*' came the answer, 'we will make it so'. He took his pencil, crossed out a name and put in Ronald's. 'You will be the tenth,' he said happily, 'it is all right?'

We never did discover who was so unceremoniously sacrificed – we thought it better not to ask!

The service was memorable, although unbearably lengthy. I had a most comfortable seat in a cosy little corner where I could hear and see everything. I was also able to have a surreptitious nibble at a bar of chocolate and push a piece across for Ronald and his chaplain. We were all absolutely famished.

Ceremonies of all kinds continued throughout that day but the great day, the Reformation Day, was Tuesday, October 31st, the anniversary of the day on which Martin Luther nailed his theses to the door of the *Schlosskirche*.

We left for Wittenberg even earlier than usual and went to the Augusteum to take our places in the procession. I had only discovered on the previous day why it was that the people of Wittenberg seemed to take such an interest in my appearance. I was wearing a scarlet cloak; they had never seen such a thing before and evidently thought I was a fanatical follower of Lenin. I had no other overcoat with me so I was obliged to wear it for the procession – no doubt I was judged to be the only communist present.

There was a scene of intense excitement in the garden of the Augusteum as the representatives of all the different churches arrived in their robes – it was the most colourful procession one could imagine. We walked slowly up the main street where crowds had gathered to watch. I was paired with the youth leader, which pleased me a lot. As we walked the great bell of the *Schlosskirche* tolled solemnly; we entered through the very door on which Luther nailed his thesis; I felt as if we were living the sixteenth century all over again. It was another long service, but Bishop Jänicke of Magdeburg preached a wonderful sermon of which I could understand almost every word and the last chorale was Luther's great and famous hymn *'Ein Feste Burg'*. Ronald had Luther's grave *and* Melancthon's almost within touching distance.

I slipped out of the procession on the way back and ran down to the porch of the Augusteum to see them all come in. I could hardly believe that I had been part of this great celebration which had been talked of for so long and which meant so much to so many.

Between the service and lunch there was just time to spend our precious 'pocket money'. Ronald bought a picture of a panel from an altar piece by Cranach. I got some lovely Christmas candles.

That afternoon a group of us had to leave for home. There were five of us – the Bishop of Bangor, John Todd (a Roman Catholic

layman) Owen Chadwick, Ronald and I. To our surprise the train
to East Berlin was quick and comfortable; over tea we discovered
that we were all booked in at the Hotel Windsor in West Berlin;
we decided to celebrate our safe return through the Iron Curtain;
always assuming that we all got back.

Anything more utterly soul-destroying than East Berlin I have
yet to see. It was dark, only a few dim lights could be seen even in
the main streets; shops were shabby and half empty; so few
people were about that their footsteps echoed as they walked. I was
longing to get away from it; I felt anything could happen; if ever
I was really aware of the unseen presence of some devilish power
it was then. We waited interminably for taxis; the one we eventually got was obviously about to disintegrate. We asked for Checkpoint Charlie; the driver took us as near as he was allowed to go.
We dragged our luggage to the East German sector post. Inside
we found the rest of our party looking slightly anxious.

'Anything wrong?' asked Ronald.

'John can't find the ticket they gave him for his passport,'
volunteered Owen.

'But you couldn't have *lost* it,' I exclaimed clutching the tiny bit
of paper, the size of a postage stamp, they had given me in exchange
for mine.

'Oh yes I could – you don't know me.'

'What's that?' asked Ronald pointing to a ragged scrap of paper
on the floor. John grabbed it as if it was his most precious possession – as indeed it was at that moment.

An official put his head out of a door and called a number. It was
mine, I walked forward with a friendly gesture. The man eyed me
as if I was something the cat had brought in.

'I weesh a gentleman,' he snarled. Ronald rushed forward, exchanged papers with me and was rewarded with his passport. I had
to wait a long time for mine. At last we were released and with a
whoop of delight struggled into the American sector. Formalities
were finished in a matter of seconds. A cheerful taxi driver picked
us up. Would we like to see the Berlin Wall? Would we like to go
up on the platform? We were game for anything now we were in
friendly territory. The Wall is extraordinary; I had expected
something much higher and more massive – it looked almost puny.
But every section of it was watched and barbed wire bristled every-

where. Up on the famous platform we looked down on Hitler's bunker and Goering's Luftwaffe building. Away across the bleak streets we could see the Brandenberg Gate, once the pride of Berlin, and *Unter den Linden*, regarded before the war as one of the most gracious streets in Europe. Everywhere it was black and derelict as if a curse lay upon the place; the only ray of hope was the illuminated newscaster erected in the West which day and night flashed continuous news to the marooned population in the East.

We did not stay on the platform long, because Ronald thought we made too good a target for anyone with a weapon, so we bade the driver take us to the Hotel Windsor. The light and beauty and effervescing life of West Berlin takes one's breath away after a dose of the Eastern Sector; it was another world, a different mode of existence. We luxuriated in hot baths, the first since we left England, and joined the rest of the party for drinks. Two of our men had a tale to tell about their room. There was a great shortage of rooms apparently; they found themselves dumped in a kind of bridal suite! We asked the barman to recommend a typical German restaurant; he suggested the *Hecken Deele*, and it proved to be just what the doctor ordered. We had a marvellous evening; mushroom soup appeared and was followed by *Wiener Schnitzels*. At that point I had to stop – there was no more room to put anything inside me – but the men went on to exotic-looking ices and we finished up with delicious *café crême*.

We had not much time to enjoy our comfortable beds at the Hotel Windsor – we were called at 5.0 am the next morning to get our plane. We drove through the celebrated streets of Berlin and I got a real thrill from that. For years I had longed to see Berlin and never expected the chance would occur and now we were crossing such places as the *Potsdammerplatz* and the *Kurfurstendam*. I felt like someone in a novel; it was almost unreal.

Tempelhof airport is everything that Schönefeld airport is not; it has a positively regal appearance and causes one to feel quite self-important at take-off. We touched down at Hanover and were soon airborne again, bound for Heathrow. It was raining when we arrived, but nothing could damp our spirits. We reached the House of Lords in time for lunch, and for Ronald to take prayers. I slipped into the Abbey and the Dean's verger gave me a copy of the Malcolm Sargent Memorial Service. When I returned Mr Green was waiting with the car to take us home. We were sleepy from travel and excitement but we hardly stopped talking as we whizzed up the MI. After all we *had* been behind the Iron Curtain – and returned!

In these days of change and earth-shaking events it is not often that a chain of circumstances whose origins lie deep in the distant past finds fulfilment after the passing of years. Just occasionally the wheel that began to turn in childhood comes full circle in middle age. I was considerably astonished when this very thing happened to me.

When my brother and I were children we developed a tremendous affection for the vicarage family of our parish church. For the vicar himself who was an elderly and rather forbidding canon we perhaps had more respect than affection – he intimidated us at times. But his son Maurice, who was his curate, and his daughter Theodora, had a lasting influence on us both; they were of our parents' generation but they had a touch with young people which worked like magic; we were prepared to believe anything they said and to do anything they desired. This passionate devotion inevitably did not last long; it developed into a deep and lasting friendship which continued over the years. We children grew up and married – and how delighted Maurice and Theodora were that I married a parson. Very soon the war came and at about the same time there was news that Maurice's health was becoming very precarious. On the night of the great blitz on the London docks he died suddenly down in Dorset. Geoffrey, my brother, was in the Navy; Ronald was at the Ministry of Information; I was in the Transport Corps. None of us could be there to pay our last tribute at his funeral. Two years later a memorial was put up beside that of his father in their old church, and to our very great joy Theodora asked Ronald to dedicate it. We were still young; we hardly seemed to be senior enough to be engaged in the dedication of memorials. But Theodora wanted someone who was representative of the young people Maurice had loved so much and Ronald gratefully accepted.

The years went by; Ronald became a bishop and one of the most understanding letters I received at that time came from Theodora. During our first ten years in Leicester we lost all four of our parents; Theodora still remained and it was always to her that I turned when I wanted assurance or advice from someone of that generation. And then suddenly, quite unexpectedly, she died. Once more engagements prevented my getting to the funeral. I felt strangely bereft; her presence had tided me over the loss of my parents; now there seemed no one left. However I knew there was no real cause for lament; she was well on in her seventies. It was just that I had not expected to lose her – it was the end of a long, long chapter. More than a year went by and a letter came from a lady I had not met for twenty-five years; she was an old friend of my parents and of Maurice and Theodora and I remembered her gratefully for the glorious rides I had on her pony Teddy and for the wonderful tennis parties we had on her court. She wrote to say that a memorial to Theodora was to be placed in the Lady Chapel beside those of her father and brother, and the whole parish wanted us to come down for Ronald to dedicate it. Nothing could have pleased me more; I had always felt that there was an incompleteness about Theodora's going; now it would all be happily tidied up. We went down for a lovely little service one November evening and met lots of friends I had not seen for years. When Ronald dedicated the memorial I felt that the coping stone had been put on this long and wonderful friendship; and it was a new beginning rather than an ending; there would be an even closer unity in the life to come.

Our diocese has one distinction enjoyed by no other – Archbishop Lord Fisher was born and bred here at the vicarage of Higham-on-the-Hill. The living has remained in the gift of the Fisher family; towards the end of the year there was a vacancy there; a new vicar was appointed and had to be inducted. It occurred to us what a joy it would be to the village if Archbishop Fisher would come for the service. Ronald wrote, but not too pressingly; after all Archbishop Fisher was eighty, and he might find the journey too much in the winter. We entirely misjudged his capacity; certainly he would come and would be delighted to preach.

He arrived on a bitter night and we warmed him up well before we started out. The church was packed to capacity; the whole village had turned out and visitors from surrounding hamlets as well. It was a marvellous sermon; not the sermon of an old man but words from the long experience of someone still bubbling over with life. We thought we should never succeed in extricating him from the bun-fight; we no sooner got him in the car than he saw someone he absolutely *must* contact. When we eventually got him home there was no question of going to bed; for another hour he expatiated on politics in general and the virtues of the Prime Minister in particular! His visit was a tonic to everyone; after all, if one could be like that at eighty, old age would not be such a bleak prospect as it sometimes appears.

CHAPTER VIII

Gibraltar, Holyrood House, Lambeth Bishops

'A bad year all round' – that was the heading of a leader in one of the national dailies at the end of 1968. When I read it my first impulse was to agree whole-heartedly. Such a frustrating twelve months: apartheid; the Pope and the Pill; barricades in Paris; starvation in Biafra; protest marches in London; devaluation deflating the meagre travel allowance further; deliberate invasion of Czechoslovakia by Russia and a cold, wet, sunless summer just to top off everything. A pretty ghastly record for the nation, the world and the human race as a whole; even our personal lives seemed to have had some pretty black patches – or so I thought to myself as I looked back gloomily.

Of course it was not as bad as that – not in our own lives at any rate. If there were a good many dark valleys there were certainly some shining peaks rising above them. If there were some things one would prefer to forget there were others that one would want to remember. How warped can one's vision become! 1968 is a year worth recording after all and even the seamy side has its place; without it we might not have realized the urgency to stand up for the right as we see the right.

At least we made a good start, with the arrival in January of some very old friends, Desmond Treanor and his family, to take up residence in St Anne's vicarage. The story of our friendship goes back a long way – right back to the arrival of Dorothy, Desmond's wife, at sixteen and a half. She was our first secretary when Ronald became Principal of St John's, Durham, at the end of 1945. After a few years Desmond joined us as an ex-service student. When we left for Leicester in 1953 Dorothy and Desmond were engaged and in 1954 we went back for Ronald to marry them in the college chapel. After two curacies and two livings they eventually found their way to the diocese of Leicester complete with three lively young Treanors, the eldest of whom, Christine, is my goddaughter. The induction service was a real gathering of the clans; there are not a few ex-John's men in our diocese and on this occasion they knew not only the vicar but also his wife.

When Joost de Blank had to resign the Archbishopric of Cape Town for reasons of health, we hoped and indeed expected that he would have a long and useful ministry at Westminster Abbey. As it happened his years in London were to be very few but in the short time allowed to him he accomplished much. His early death on New Year's Day was a sad blow to the Church and left a big gap in the hearts of his friends.

Joost had been part of our lives even since Cambridge days; he and Ronald were up together and he was still around when we were courting. Then came the war and once more we were in close touch in London. When eventually the paths divided and Joost went off to South Africa, we were proud that it was one of our Leicester curates who went with him as his chaplain.

Now he was gone and on a bright January day Joost's friends gathered in Westminster Abbey to pay grateful tribute to his memory. Joost was powerful and compelling in his life; he was not less so in his death – there was something almost Churchillian about his memorial service. Every moment breathed hope of eternal life: as the casket containing the ashes was committed to the burial place near the Unknown Warrior's Tomb the lovely words of Bishop Brent's prayer 'We give them back to Thee, dear Lord' were read; as the little procession of personal relations and friends returned up the nave the great congregation almost raised the roof of the Abbey with Peter Abelard's hymn 'O what their joy and their glory must be'. Memories of another great funeral came back as we joined in 'Mine eyes have seen the glory of the coming of the Lord'. Joost was a great padre – it seemed as if this last hymn might be his final battle cry, and just because he had been a great soldier the Chaplain-General walked in the procession and the trumpeters of the Coldstream Guards sounded a fanfare. As the last notes of Vaughan Williams' arrangement of the 'Old Hundredth' died away and we came out of the west door to the muffled peal of bells we felt satisfied rather than sad – Joost was with the Church triumphant.

The Women's World Day of Prayer, which takes place each year on the first Friday in Lent, involves Christian women of all denominations all over the world. It is a remarkable institution; the same service is used in all countries; it begins at daybreak in the Pacific Islands; all across the world the different countries take it up and it ends on the Pacific coast of America as the twenty-four hours run their course.

Leicester Cathedral was the first cathedral to have a service for this great day; every year several hundred of us gather there in the morning before going off to take part in later services in churches and chapels all over the county. This year I was more than usually involved: our local radio asked me to talk about the Day of Prayer at 'ten to eight' and I had also promised to lead the service in the cathedral – quite a big assignment for one still not used either to conducting services or to preaching! However I survived; it was inspiring to feel I was just one of hundreds of others taking up the task all over the world as the day wore on.

I chose the season of Lent to indulge in a thoroughly vicious attack of 'flu. I had almost forgotten what it was like to feel really ill, being one of those lucky ones who are usually only fringers as far as epidemics are concerned. My private theory that mind must always triumph over matter suffered a sharp set-back. I was sure that the sooner I got about again the sooner I would forget my troubles, but somehow it did not work out like that. I drooped around the place trying to cope at home and keep up with as many public engagements as possible; I looked and felt miserable, and when in the middle of March my horrible hollow cough was still echoing round the house, Ronald decided that a dose of the sun was essential – especially as our summer holiday was going to be late and very short on account of the Lambeth Conference.

There were hazards of all kinds to be overcome: time, place, not to mention the ever-present problem of foreign currency. We had only five clear days after Easter; Malta was too far; the south of France was too expensive. Suddenly we thought of Gibraltar and the wonderful afternoon we had spent ashore from the *Venus* the previous year. There should be sun and it was in the sterling area

– could we afford it? An enterprising agency quoted us a surprisingly low package price and the deal was done.

I had just told myself that at last the tide was beginning to turn when there occurred one of those sad and baffling experiences that are inevitable and inescapable in the complexities of human life, but which hit you hard if you are one who tends to love very dearly.

There were few people in Leicester whom I, and many, many others, loved more than the head verger of our cathedral, Cyril Innocent. For us he *was* the cathedral. On Palm Sunday he was not well but assured everyone it was nothing and only reluctantly accepted the advice of our Provost, John Hughes, that he should go home to bed. As far as we could tell it was nothing serious, but on Good Friday when we came out of the cathedral after the three hours' service we heard that Cyril had died from a sudden heart attack only an hour before.

No one could believe it – even the doctor could hardly believe it had happened. It seemed incredible that we should never see Cyril in his place in the procession again. Things like this are happening every day; it is only those who are nearest to the scene who know the mystique surrounding the person concerned, who can fully understand what such an event means.

Cyril had spent forty of his seventy years at the cathedral; his title was 'Provost's Verger' but he was the servant of all and the friend of all. He loved the cathedral with every fibre of his being; visitors invariably commented on its perfect appearance; all the many organizations who came to arrange great services knew that they would have a kindly welcome and that everything would go without a hitch just because Cyril was there. Those of us who arrange the cathedral flowers would find the vases and the water put ready and when the task was done Cyril would be lurking in a corner ready to help clear away the rubbish. When we arrived for a service he would be at the door to carry Ronald's case; each successive provost found his cassock warming on the radiator on winter mornings; he always escorted me to my seat on every occasion.

Cyril met and mixed with everyone who came to the cathedral from royalty, archbishops and lords lieutenant down to young people from the smallest youth organizations. Again and again people wrote to the bishop or the provost commenting on our 'wonderful verger' and one of his most treasured possessions was the 'Thanks Badge' given him by the girl guides for all the help he had given at their services over the years.

Cyril was not just a magnificent verger; he was a holy and humble man of God who loved to worship in the cathedral as well as to serve it. The little home with his wife and daughter whom he loved so much was a truly Christian home – a benediction to all who visited it. Nor was he just good, he was gay as well; having turned a stern eye on an erring chorister he would afterwards tell us with a chuckle the particular prank the young man had been up to. He was an ardent and lifelong supporter of Leicester City soccer team and on Saturday nights after choir evensong we would always have a 'city session' in which we rejoiced or condoled with him according to the result of the match.

Cyril and I had been rather special friends since the day we first met – the day on which we came to Leicester for the first time to meet the diocesan staff and see our cathedral, when we were on our way to Canterbury for Ronald's consecration. Ronald had warned me that the Verger's name was Innocent and that I was to keep a straight face. Of course I thought it was a most amusing name for a verger and so far forgot myself as to reveal my feelings. Cyril understood how it struck me and took no offence and from that day forward a special bond existed between us.

Suddenly he was gone – so swiftly, before any of us could tell him what he meant to us. It was rather wonderful that it should be Easter Sunday when John Hughes told the crowded congregation the news and that Ronald should be able to incorporate his tribute to Cyril in his Easter sermon. Everyone seemed involved; the choristers and songmen sang their hearts out on the Easter hymns; triumphant notes pealed from the organ under George Gray's expert touch; the whole congregation proclaimed that because of the Resurrection we could rejoice that Cyril Innocent would be waiting for us on that other shore.

With the memories of that poignant Easter Sunday still fresh in our minds we drove down to Heathrow through a blustering gale and torrents of rain – there was absolutely nothing to suggest that we were setting out on a spring holiday.

From the moment of take-off all was changed. We rose above the clouds and over France the stars met us; soon it was dinner and

the lights of Bordeaux below us; then came the floodlit battle-
ments of Madrid; a gleam of lights reflected on the sea was Malaga;
we fastened our seat belts; earlier I had been worrying about the
tricky landing now necessary to avoid violating Spanish air space;
I forgot about it in the pleasure of the flight – there was nothing to
remind me of it, the touch-down was all that it should be.

The velvety warmth of the Mediterranean night wrapped us
round as we stepped out of the plane; the mighty floodlit Rock rose
abruptly above the tiny landing stage; the Moorish castle glowed
green above the lights of the town; it was perfect – we knew we
had chosen the right place at the right time.

One of the joys of Gibraltar is that it is one of the few places one
can get to know in a few days. We had chosen one of the cheapest
hotels but it boasted a tiny swimming pool with a bar and sun-
bathing facilities. When we were not exploring the Rock we
were lying prone in our swimsuits grilling ourselves to a nice
even tan.

The weather was glorious and we seized the very first day to
make a voyage to Tangier. Back in the 'flu period we had decided
on this for my birthday present; a day trip to Africa had seemed
almost too much to hope for in those depressing days. We sailed
on the *Mons Calpe* (the Latin name for the Rock); being so early in
the season there were very few passengers; the sun poured down
upon us and I lay on the deck and sizzled. The spires and pinnacles of Tangier were etched on the skyline; we sailed out of the
Mediterranean and into the Atlantic; very soon we found ourselves in Africa.

A determined little man wearing a fez captured us and appointed
himself as our guide. He was a pest and his fee was exorbitant but
he made himself extremely useful. The centre of modern Tangier
is gay and exotic, glamorous boutiques and streamlined hotels
abound; one felt it could have been Cannes or Monte Carlo or any
other Mediterranean resort. A stroll through the old city and the
souk took us into an entirely different world, a world of sun and
colour – in some ways reminiscent of the Middle East and yet
unmistakably African. There were veiled Moslem women and
Moors and Arab men wearing the *keffiyeh*; but there were also
dark-skinned vendors of exciting commodities clothed in the brilliant colours beloved by the Africans and wearing hats so wide-

brimmed that they had to stand yards apart from each other to secure breathing space. The noise and the heat, not to mention the smells, were unforgettable but they proclaimed the real Tangier and this was the picture we took back with us across the Mediterranean to Europe.

One morning we took the local bus out to Europa Point. A bus trip in Gibraltar is not the last word in comfort but it is a reminder that good manners still exist; men stood back to allow ladies to board first; the young gave up their seats to the elderly. Europa Point is the last outpost of Europe; as we lazed on the warm rocks above the sea, looking across to the African coast, we remembered that it was from Gibraltar that General Eisenhower led the Allied armies out to North Africa and to subsequent victory at El Alamein. The Mediterranean cradles a large slice of the world's history; perhaps none of the many epics which its shores have seen were more vital for the future of mankind than the departure of the great modern Armada that slipped silently out of the harbour below the Rock in 1942.

One almost breathes British naval history in Gibraltar. We walked back from Europa Point by the road that runs round Little Bay to Camp Bay and brings one at last to Rosia Bay – a tiny, tranquil spot today. But it was here that Nelson's body was brought ashore by his sorrowing sailors after Trafalgar and as we walked on into Gibraltar, just before the South Gate, we came upon the little Trafalgar cemetery where rows of tombstones, bearing proud inscriptions, tell the names of those who perished with their leader.

We went by cable car to the top of the Rock and scrambled about on the tiny tracks that creep across the summit. We came down to the apes' den – not for nothing had I begun to read Paul Gallico's enchanting book *Scruffy* on the plane. I knew exactly where to look for everything connected with the apes and there are few books that give you a better picture of the Rock. Let into the wall near the apes' cages is a plaque which explains that in 1954 the Queen and Prince Philip made friends with the Rock apes and introduced them to Prince Charles and Princess Anne – a nice touch which instantly makes the hairy fellows part of the British family.

Worn out with our sightseeing we limped into the Rock Hotel

for tea and felt restored almost before we had sat down – it was a real home from home. On a veranda dripping with wisteria we enjoyed a thoroughly English afternoon tea – hot buttered toast, fruit cake, gallons of tea. Across the Mediterranean the coast of Africa shimmered in the sun.

We had some interesting invitations while we were in Gibraltar – brought about by the then Dean who was the one person we knew on the Rock. We had lunch with the surgeon-commander on the veranda of his lovely house on the Europa road; the sea below us was alive with shipping from every corner of the world and we virtually ate our lunch with a telescope in one hand, so exciting were the discoveries to be made. One evening we had drinks with the captain of the dockyard – whose more picturesque title is the Queen's harbourmaster. He lives in an old Georgian house near Rosia Bay. It was he who showed us the house in Rosia Parade where Nelson's body lay, pickled in rum, until he was taken home for the state funeral in London. Up the steep hill above is the old naval hospital where his wounded sailors were cared for.

We got to know Gibraltar and we came to love it. There is the rather lovely cathedral and a magnificent old peoples' home where we went to visit the patients. There is John Mackintosh Square, an arcaded, traffic-free area with the badges of famous regiments set in mosaic in the pavements. Last but not least there is the governor's residence, known as the Convent, with the historic little King's Chapel beside it. We wandered up the steep alleys and flights of steps behind Main Street and realized as never before the intense love of the people for the British. Even the buildings were painted red, white and blue; there were slogans everywhere and people stopped us in the street and on the buses begging us to 'put in a word for us with your government at home'. How the words ring in my ears every time General Franco aggravates the situation further. At night we used to watch the *Paseo*, the evening promenade, when all Gibraltarians stroll in the street arrayed in their best.

Better almost than anything else we saw were the unforgettable sunrises and sunsets of Gibraltar; dawns that break in a slow, silvery, light, revealing the snows of the Sierra Nevada away to the north east in Spain; multi-coloured sunsets when *Mount Abyla* in Morocco glows pink and gold and fades into the mist; the magic moment when the sun goes down like a flaming ball, turning the sea into a plate of gold.

On our last night we had dinner with the Dean of Gibraltar and his wife in their flat in the old naval hospital and heard all the stories about life as it is lived on the Rock. While we were there we had a glimpse of the Levanter – the great cloud of mist which settles on the Rock from time to time, sometimes for days on end. Fortunately for us on this occasion it moved out after only half an hour and the kindly Worsleys drove us to the airport under a clear sky.

We were too excited to sleep on our night flight: there was so much to talk about; so much to remember and reflect on; so much to give thanks for – not least the complete disappearance of my cough and the acquisition of a healthy tan!

It was good, since we were feeling so refreshed, that our first engagement when we got home should be a demanding one. This was a weekend visit to a whole deanery to which we were much looking forward. The project had grown out of the Ruby Year Celebrations when the different deaneries had enjoyed the visits of the Bishop and Provost and one; Akeley West, with Ashby-de-la-Zouch as its centre, had asked for more. We agreed to spend the week-end in the deanery and see every aspect of life if that proved possible.

Our entry into the district was certainly thrilling. We were met at the boundary by a team of ton-up boys, motor-cyclists who had offered to give up their Saturday afternoon to escort the Bishop's car into Ashby. It was a generous gesture by tough chaps who would certainly have preferred to be tearing round the country-side at some phenomenal speed. They did their job magnificently and as one of them pointed out, the police could not get them for not having silencers when they were escorting the Bishop!

The arrival with our outriders got the weekend going in splen-did style; in fact, to pay the highest honour that modern jargon accords, it really did swing. We had tea with the people of Ashby and chatted with the hard-working men and women who look after the town's civic affairs. We visited a youth club that was cer-tainly swinging in every sense of the word. We found them friendly, anxious to take us round and very ready to sit and talk more seriously. The only event that created some hesitancy in their minds was the Saturday night dance – could we possibly stand the noise? We explained that Saturday night hops had been a feature of our courting days and that we were prepared for anything, in fact we would hate to be deprived of a visit. As soon as we got inside we realized that things have changed a bit since our day. The noise was indescribable; it was quite impossible to speak; but nobody wanted to; nor did they want to dance; they had their partners and it seemed that they just stood around with them. Meanwhile the band made up for any lack of energy elsewhere; drums thundered, guitars hummed; a gent with flowing locks and a beard sang – very melodiously I thought – the latest top pop. It was very dark, in fact the whole effort seemed to be taking place in a dimly lit cavern. It was not exactly my idea of a dance; I still, I'm afraid, want to dance every dance. But then I am not seventeen in the late 1960s; if I were I have no doubt I should enjoy it as much as anyone. They were a fine group of young people and they were just as willing to drink coffee with us as they were to stand around by the band.

We were up betimes the next morning to drive to the Rural Dean's church for an early celebration with breakfast after. There followed Matins, in another country church and a visit to a hospital. The afternoon brought the civic service in Holy Trinity, Ashby, and in the evening there was compline at Donisthorpe.

On Monday morning Ronald went off for a celebration, breakfast and conference with the deanery clergy followed by a visit to a coal mine – this being one of our deaneries where mining is still a thriving industry. I met the deanery wives for coffee and we toured a cheese factory – slightly less exacting than a pit. At midday we were reunited to meet the WRVS with their meals on wheels service and to visit a comfortable home for the elderly. Our last event was lunch with the National Coal Board at Cole Orton Hall where there was much talk about Ronald's visit to the pit and his interesting appearance when decked out in mining gear.

And then we drove home. Everyone thought we should be exhausted; as it happened we were thoroughly exhilarated. We were closer to the clergy and the people of the deanery than we had ever been before; we could visualize the daily life of that area in quite a new way. Meanwhile our physical comforts had been cared for so lovingly by George and Marjorie Curtois, who received us into their comfortable home for the whole weekend, that we really felt completely spoilt.

How lucky bishops are – and their wives too. Or at least how lucky *we* are; perhaps it is wiser not to generalize! There cannot be many jobs in which one can get so close to people; to try to help them; to learn from them; to see life from so many aspects – and then find everyone so grateful for what one tries to do.

This deanery visit was an experiment; it proved to be a success. It has started something; already the programme has been completed for a weekend with another deanery; in a few weeks we shall be in the midst of it; it is a challenging and a heart warming prospect.

One night the telephone rang rather late. There was nothing unusual in this; our telephone seems to ring most of the day and at all times of the night. Ronald went to answer it and when he came back I knew this was a call with a difference.

'How would you like to spend a night in the palace of Holyrood House?' he enquired casually.

'Why? When? Where? How? Tell me quick!' I couldn't wait to answer his question.

'That was Lord Reith on the phone; he wants us to go up for the General Assembly of the Church of Scotland. That means a night at Holyrood and a morning in the Assembly.'

'Can we?' I hardly dared to hope it would be possible.

'We must, it's almost a command, but I think we can do it. We shall have to leave at lunch time. I've got a confirmation that night, but he says that will be all right.'

I was all agog to know every detail, of course, but there was very little to know, except the date, until our instructions arrived a few weeks later.

It was years since I had travelled to Scotland by day, so even the journey was quite a thrill. The car took us to join the train at Grantham and we were soon on our way to Edinburgh. At Waverley station we were to wait at the North British Hotel until our escort arrived. He was not long in coming and there was no mistaking him – a magnificent young officer of the Black Watch wearing the kilt and all that goes with it. We became friends at once and he suggested we drove up to the castle as there was time to spare. We had been to Edinburgh castle before but never in an official car flying a pennant which sentries saluted as we swept on into parts not open to the public. We prowled about the top of the castle looking out over Edinburgh and enclosed among the bastions I found a spot after my own heart – a little cemetery for soldiers' dogs. Each tiny grave had a headstone; on each there were grateful words of remembrance.

We came down from the castle and drove down the Royal Mile to Holyrood House. There Lord Reith's daughter and a delightful young maid of honour were waiting to receive us. As representing the Queen, the Lord High Commissioner is accorded the honours usually reserved for royalty – ladies-in-waiting, aides-de-camp, maids-of-honour, the lot!

We were taken to our rooms, one each, opposite each other in a long corridor. They were comfortable, completely Victorian and full of memories, if not of ghosts. The bathrooms had to be explained to us, being of not very modern design. One had so many curious gadgets – you could even produce waves in the bath – that it looked like a miniature steam engine.

At tea we met our fellow guests – about twenty were staying in the house – and soon there was a great stir as 'The Lord High' was announced. The abbreviation seemed to be his usual title. The ladies curtsied, the men bowed, and our host and Lady Reith came round to greet us all.

When we went up to dress for dinner I soon realized I was staying in a royal residence. My long frock had been carefully pressed and everything was laid out in readiness for me; I was fascinated. I popped across the corridor to see how Ronald was faring.

'You did pack that new set of pants and vest, didn't you?' I asked anxiously.

'Of course I did. There they are, spread out in great state.'

Sure enough there was one nylon vest and one pair of gents terylene underpants laid out as carefully as I lay out Ronald's cope at home.

My trip to the bathroom provided great adventures; I collided at the door with Yehudi Menuhin who insisted on my having first turn and also stayed to help me work the gadgets. We produced quite sizeable waves before we had finished.

We assembled in the west drawing room with the other guests until we followed Their Graces into the great hall where they were to receive about a hundred dinner guests. As we made ready to process into dinner each gentleman had to discover his partner. Ronald took in Lady Hughes and I followed on the arm of the Primus of Scotland. The dining room was an unforgettable sight with candles burning and kilted pipers marching slowly up and down playing their bagpipes. The dinner was excellent, with not too many courses, so that there was ample opportunity for conversation.

Later in the drawing room we discovered quite a number of people whom we knew, an unexpected piece of luck which made a superb occasion seem even more delightful.

While we were going to bed we heard Yehudi Menuhin playing his violin in the room next to Ronald's; we listened enthralled for half an hour. It was only next day that we heard that he went downstairs again to give a short recital; it was a pity we missed it but after all we had had our own private concert upstairs!

I lay in bed listening to the gentle May breezes wandering among the trees by my window. I wondered who had slept in my bed, what stories my predecessors could have told; I felt myself caught up in Scottish history as I slipped slowly off to sleep.

When a tray of tea arrived the next morning I ran across to ask Ronald to come and share it. I found him halfway through his second cup but I made him bring it to my room to enjoy with me the view of Arthur's Seat which climbed up to the sky so close to us that it seemed one could touch it.

We attended family prayers, a homely occasion conducted by Lord Reith's chaplain, who was his son-in-law. I can never forget his all-embracing *ex tempore* prayer; his language was as poetic as it was sincere.

At breakfast I was seated next to Sir Michael Adeane, the Queen's Secretary. I had long wanted to thank him for a small but very important kindness he had done me. Someone who read my first book remembered that during the war when, as a transport corps driver, I was waiting in the Chinese drawing-room at Buckingham Palace to collect an important passenger I had put a piece of royal notepaper in my shoulder bag as a souvenir. My conscience soon smote me, however, and I replaced it; there was a thick November fog outside – suppose I had an accident and someone found I had pinched a piece of notepaper from Buckingham Palace!

This event evidently stuck in the mind of the reader of my book. He mentioned it to Sir Michael Adeane who straightway sent me not only a piece of notepaper but also an envelope from the reign of George VI. At last I had an opportunity to thank him personally; he remembered the incident and I thoroughly enjoyed my breakfast conversation with him.

When the time came to leave for the General Assembly we found our Black Watch officer waiting for us in the motorcade. He explained that he was to bring us back for an early lunch – a totally unexpected kindness on the part of Lord Reith.

The General Assembly was intensely interesting, not least in the number of notable visitors from other churches whom we could see seated near us. I very seldom enjoy long meetings of this kind but when our escort came to fetch us I was quite sorry to leave.

Most jobs have their 'perks' – even for wives. One of the 'perks' that I value most is the opportunity to listen to debates in the House of Lords. Not that I can avail myself of the privilege very often; Ronald cannot spare many days away from the diocese to take part in debates but he seems to be asked to speak on a variety of subjects and when I can manage it I love to be there. Just to sit in the gallery and listen is an education in itself; many of the matters debated are far above my head, but always one is aware that it is the good of the country that members have at heart. Party counts for little; self advancement is unthought of; there is an atmosphere of restraint and courtesy and deep sincerity; one comes away a better person for having been there.

One reads of great debates of the distant, and not so distant, past; occasions when every seat was filled and the floor of the House was crowded – I had never expected to be present at such an exciting scene but by a piece of good fortune found myself involved.

The increase of sanctions against Rhodesia was to be debated in the Lords. Opinion was sharply divided; there was every indication that it would be a tremendous affair; Ronald was not speaking but intended to be present and suggested that I came along during the afternoon. As soon as I arrived I realized that this was something quite different from most debates. I just managed to squeeze into the last half-seat in the peeresses' gallery. There was not a space anywhere; members sat where they could – on the floor, on the steps of the throne, anywhere. The bishops were there in force; their robes brightened the scene considerably. The atmosphere was tense but devoid of animosity. Speakers of all parties were at their best; there was no rivalry, indeed most of the time there was little difference between them. I am a most partisan-minded type; I seldom see two sides of any question, but on this occasion the speeches on both sides were so convincing that had I been asked to vote I should have found it impossible to do so.

The House divided and my next-door neighbour and I, who were total strangers to each other, found ourselves holding hands through sheer anxiety and excitement. At the same moment we both made the same remark, 'If only it could be a dead heat!' It was not a dead heat, nor was it a party vote. Labour peers voted against the Government, Conservatives voted with it; the bishops voted *en bloc* with the Government, but the motion was defeated. I didn't know whether to be glad or sorry; I didn't know what the consequences might be for the country or the Commonwealth; but somehow deep down I felt that good must come from so much hard thinking and sincere debate.

The Lambeth Conference was catching up with us at a record rate; it had been looming over the horizon for a long time; indeed it was in a sense the culmination of months, even years, of preparation. Even the bishops' wives had been meeting regularly for more than a year to sort out the social side. There were many differences between Lambeth '58 and Lambeth '68. This year it was to cover the whole of August instead of, as previously, July and only a week of August. This upset everyone's holidays, especially those with children, but it was inevitable and had always been accepted as such. Very many more people had been invited which was, of course, excellent, but the increased numbers meant that the venue had to be Church House rather than Lambeth Palace. Church House is spacious and equipped with every convenience but it could never produce the warmth and domesticity of Lambeth.

Of the conference itself I am, needless to say, not competent to speak, but many of the things in which wives had a part I shall never forget. The great opening service in Canterbury Cathedral – it was one of my most vivid memories of Lambeth '58; it was repeated in '68 in all its glory and was just as impressive. In fact it had an added dimension for me because in the great procession I was able to spot all those American and Canadian bishops with whom we had stayed on our transatlantic trip and whom we had not seen for so many years. There was a garden party in the deanery grounds later and before it was over I had discovered all the bishops and all the wives I most wanted to see. There was only one cloud over this service; I had to be there on my own because Ronald was taking prayers in the House of Lords. My pleasure was almost halved, but I had been commissioned to bring back every scrap of news – including the text taken by the Archbishop for his sermon. Texts have never been my strong point – I had to repeat it at ten minute intervals to keep it clear – but when I questioned a bunch of South African bishops in the train on the way back to London, I found they couldn't tell me a word of it.

My own Lambeth programme was a full one. We stayed in London at the English-Speaking Union during the week and took groups of overseas friends home for the weekend. On Wednesdays I drove back to Leicester in the morning to cook up for the week-end and do what I could to help the household prepare. I came back to London in the evening and on Thursdays I was on duty on the driving rota at Church House.

Women played a big part in Church House; the Mothers' Union staffed the enquiry bureau, which included the sorting of mail, for the whole month. They also ran the Wives' Club, assisted by members of the Women's Fellowships; this club was enormously popular with episcopal husbands on account of the television screen on which they could watch the test match. The Women's Fellowships held a series of discussions during each week which meant there was always something to listen to. Wives like myself, who like driving in London, made up the driving rota.

Each diocese had been asked to help in some way with the social side. In our diocese we arranged to bring a coach load of wives down to Leicester for a day's outing. On the night before I went home full of excitement to get ready – I had been looking forward to this for eighteen months. Of course it turned out to be a bitterly cold day with pouring rain which never let up for one minute. We put on all the fires in the house and greeted our visitors with steaming cups of hot coffee – I never saw people more grateful. My goddaughter, Christine Treanor, came to help hand round and delighted everyone. They were mostly American wives and they love our young English schoolgirls – there was quite a fan mail for Christine when Lambeth was over. Martin made everyone most welcome, wagging his tail unceasingly and willingly accepting biscuits from anyone who cared to offer him one. Mrs Bell and I showed them the house from top to bottom and they enjoyed this immensely; they could hardly tear themselves away to come down to the cathedral.

Here John and Sybil Hughes were waiting to take them on a conducted tour and then we set off for lunch at Launde Abbey. This was to be the *pièce de résistance* and in spite of the awful weather it proved to be so. To have a meal in a medieval abbey is something that can't happen on the other side of the Atlantic and they revelled in every moment of it. They even insisted on putting up their umbrellas and touring the park; I hated to think of them journeying back to London with oozing feet but they seemed to think it was well worth it. We escorted the party back to the motorway with everyone bubbling over with enthusiasm for all things English – and so ended our long anticipated Lambeth Wives' Day. A lot of hard work and organization had gone into it; our efforts were well rewarded.

For the so-called missionary weekend all Lambeth went out to the dioceses of England, Scotland, Wales and Ireland – they penetrated to the Shetlands and to the Western Coasts of County Kerry. We had a wonderful batch with us; Bishop's Lodge was bursting at the seams and Mr and Mrs Bell kindly lent a bedroom and bathroom in their flat. Other friends in the county offered hospitality and it was a remarkable weekend. It was wonderful for us to have Harry O'Neil, Archbishop of Fredericton and his wife Mardie; Hamilton and Charlotte West from Florida; Archie and Jean Crowley from Michigan – all friends who had entertained us so royally in their own homes during Ronald's lecture tour of their dioceses.

Our visitors worked hard that weekend; sometimes they hardly had time to eat the meals we had prepared for them, and the few moments of respite we had tried to organize just went by the board. But they loved it; so did we and so did the diocese; perhaps the climax came at Lutterworth when Harry O'Neil, who had worked with the Bible Society, preached at evensong in John Wycliffe's church. The whole deanery closed its churches and attended *en masse*; Harry O'Neil described it as one of the greatest occasions of his ministry. When Jimmy Good, the Rector of Lutterworth, brought Harry home to us he had to stay till nearly midnight to tell us the story.

It was a great weekend – everywhere – and certainly with us; many bishops regarded it as the most important event of the whole conference. Only a few weeks ago, more than a year after everyone had gone home, we had a letter to say that the weekend at Leicester was the highlight of Lambeth.

But there were many other great events and the social side was attractive. The Friday morning meetings laid on at Lambeth for wives were inspiring and Joan Ramsey's many supper parties, which meant that every member of the conference and his wife was entertained at Lambeth, were deeply appreciated. Joan, always a good hostess, surpassed herself during Lambeth and there must be many who will never forget her kindness and thoughtfulness.

The Lord Mayor of London gave a reception at Guildhall and gave us all an opportunity to see the city at its historic best. There was a royal garden party and the invitations were worded so that it was obvious that the party would take place even if it rained and no one would have to be disappointed. It turned out to be one of the few fine days of that dreary summer and the scene in the grounds of the Palace can never have been more colourful. The bishops wore their purple cassocks and the Queen, always sensitive to what will please people most, chose a charming pale mauve summer coat and a little hat composed of violets. This caught everyone's imagination and everywhere one could hear grateful remarks.

The great Eucharists of the Lambeth Conference will live in memories throughout the world for years to come. The opening Eucharist at Westminster on the first Sunday was a true dedication; even more outstanding perhaps was the open air Eucharist at the White City. Anyone was entitled to be present; people came from all over the country; when the then Archbishop in Jerusalem began the service there were 15,000 people present. As an aesthetic experience it was out of this world; the rows of bishops in Convocation robes; the Archbishop in his gold mitre, surrounded by his assistants; the tiered seats filled with expectant crowds; the

deepening twilight and the floodlit arena; the most famous expo-
nents of décor could not have excelled this. When it came to the
administration and the reverent figures in their red and white
robes moved silently from the flood-lit altar bearing the elements
to the congregation waiting to receive in the dark arena and
returned once more into the light it seemed to be a wordless picture of what the faith can mean to people all across Christendom.

The last week of Lambeth was just one long uninterrupted programme of work – there were times when it seemed as if it would
be impossible to have everything finished in time. 'Uninterrupted'
is not quite a true description, but the conference had been
remarkably free from protesters and other similar modern pheno-
mena. However, on the last Saturday morning, just to remind
everyone of the times we live in, a hairy type bearing a banner
came clattering along the corridors and succeeded in reaching the
door of the hall. He was pounced on by a porter of small stature
who easily overpowered him and sat on him comfortably until the
proper authorities came along to escort him out. The banner,
which this gentleman lost in the melée, landed on the lap of one of
the bishops who doubtless kept it as a trophy. Nobody minded, in
fact some bishops actually applauded the effort! One is only young
once, and the adult world has learned to live with these outbursts
of youthful exuberance; it will pass, I believe, as all epidemics
pass.

Work was over at last; Saturday afternoon afforded a breathing
space – an incredible number of purple stocks were in evidence
among the test match crowd at the Oval – and on Sunday an immense crowd gathered in St Paul's Cathedral for the final Eucharist. As in 1958 it was a moving occasion; so many people were
meeting for perhaps the last time in their lives; for some it was the
last event of their last Lambeth Conference; we had all been so
close to each other for so long that we seemed to be one great
family.

For me the most impressive moment of the whole service, and
one which I shall never forget, came during the Prayer of Consecration. The Archbishop of Canterbury celebrated at a nave altar;
round him in a square phalanx stood all the archbishops of the
Anglican communion. At the moment of consecration they all
raised their right hands in concelebration; for me it signified the

unity of the Anglican communion; if we were united in this central act surely any other minor difficulties mattered little.

We came out on to the steps of St Paul's, the bells were pealing; the sun, for once, was shining. We managed to find our special friends from overseas; the Wests returning to sunny Florida; the Crowleys to Michigan; the O'Neils to Fredericton; George Luxton and Dorothy to Huron. How good it had been to be together again – how long would we have to wait for our next meeting? Perhaps not so terribly long if jumbo jets bring down prices in the way that is promised.

Everyone went off for their much-needed holidays – everyone except us. We still had to wait one more week because Ronald had to preach the sermon at the service of the Trades Unions Centenary Congress at Blackpool. Our holiday had to be even later and shorter than it might have been but it was an interesting event and worth waiting for.

But even when we did set out for the long-delayed holiday it was with a sense of frustration. For years, nearly twenty years, we had been planning a visit to our friends Kurt and Traude in Czechoslovakia. At last it had been arranged; we had our visas, all was in order. And then, before Lambeth was over, there came the Russian invasion of Czechoslovakia and the closing of the frontiers. We felt desperate; we wrote, we telegraphed, we tried to telephone; we could make no contact at all. We set out across Europe with heavy hearts wondering how they had fared. We could allow ourselves only four days in Zermatt; it was wonderful to be there after all the vicissitudes of the summer; wonderful to have loving, understanding friends around us; but even the beauty of the mountains could not banish our sadness and anxiety. And then a letter arrived sent on from England. It was from Kurt and Traude; they had been on holiday in Italy when the invasion took place; they were now with relations in Western Germany, undecided whether to return home or remain. They had no idea where we were but they wanted us to know that for the present they were safe. It is extraordinary how all problems seemed to get solved, or partially solved, in Zermatt. A load was lifted from our hearts; I stood at our bedroom window looking up the moonlit Matterhorn, its presence was a benediction; I was sure that somehow, somewhere we should make contact with Kurt and Traude.

We had only five days holiday left but we decided, of course, to spend it looking for our friends. The address they gave was Bischofsheim – a place we had never even heard of. We found it on the map up by Fulda near the East German border. It took us three days to get there and we eventually arrived at a tiny hamlet where no one had even heard of the street we wanted. An obliging man at a little garage thought it might be Bischofsheim-Hanau, near Frankfurt – a hundred miles further south and almost exactly where we had come from. We were getting anxious about our foreign currency, petrol is not cheap and we seemed to be using it up at a catastrophic rate. We arrived in Frankfurt in the rush hour – one of the most exasperating experiences that can befall any motorist. Once more it was the wrong Bischofsheim; we were advised to try Bischofsheim near Mainz, thirty miles west. Third time lucky, we said to ourselves trying to keep up our spirits. We were right; our luck was in at last; the joy and astonishment on the faces of Kurt and Traude when they opened the door more than repaid our weary travels.

We were shocked beyond words at the state in which we found them; they were far more shaken, in much lower spirits, than they had been in London twenty-nine years earlier. This was the second time they were refugees; the second time they were parted from home and family. And they were terribly torn in mind; here in the West there was freedom; they would be poor but people were friendly – they had been promised small jobs. But their son Peter was in Czechoslovakia, and his young wife, and Traude's aged mother. It is one thing to leave your country in your late twenties when there is little to keep you there; it is a different proposition in your late fifties when ties are much stronger. Greatly daring, Ronald advised them to return. They told us they would be in no danger and there at least they had a home, a job and the family. We said goodbye to them wondering if we would ever meet again. On the night that we sailed from the Hook of Holland they crossed the Czechoslovakian border – how very, very different their future looked from ours.

We almost breathed a sigh of relief when we got back to Leicester to start the winter's work. What with Lambeth and the late holiday and the inevitable late return it seemed a long, long time since we had been able to settle down to the regular diocesan routine. But we were soon completely immersed and everything was as enjoyable and interesting as always – perhaps even a little more so after the long gap.

It was good to be firmly established in Bishop's Lodge again; to get down to household chores and the little extras, like feeding the birds, pickling the beech leaves, hanging up a string of onions; to say nothing of taking Martin for exciting walks among the drifting leaves. I love this time of year when new projects abound and everyone meets up again after the holidays and you can almost hear the stealthy approach of winter as the wind gets wilder, the nights darker, and the mornings crisp and crackling.

Leicester is conveniently sited being almost equidistant between Oxford and Cambridge; when there are jobs to be done in either place they can be carried out with the minimum of inconvenience. This autumn Ronald and I both had assignments in Cambridge on the same evening – a most happy coincidence.

Ronald was billed to address the Research Club of Kings with opportunity after for dialogue with the Provost, Dr Edmund Leach. He found things greatly changed since his own undergraduate days – no gowns, no dinner in hall and women as well as men present at the lecture, some of them married! It was a stimulating evening; unfortunately, Dr Edmund Leach found himself in such complete disagreement with nearly every word Ronald had said that he declined to indulge in debate. But the rest of the party, including the Dean, David Edwards, were extremely articulate and a good time was had by all.

My little effort was totally different. A second year undergraduate at Girton, reading Geography, proposed to write a thesis on the Zermatt valley and its people and wrote to me for advice and titles of suitable books. I arrived at Girton with a case crammed with books and names and addresses of contacts. Girton must have changed much less than Kings; it seemed to have retained all the best things I remember about it when Ronald and I used to visit there when I came up for May Week. Judy, my correspondent, met me full of enthusiasm and escorted me to her room which was cosy and colourful. We sat on the floor consuming enormous éclairs and innumerable cups of coffee while we discussed every aspect of the thesis. Judy's friends drifted in and out; like her they were modern, mini-skirted misses, all of them so full of high spirits, so well-mannered and friendly. Some came to share our feast; others to collect for Shelter or World Poverty. One thing was common to them all – they loved Cambridge, they loved Girton and thought themselves privileged to be there. There was no talk of rights, or demands, or participation; they were happy, hard-working, dedicated young women; they gave one great hope for the future; it was a wonderful evening. When Ronald and I joined up again in the car our stories were a complete contrast.

Not long after this came the long-awaited, much advertized protest march through the west end of London to Hyde Park. Ever since the summer certain sections of the community had been trying to make the public's flesh creep with suggestions of the enormities that were to be perpetrated – an effort, one supposed, to outshine, if possible, the disgraceful events in Paris in the previous May. As it happened, the march did far more good than harm to all sections of the community. There were very few rowdy scenes; the marchers on the whole were in a good mood, our London police were even more benevolent than usual. The rest of the world was amazed; England was the only place in which such an event could have taken place; we were the envy of the western world. Contributions poured in for the police who had given up their Sunday afternoon leave to keep the peace. I took our mite personally to New Scotland Yard and had an entertaining conversation with a most charming and grateful recipient who, in spite of his exalted position, spared the time to come and receive my paltry envelope personally.

At the end of the year a great transition was to take place at our cathedral – our beloved George Gray, who had reigned as organist for over thirty years, was resigning. The news shattered us all; it was not easy to imagine the cathedral without George. But just as our spirits reached their lowest ebb our mourning was turned to joy – the Archbishop of Canterbury announced his intention to confer on George the Lambeth degree of Doctor of Music. The transformation of outlook was instantaneous: we all forgot that George was resigning; we could think only of his new honour.

Quite a party of us attended in Lambeth Palace Chapel to see George receive his degree; there was a sherry party after given by the kind Ramseys and then we all went off to a festive lunch to celebrate the great event.

When the choir procession entered the cathedral for his last Christmas Eve carol service, George was present wearing his Doctor's hood; what might have been a sad event was an occasion of great rejoicing.

CHAPTER IX

Cruising Again, Methodist Crisis, Czechoslovakia at Last

THIS chapter is being written close to the screen. I am so near to the events being described that the picture may be slightly out of focus; there has not been much time yet for reflection or for getting things in proportion. On the other hand impressions are very vivid; nothing has faded. Perhaps that is why it seems at the moment to have been a good year, a year when things went right, when plans materialized and projects came to fruition. A year too that has proved to be particularly rich in the revitalizing of valued friendships, the reforging of links worn thin by time.

In the Midlands, and particularly in Leicestershire, we had a severe winter. I rejoiced inwardly and commiserated with everyone else publicly. Not for nothing have I attended the Dry Ski School in London regularly for the last four years. It has kept me fit and supple, which is the main object of the exercise, but always I hope secretly that there may be a smattering of snow; enough for me to try out my prowess on my own skis. At the ski school the diligent efforts of Anni Maurer have produced a miniature artificial slope for aspiring pupils; having taken one or two nasty tosses on this slope, I felt I had earned a taste of real snow.

Well, I had it – with a vengeance. Every day the white covering grew thicker and thicker, then one night a blizzard raged for hours. We woke up to find bushes, paths and steps obliterated; our garden was almost unrecognizable. I put on my Wellington boots to take Martin out before breakfast; he disappeared into the snow and only his head and the tip of his tail were visible – a difficult situation for a dog endeavouring to do his morning duty! Feeding the birds was quite an experience; the snow round the bird table came over the tops of my boots and they became so heavy I could hardly walk.

Skis, of course, were just the job for getting about and the drifts in the garden made miniature runs and gave me great joy. As always, the more macabre side of things was much more obvious than the light relief – which could only be a sideline anyway. Twice the traffic in the city of Leicester seized up completely; poor Mr Green bringing our car back from the garage took an hour and a half to cover a quarter of a mile. One night the county caught it badly just as the rush-hour traffic was at its height; cars were abandoned all over Leicestershire; school buses were marooned and householders in the villages became hosts to unknown guests stranded without transport.

We have always thought that our house, being Victorian and therefore solidly built, was pretty well proof against storm and tempest, but we had been living in a fool's paradise. I stepped out of the bedroom to make the early morning tea and found icy water cascading in all directions on the first floor landing. My howl of dismay brought Ronald rushing out; we abandoned the tea and set to work with buckets and mops to assuage the flood. After these exertions a further effort for a pot of tea seemed a good idea; once again we were foiled, this time by ominous drippings coming from the direction of the flat. Mr and Mrs Bell were away; we discovered a miniature mountain torrent descending their stairs. Out came the mops and buckets; we did not mention tea again – it seemed to be asking for trouble.

This particular day proved to be something of an epic. One of our much-loved country vicars had died and the funeral was arranged for this afternoon. Ronald was determined to get to the church at all costs to support the wife who had a special place in our hearts. The village was remote but only about fifteen miles away; we allowed ourselves two hours, which we hoped would suffice for all hazards, and set out, a party of four – Mr Green, the Archdeacon of Loughborough and ourselves. I had suggested wearing my ski suit under a coat but Ronald thought this looked disrespectful. Our progress was painfully slow but we did at least keep going while we were on the main road. When we had to take to the country roads problems increased but we struggled on and were actually within sight of the village when disaster overtook us.

P   229

A land-rover and a car stuck fast in a drift blocked the whole road. Soon we too were stuck; three cars, also on their way to the funeral, piled up behind us. Mr Green and the other drivers decided to stay with the cars while the rest of us tried to walk to the village. Carrying robe cases the curious cavalcade of clergy, and I, stumbled across the fields. The gale was blowing the snow horizontally across our path; I have been in a good many blizzards in the Alps but I was never so terrified as on this occasion. It was difficult to keep any sense of direction, and we found ourselves wandering and then someone would shout that the church spire was to the left or the right. Somehow we made it and our battered little party stumbled up the path only to find that we were almost the first arrivals. A more ridiculous figure than myself could hardly be imagined – Wellingtons, fur jacket, black funeral hat, all tastefully decorated with caked snow and icy sprigs of hedgerow. The vicar's widow was a model of courage and self-control; the number of clergy and people who managed to get to the service, some of them very late, was proof of the affection in which the vicarage family was held.

It was a beautiful little service in spite of everything and just as it finished to our great relief Mr Green and the other drivers appeared – the cars having been pulled out by an obliging tractor driver.

The police brought a land-rover to lead the cortège into Leicester and asked car drivers to form up in procession behind – all the roads out of the village being perilous. Even these precautions did not succeed entirely; one after another the cars slid off the road into the ditch; police, undertakers, passengers dived in and out pushing and shoving. My heart ached for the sad relations but they never once allowed it to get them down. At last, after what seemed hours, we reached the main road and very slowly, very cautiously the cars went their own way. I was never more thankful to reach home.

That night there was another blizzard but it did not come until most people were safely indoors. The next day at lunch time, when I hoped most people would be too preoccupied to notice me, I took my skis out again. The sun was shining and the snow had blue alpine shadows about it; it was too good to miss and probably it would soon be gone – it was, to everyone's relief!

The recurring miracle of spring makes a bigger impact after a hard winter. Snowdrops and crocuses blossomed beneath the melting snow and stood revealed as it disappeared. Patches of aconites brightened the frozen earth and the birds gathered in little groups on the branches of the oak tree. It was good to be alive; there were still the harsh winds of March to encounter and plenty of disappointments might occur before winter was finally vanquished but once more there was the scent of hyacinths in the house; in a few weeks there would be almond blossom and daffodils in the garden and spring would be established.

For us there was a special magic about this particular spring. Ronald had agreed to lead another cruise-pilgrimage and a group of friends were to join us. We had had to say no to so many of Morris Perry's kind invitations to lead parties – much as we longed to go – but this trip came at just the right time and it was possible to accept.

An added pleasure was that Netta Mayston was coming with us; Dick had always hoped that one day she would visit the Holy Land where he had been stationed in the troublous days before the war and now the hope was to be fulfilled. It very nearly was not; Netta became seriously ill only seven weeks before we were due to sail and it was not until almost the last moment that we knew she would be fit to come.

On a mid-April morning the party of two hundred met at Victoria station to travel overland to Genoa to join the ship. Most of the company were total strangers to us but it was great fun discovering well-known faces from Leicester among them and their cries of joy on seeing us were heartwarming. Netta, of course, travelled *en famille* with us; another close friend from London, Edie Burt, who has shared many climbing adventures with us, joined the group, so we were a happy party of four.

I enjoyed travelling across Europe but I seemed to be the only one who did. Most people prefer air travel but there is so much more to be seen from the train. The white cliffs of Dover fading away astern and the French coast growing clearer on the horizon still give me a little thrill. *Sacré Cœur* brooding benignly over Paris revives happy memories of gay happenings long ago; even climbing into my bunk in the sleeper gave me pleasure – after all, we were avoiding twenty-four hours of misery in the Bay of

Biscay even if the train did lurch and roll nearly as ferociously as a
ship. The early morning was the high spot for me. We woke up
rather the worse for wear as the train was leaving Turin. Ronald
called to me to look out of the window. I pulled back the curtain at
the foot of my bunk – clear-cut like a frieze spanning the whole
horizon were the Alps, gleaming pearly pink and pale gold above
the early morning mists. It made my day; for minutes I sat and
feasted on what I saw. But we couldn't keep it just to ourselves. I
slid down the ladder on to the floor and rushed into Netta and
Edie next door – Ronald throwing his dressing-gown over me in a
despairing gesture for decency's sake. They were already trans-
fixed at the window and we shared the experience together. It
seemed a good omen; I was sure it would be a grand trip after such
a beginning.

Genoa is a story-book setting for a magic carpet kind of voyage.
The *Regina Maris*, a splendid, modern German ship, sailed just
before midnight; we were all on deck for the departure and heard
for the first time the voice we came to know so well: 'Will all
visitors go ashore now please – *Regina Maris* is ready to sail'. It
was our signature tune as we left each successive port. The many-
coloured lights of Genoa climbed up the hillside; there were great
floodlit churches and the softer glow of quiet Italian homes; lights
lining the waterfront danced in the wash of our ship. We were
sailing for destinations we had never seen before; the ghost of
Christopher Columbus, the pioneer of long sea voyages, hung over
Genoa.

Corsica, Sicily, Malta – that was how we set our course for the
first few days. Corsica was building up mammoth celebrations for
General de Gaulle in honour of the bi-centenary of Napolean's
birth on the island. Unfortunately for *le Général* he was deposed
before the great day arrived and his successor received the
honours. Taormina in Sicily was impressive, with views of snow-
clad Mount Etna at the corner of every street; it was somehow
easier to enthuse over Etna than over Napolean.

Malta is one of our favourite haunts. When we first went there,
years ago, we sailed into Grand Harbour to find the ships of the
Royal Navy everywhere and the Union Jack flying from the
famous forts. It is different now and we were nostalgic for the
things that had been; but the British people will always remember

what Malta has stood for in history and no one of our generation will ever forget the epic of Malta GC in World War II.

We had a great tour of the island seeing places such as Medina and Mosta which were new to us and revisiting spots like St Paul's Bay which we knew well. The tourist development round this bay is remarkable: hotels, villas, blocks of flats – all the evidences of modern mushroom growth. But it never loses its Bible-story appeal; the 'place where two seas meet' is so unmistakable that one can almost see the ship breaking up and St Paul and his party coming precariously into land on the 'broken pieces of the ship'.

After Malta there were several days at sea; this was exactly what everyone needed after three days sightseeing. The weather did us proud; there was ample space for sunbathing on the *Regina Maris* and pale, *après*-winter faces were gradually transformed. There was plenty to do from early morning onwards; Ronald and Bishop Corson, an American Methodist bishop, conducted services together at eight o'clock each morning and the Roman Catholic padre said Mass at the same time in another lounge. Most days there was a lecture on the places we were to visit; this time our lecturer was Tony Gilkes, lately High Master of St Paul's, and his talks were superb; it was almost impossible to find space for everyone when he was billed to speak. In between these events we played endless table tennis and there was always the swimming pool to cool off in. In spite of all these activities there was still time to settle down lazily with a book – something I can hardly ever do at home except in bed. Ronald had given me for my birthday the Earl of Birkenhead's *Life of Walter Monckton*; it was a big book to take on a cruise but I loved every line of it. It is a very frank biography; some parts made me sad, other parts gave the answer to questions that had troubled me for years. Much of it I found inspiring and much of it brought back thrilling and precious memories. When I finished it – on the last night on board – I found that for me Walter Monckton was still the hero he had been for nearly thirty years.

The *Regina Maris* was nearing Haifa and excitement rose rapidly among the passengers. For us it was our first visit since the Six Days War; we wondered rather anxiously how much things might have changed. The ship was to be our home during our visit to the Holy Land; she anchored in the harbour at Haifa and every day we went ashore and were taken by coach to Jerusalem or Galilee.

Our trip to Jerusalem was memorable – it coincided with the Israeli Independence Day. It was not perhaps the best time for a visit to the Holy City but it was interesting and very exciting. The roads were full of people in coaches, cars, on foot and on donkeys, all on their way to the celebrations. For the first time in twenty-one years the great day was not to be a military occasion; instead there was an immense march past of six thousand Israeli youth.

We approached Jerusalem from the west and as we got our first view our driver managed to find a spot where we could stop and watch quietly while Ronald read Psalm 122. As the gay excited crowds went milling by, the words seemed strangely relevant. We went in through what we had in the past called New Jerusalem; past the King David Hotel and the YMCA building until we came to the magnificently decorated balcony where the President, members of the Government and the Diplomatic Corps were to be seated for the march past. Police and troops were everywhere; armed soldiers crouched on the roof of every building; it was not exactly a comfortable situation for pilgrims like ourselves. Our guide decided to go on to Bethlehem and try to get back to Jerusalem before the streets were closed at three o'clock.

We were anxious about Bethlehem; there had been fighting and damage there during the war. Fortunately everything that really matters is still just as it always has been; the Church of the Nativity and the crypt below are unharmed. There were signs of damage near by, but as we gathered round the star in the floor of the grotto we gave thanks that the most precious places had been spared.

The road back to Jerusalem was new to us; previously it had been no-man's-land, and the journey was then much longer. Now we had to travel only five miles; we must have covered the distance in record time so determined was our driver to get us to the Old City while the streets were still open. He tried every gate without success but at the last moment our luck turned. We approached a street leading to the Jaffa Gate. The policeman on duty stopped us as usual; then he recognized our driver as an old friend. Many signs entirely unintelligible to us passed between them, to the noisy astonishment of the crowd our coach swung across the road and came to rest by the gate. We tumbled out in haste before the policeman could have second thoughts and in a matter of minutes we were filing through. To enter Jerusalem by the Jaffa Gate was a fresh experience for us; it has only been re-opened to the public since the Six Days War.

Once inside the gate all thoughts of processions and wars and armed men were banished. The old city seemed quite unscathed and, apparently, quite unaffected by all that had happened. The *souk* was as crowded and as noisy as ever: loaded little donkeys and swaying camels jostled each other in the Via Dolorosa, Arabs shouted their wares in David Street. Gradually we became aware of differences: there were Israelis to be seen in the *souk* – they had never been there before. When we reached the Wailing Wall a complete transformation greeted us – the little old Arab dwellings had disappeared; there was a wide space in front of the wall and, for the first time in our lives, we saw Jews wailing there. Meanwhile the Cry of the *Muezzin* came from the minarets calling the faithful Arabs to prayer. One felt Jerusalem must be seething with discontent – but among the ordinary folk there seemed to be little hostility between Jew and Arab.

More than two hours later we rejoined our coach outside the Jaffa Gate; everyone was in grateful mood – in spite of everything we had been able to see all that had been included in our itinerary. As the coach moved off we could just see the great procession of youth winding its way back to the dispersal point outside the city. All was peaceful; there had been no incidents of any kind; it seemed a miracle in this explosive country. We drove back to Haifa through Tel Aviv; our Israeli driver could not resist taking us on a tour of the city which was *en fête* in a big way. Tel Aviv is a great modern city and had few attractions for us, but to our driver it was a symbol of all that Israeli independence meant; we tried not to disappoint him in our reactions.

The trip next day to Galilee was a complete contrast; there was even time for a swim and a picnic by the Sea of Galilee. Ronald and I loved it as much as always; perhaps this time we loved it even more. In Jerusalem we were recording impressions almost minute by minute; here in our Lord's own country there was time to think and to sort things out.

From Haifa we sailed to Rhodes – an island about which we had heard so much that we felt we were almost certain to be disappointed. The reverse was the case – it was even more breathtaking than we had been told. The most hardboiled, sophisticated globetrotter could not be disappointed in Rhodes – it is exquisite.

Mandraki Harbour is small, too small to take our *Regina Maris*. We lay outside and went ashore by lifeboat, watching as we went the windmills that decorate the harbour. Even from the boat we could see why Rhodes is called the island of roses; everywhere we looked there were flowers, blue sky, blue sea and lovely buildings – that is how I shall always think of Rhodes. There is nothing out of place, no jarring note anywhere. The Greeks are artists in their way of life and this permeates everything.

We went through the city walls and spent nearly all our time in the Street of the Knights, where each building is a medieval *auberge* belonging to a different country – Great Britain, Germany, France etc – and built by the Knights of St John coming from that country. We could hardly tear ourselves away; I long to go back with time to absorb the beauty and the history and be enriched by it. The little time we had left we spent in the rose arbour of a gracious little restaurant drinking lemon tea and feasting on mouth-watering cakes while we watched the swimmers plunging into the blue waves from the clean, sandy beaches.

I had thought there could be nothing more perfect than Rhodes, but when I looked out of our porthole the next morning I found myself wondering. The first sight of Patmos in the early morning sun is almost past description. Patmos is *petite* – a pearl of great price; everything is in proportion; just one big mountain dotted with vivid green vineyards and crowned with a gleaming white monastery; one pretty little town perching halfway up the hillside; one busy, colourful little port all agog for visitors. It is like a perfectly-fashioned child's toy.

We went ashore by lifeboat and landed at Scala. Here our guide stood on a soap box calling, 'Taxis to the left, walkers to the right, riders straight on'. We had of course decided to ride; donkeys were to be provided and the local way of reaching the summit seemed to us just right. A large crowd of donkeys was assembled for our inspection; Ronald was introduced to a mule as being a more suitable size for him; Netta and Edie were somewhat unceremoniously hoisted on to their mounts and I found myself

astride the nicest animal I have ridden for years. Her name was
Alexia; we liked each other from the start. She was an individualist;
we had only gone about fifty yards when she decided to detach
herself from our little party and take me on her own private way to
the summit. The man in charge shouted, and probably swore, but
Alexia turned a deaf ear; I could do nothing about it and so we
continued on our lonely way. Every now and then I waved to the
others; I could just hear Netta telling her lethargic animal that he
was a lazy brute; Edie was manfully trying to plot a course up the
middle, rather than the edge, of the precipitous path; Ronald
appeared to be talking Greek to the donkey-man.

The path wound up the hill among scrubby trees and through
the tiny town of Chora; out to sea were the countless islands of the
Dodecanese; far below us the spotless white *Regina Maris* rode at
anchor. There was no need to call our steeds to a halt; they knew
exactly where to deposit their burdens; Alexia looked round and
nudged my knee; I leapt off with alacrity – she was a determined
little donkey and I was not too keen to find myself descending the
mountain at top speed.

The treasures of the monastery were displayed and explained
by the priests who lived there; they made it come alive for us just
because they loved it so much. St John, they explained, did not
write the Book of Revelation here, but in a tiny grotto half-way
down the mountain. They pointed out the winding path and we
made our way down. St John must have had the mind of an
artist; as we looked out over the 'glassy sea' we realized how perfect his pen pictures are. I have always loved the Book of Revelation; now, when it is read in the Lesson, I can hardly wait to hear
what is coming next. Back in the port of Scala we gathered round
tables in the square for drinks while gentlemen with a sharp eye for
business brought round photos of ourselves on our donkeys. They
were hardly works of art but of course we all bought them. 'Me on
my donkey at Patmos' must be an entry in at least two hundred
photo books of 1969.

As if Rhodes and Patmos on consecutive days had not almost
saturated us with beauty, we landed that same afternoon at
Kusadasi to explore Ephesus! This was a very special treat,
especially for the New Testament scholars among the party. It was
naturally news to an ignoramus like me that there were five

different Ephesuses in the course of history. I got greatly confused on being taken to Ephesus I and Ephesus V; it was quite a relief suddenly to see two enormous storks' nests with storks sitting on them – it seemed to bring one back to reality a bit. Ephesus III is the most famous and best preserved and this I loved; it was a great experience to walk down the wide marble street where St Paul himself actually walked and taught; shops and houses stand on either side, and at the end we came to the theatre which St Paul tried to enter, but where his friends prevented him from risking his life. Ronald read the story from the Book of Acts.

From Ephesus to Athens – it sounds like one of St Paul's journeys! Just to keep our sense of elation in proportion we had a horrible night crossing the Aegean. Kwells, Dramamine, Sea-legs – every kind of pill was swallowed on the ship that night; but when we woke to find ourselves in harbour in Piraeus our woes were soon forgotten. I could never tire of the Acropolis: undiscovered treasures are revealed on each visit. This time it was something entirely different I wanted to see. Right at the far end of the Acropolis is the Belvedere – a rocky eminence with a deep drop below it. Here in 1941 when Nazi troops took possession of Athens the Greek flag was still flying. A young Greek soldier was ordered to haul it down; rather than surrender the crowning glory of his country to the hated invader he tore the flag from its mast, wrapped himself in it and threw himself over the precipice. Tony Gilkes' story of this incident, which he told during his lecture on Athens, was so moving that I felt it was somehow a natural part of the Greece I love so much.

To see Sunion had been one of my secret wishes ever since I first went to Greece; on this trip my wish was granted. It was worth waiting for. We followed the rocky coastline round innumerable bays; we passed luxurious villas; they included, we were told, the abodes of Maria Callas and the famous Mr Onassis. Behind us were the Greek hills, before us tiny islands were scattered about the sea. At last the great columns of Sunion appeared on a cliff jutting out into the water. There was everything to make a perfect picture: sun and sea; a riot of flowers; the incomparable grace of the columns; and lovely Greek children pressing pistachio nuts upon us. We were drenched with aliveness and beauty – the two most vital attractions of Greece.

After a great evening with Roger Stafford and his Greek wife who live in Athens, we sailed away and had only one more port of call on our homeward journey – Gibraltar. We were to be three days at sea on our way there and this was the time for all the final merrymaking – nothing could be planned for the final stage after Gibraltar lest the Bay of Biscay should be in bestial mood.

What fun we had – table tennis and the swimming to our hearts' content – the fancy dress ball and the ship's concert in the evenings. The fancy dress concerned everyone – those who were not actually parading were roped in to applaud, to judge and to lend props of all kinds. All the outfits were of the do-it-yourself variety and caused immense hilarity. The first prize went to Tony Gilkes and his wife Ruby as General de Gaulle and *Vive La France*. Anything more exactly resembling *Le Général* than Tony could not be imagined; his only props were a peaked cap and a large notice pinned on his bosom – '*Après moi*' – but his appearance brought down the house, or nearly overturned the ship. Leicester covered itself with glory by carrying off the second and third trophies. Maurice and Barbara Millard with David and Vera Holmes produced a wonderful pageant of four of Chaucer's Canterbury Pilgrims *en route* for the Holy Land. Netta, Edie and I in shorts, frilly red gym tunics, white socks and school hats, described ourselves as 'three little maids from school'; the verdict of one elderly gentleman, that we represented St Trinian's at its worst, did not prevent us being awarded third prize.

The ship's concert revealed a mine of undiscovered talent; the most unexpected people sang, danced, recited and cut all manner of capers. There were encores and congratulations all round but the biggest roar of all went up when Maurice, David, Ronald and a nice young man called Adrian clad in red-and-white jerseys and sailor caps gave a spirited performance of 'Four Jolly Sailormen', preceded by a rather heavy-footed hornpipe.

The bad weather predicted for the Bay somehow caught up with us before Gibraltar, which delayed our arrival until the evening. However, there are few more attractive sights on the whole Mediterranean coast than Gib by night and no one minded exploring under the stars on a mild spring evening. Our party of four made merry at the Rock Hotel and strolled back to the harbour along Main Street, reviving our memories of our short stay the previous year. No one went to their cabins until well after midnight; all decks were crowded to see the magnificent sight of Gibraltar as we sailed slowly out. The Gibraltarians had stopped us in the street, and even as we boarded the ship, begging us not to let them down with General Franco. As we watched the twinkling lights of the town and the mighty Rock floodlit above, we seemed to sense how much the ties with Great Britain mean. In this nuclear age Gibraltar would be of little use to us or to Spain or any other power as a base. It is the people that matter; the people are part of the Commonwealth and long passionately to remain with us. Surely we cannot and must not let them down.

The Bay of Biscay belied its evil reputation and was as calm as the proverbial mill pond. It provided us with one last exciting experience. During breakfast we realized that the ship's turbines were no longer in action, the *Regina Maris* was drifting slowly northwards. The Captain's voice came over the tannoy, 'It is seldom in these days that we have the opportunity to see a five-masted schooner. In a few moments we shall pass our German training schooner the *Gorch Fock*. I hope you will admire her.'

Knives and forks were dropped with a clatter; everyone rushed out on deck. There she was, a glorious great sailing ship, gliding silently over the smooth sea, her white sails and masts clear-cut against the blue sky. A chorus of cheers went up from our ship; the *Regina Maris* sounded her sirens; the *Gorch Fock* replied on a lighter note. Friedrich, our dining-room steward, welcomed us back to breakfast waving a ten DM note – on it was a picture of the *Gorch Fock*. It was a great climax to the end of our long and lovely voyage, as we began our packing up.

How different everyone's luggage looked after visits to so many countries – Greek bags, Arab headdresses, trophies from all nations surmounted prosaic-looking British cases.

Only one small incident marred our homecoming. We were later than expected at Southampton; to help get us away the Captain had asked the German stewards to begin getting our luggage off the ship. It was promptly ordered back by the dockers as union rules did not allow work to begin for another hour. The Germans stared incredulously, we waited, silent and ashamed – sad for our own beloved England. It was the twenty-fifth anniversary of VE Day.

We came home to what will live in the minds of many as the 'Methodist summer'. Plans had been worked out during several years for a scheme of union between the Church of England and the Methodist Church. This year voting was to take place – it was the major event within the dioceses and the Church as a whole; it meant much work, much thought, much heart-searching for everyone.

We had one breathing space during June – just for one day. The son of a famous cricketer of former days, Gilbert Jessop, is Rector of Kegworth in the Leicester diocese. As a member of the MCC he presented us with tickets for the members' stand for one day of the test match at Lords. Lords is an old and favourite haunt of ours but never in our wildest moments had we expected to find ourselves in the members' stand. The cricket could perhaps have been better – the next day when we were not there, it was – but that did not really matter. The glorious summer day; the white figures against the green of the ground; the gay crowds completely filling the stands; it all stood for something very, very English; something both of us cherish dearly, something which, in spite of the cynics, will never perish. It was a great day out, and it ended with a meeting outside the pavilion with Frank Woolley.

The day of decision for the Anglicans and Methodists was to be Tuesday, July 8th. Already in May a preliminary vote had been taken and in June the referendum in the dioceses had taken place. So far there seemed to have been no very decisive evidence in either direction. The voting in our own diocese almost exactly matched the average – 63 per cent in favour of proceeding with stage one of the scheme for union. I only occasionally go up in the gallery at Church House to hear what is going on – I am not a meeting-minded type by nature – but on this occasion I arrived with Ronald at 9.30 am, determined to sit it out until the end. Quite a few wives had decided on the same course. Although the issue was vital to all of us I do not think that was really what brought us there; it was our loyalty to our husbands, and the knowledge that for many of them this would prove to be an agonizing day when perhaps our presence might produce a little comfort. I did not know how Ronald would vote; I knew he had voted for the scheme in May and in our referendum, always with certain misgivings in his heart. But now he was faced with leaving nearly half his clergy behind him if the proposed service of reconciliation took place. It was a cruel choice and Ronald was by no means the only bishop in that position. The day wore on; we went out to lunch together but somehow we could not eat anything. Many of the speeches in the morning and in the afternoon were very fine indeed. My head ached in a dull kind of way; how I wished that the choice was clearer; everyone spoke with so much sincerity and purpose; whatever happened there would be some disappointed, frustrated and anxious; there might even be a few broken hearts. I longed for seven o'clock, the time of voting, to come and put us out of our misery. It did come, at last, and Ronald was one of the five bishops who voted against the scheme. I knew he had made the choice for the sake of his diocese; I sent up a little prayer that all would understand and that at least some would be grateful. During the next few weeks I think that prayer was answered. The House of Clergy voted with 67 per cent in favour – 8 per cent short of the required number. The Archbishop of Canterbury announced very steadily that the scheme would not go forward; the Archbishop of York quietly gave the blessing.

Many of us were in tears, we hardly knew why; it had all been such a strain; everyone had tried so desperately hard to do right. Why do things have to be so difficult? Perhaps it is in the measure of their intrinsic value.

I have never felt more exhausted and I knew Ronald must feel far more so – he looked positively ill. I persuaded him to take me to dinner at his club, using the argument that I was too tired even to go back and change. The device worked and when we got there we found two more episcopal couples, John and Margaret Taylor from Sheffield, Eric and Beth Gordon from the Isle of Man. We were all old friends and it was a joy to be together. Gradually we all relaxed; by the end of the evening our sense of proportion had returned slightly; our menfolk looked less drawn and we wives began to introduce a lighter note.

During the few remaining weeks before the holidays people seemed to talk of little else than the scheme and its rejection by us and its acceptance by the Methodists – by just 2 per cent.

But I was struck by the charity and generosity of everyone; some of Ronald's friends would have gone along with him; the majority of them took the opposite view. But whoever we met and

whenever we met, there was nothing but affection and understanding; it was good to feel that friendship goes far, far deeper
than personal points of view, however convincingly held. I was
glad when everyone dispersed for the holidays – the Church and
the people, and most of all the bishops and clergy, needed a
breathing space and time to think again. Even the humble wives
were glad to be able to talk on other topics; unless one is something erudite, a DD perhaps – and not many of us are – one tends
to look at these things more simply, too simply perhaps. I know in
my heart that what I would like is unity, with *all* churches, but not
uniformity; mercifully, for the sake of the Church and the world,
no one is likely to take the slightest notice of my opinion.

The holiday this year was a continuous success. It began with
cricket at Canterbury and on our way there we made what Ronald
described as a 'Monckton pilgrimage'. The biography had revived
my memories so vividly that I wanted to catch up on a lot of minor
details. Kent was looking its loveliest in this blazing summer; it
had been a great talking point with Walter Monckton – his Kent
was my Kent and, incidentally, it was Ronald's too, so the détour
we made was sheer joy.

We slipped off the throbbing A20 down a leafy lane to Ightham
church; here at the steps of its wide chancel Walter was married
and here, in later years as a lay reader, he preached from the old
oak pulpit. We went down into the valley and up the hill on the
other side past Ightham Warren, Walter's home for twenty-four
years. Down a deep, steep, lane we found Ightham Mote, as
serene and lovely as it was when my brother and I used to bicycle
past it as children. It was here that Walter did his courting – even
before he left Harrow. We followed the road for Tonbridge to
Plaxtol, that sturdy English village where Walter was born at Reed
House. We have both known Plaxtol for most of our lives; neither
of us had previously bothered to look for Reed House. It looked
derelict and uninspiring but finding it was a triumph and it fitted
into the story we were piecing together. It only remained to find
Brenchley where Walter had elected to be buried – it seemed
rather a far cry from Ightham and Plaxtol. We understood why he
chose it when at last we reached Brenchley – an incomparable
village with a glorious old church. The churchyard is full of
Monckton graves dating back hundreds of years; here Walter lies

among his forbears, beneath a dignified, restrained stone bearing only his name, his honours and his coat of arms. We left him in the peace of the lovely churchyard and went on our way to the cricket. My picture was complete – I had seen the beginning and the ending of a great life and when, as sometimes happens, my thoughts turn to Walter Monckton for inspiration, I have the book and the pageant of that summer pilgrimage to refresh my memory.

Back again in Zermatt, I returned to the heights at last. Since Bernard died I had not been able to bring myself to fix up with another guide, although I know and admire most of the guides of Zermatt. I had never climbed with anyone but Bernard; it was a unique relationship; it seemed as if the climbing and even the mountains could never be quite the same again. And yet I longed to be up on the tops; Ronald and I have wonderful walks in the mountains; we usually get a certain amount of rock scrambling; twice I had taken friends to the summit of the Stockhorn. It is 12,000 feet and a nice snow walk, but we had not used the rope or cut steps or done any of the things that spell climbing; I felt lopsided and rather bereft.

For the last three years, of course, there has been another hazard – the iniquitous and beggarly travel allowance; I could scarcely afford to take a guide. Then one evening outside the guides' office I saw a notice advertizing guided parties to some of the lesser peaks for quite a small sum. I ran my eye down the list; most of them I had done; and then I noticed 'Traverse of the Theodulhorn' – the one bit I had not achieved of that always inviting ridge that fills the sky line between Testa Grigia and the Matterhorn. Twice we had attempted it; twice we had been foiled by bad weather; it would be fun to complete that ridge, but could I possibly enjoy it under such different circumstances?

Of course the mountains won – the mountains and Ronald. The pull of the heights is too compelling for me – I just cannot resist it. Ronald saw to it that I did not.

'You know you always go home hungry for the hills,' he said firmly. 'For goodness' sake go and take what you can – you know what Bernard would say.' I did indeed – I could almost hear him saying it!

I popped inside the bureau, signed my name, paid the fee and the deed was done.

Things could hardly have worked out better. Ronald was already engaged to go down the valley to Visp to see a young Englishman in hospital with appendicitis, at the behest of the British Consulate in Geneva who take immense care of their countrymen in trouble. I was sorry for the invalid but glad Ronald did not have to spend a lonely day. All the old thrill and enchantment was there: a call at 5.30, breakfast left ready for me in a corner of the dining-room, boots laced tightly, anorak zipped up, rucksack slung on my back, my ice axe tucked under my arm. My feet had wings as Ronald kissed me goodbye and sent me on my way. I passed the cemetery; just below me was Bernard's grave; I felt he knew and was pleased; the summit of the Matterhorn rose out of the mist, painted gold in the morning sun.

There were only five of us and our guide in the party. The guide was an old friend of Bernard's whom I knew well; my fellow-adventurers were Swiss and German without a word of English between them; it was excellent linguistic practice for me, especially on the more tricky bits of the climb!

We cut our way up the glacier; I was almost trembling with joy to feel the rope round my waist. The Almighty had produced the perfect mountain morning for us. Below, thick white mist shrouded the valley; around us cotton wool clouds clung to some of the mountains; above, the peaks stabbed a clear blue sky. I hope my little pæan of praise and thanksgiving was heard somewhere up there.

We reached the Italian hut and sat outside in the sun. Oscar, the guide, gave the signal to move and the rock work began. I can never forget the feel of the warm rock ledges under my fingers and the friction of the wall of a chimney on the back of my anorak; it seemed as if I had been born again. On the summit we solemnly shook hands and, according to time-honoured custom, devoured our second breakfast. All around was the great panorama I had seen so many times before – Grand Paradiso, Grivola, Mont Blanc, Grand Combin, the whole of the Oberland range and every one of the Zermatt mountains. It had all been given back to me, I whispered to myself Geoffrey Winthrop Young's famous line 'I hold the heights – I hold the heights I won'.

The descent was over steep snow, followed by snow covered glacier; we travelled remarkably quickly with no untoward events;

by midday we were back in the refuge at *Trockener Steg* drinking onion soup laced with slices of cheese and great chunks of bread. I had had everything I could have desired – snow, rock and glacier; sun and pleasant companionship; above all the unutterable beauty of the mountains.

I met Ronald at the station at three o'clock; we took some autumn crocuses to Bernard's grave; he had been very near me on that little climb. It took the rest of the day to hear Ronald's story and tell him mine and thus the joy was doubled.

From Zermatt via Berne, Lucerne, St Gallen and Munich to Czechoslovakia. We could hardly have taken a journey containing greater contrasts: Switzerland democratic, peaceful, orderly, steeped in history; Germany powerful, thriving, enormously hardworking, completely rehabilitated; when we had last passed through Munich it was still lying in ruins. And now we stood on the threshold of Eastern Europe, waiting to squeeze through a chink in the Iron Curtain.

We waited with a certain amount of trepidation; only a few days before, while we had been in Zermatt, there had been violent scenes in Prague when the date of the anniversary of the Russian invasion arrived. But we were determined to get through if it was at all possible. A year ago, during that sad meeting in Western Germany, we had promised Kurt and Traude that if we were granted visas we would come. We had the visas; it only remained to implement our promise.

Although the wait at the Czechoslovakian frontier was long we crossed without incident and were treated with complete courtesy and friendliness. The car was searched, of course, but the only articles questioned were a couple of Swiss calendars. When we opened the packet there was great amusement and handshakes all round. Even the changing of money produced no difficulties.

At last we were released and sent on our way with smart salutes from all the frontier guards – there was even a duplicate post half a mile down the road. It was quite a thrill; we were breaking new ground in a strange country where the people lived under a régime utterly alien to us and where we knew not one single word of the language. Even the signposts were difficult to understand, but we knew we were making for Pilzen and we did know that was spelt 'Plzen'.

The road surface was quite good; we travelled mainly through sparsely wooded country; there seemed to be very few towns. In Pilzen we were to find Kurt who had left home at six o'clock that morning in order to meet us, take us to Prague and eventually guide us to his home. We had to find the Hotel Slovan; Traude had sent us a sheet of paper on which she had written '*Hledame Hotel Slovan, Plzen. Kopeckeho Sady*' –in other words, 'We are looking for the Hotel Slovan'. She had said that if we held the paper against the windscreen people would flock to help us. It happened exactly as she had prophesied; an elderly gentleman flagged us down, shook hands, took our piece of paper and drew a map. He then gave us further instructions in German, explained how delighted he was to meet British tourists and waved us farewell. At the Hotel Slovan we found Kurt already ordering a meal for us. There were no parking problems – there are scarcely any cars – and within minutes we were exchanging our news while we devoured a delicious fish lunch. Kurt's joy at being able to welcome us to Czechoslovakia was wonderful to see and we were no less pleased to have achieved our long-delayed objective. The hotel was a rather heavy German type of building, but it had an air of prosperity and I was fascinated by the waiters who were turned out in dinner jackets – a touch of sartorial elegance that I certainly had not expected in this communist state.

With Kurt sitting next to the driver we set off for Prague, sixty miles away. This is a city we had both been longing to see for many years; there is a romantic ring about the capital of Bohemia. We found it to be, for us at any rate, a city of dramatic contrasts. High on the hill stands the famous castle with the Cathedral of St Vitus rising behind it; below is the wide river, the Moldau, spanned by the truly beautiful Charles Bridge. We saw it in a lovely setting – ever since we left Switzerland rain had been falling in torrents; by the time we reached Prague it was fine at last and a pale gold sun was flooding the castle, and the river. It was a glorious sight: there was a kind of tragic eloquence about it; an unspoken plea that here was the spirit and the soul of the real Prague – Prague as it had been in the past and as it would be one day in the future.

We were conscious of this as Kurt took us about the city. It is a sad, sad city where beautiful buildings are decaying through lack of care and where shops are only well-dressed windows with nothing behind them. In Jan Huss Square people sat silently under the trees; their children sat beside them; their dogs lay listlessly at their feet. No one spoke or moved about. No one looked underfed or badly clothed; there was just no incentive to do anything, a kind of hopelessness hung over everything. Kurt took us to see the famous Wenceslaus Square, so lately the scene of trouble. It is more like a street than a square but beautifully proportioned and pleasing to the eye. The Wenceslaus monument stands at the top with the National Museum behind it. The spot where Jan Palach, the young Czechoslovakian student, burnt himself alive is unmarked but not unremembered. Only the reigning authorities find it convenient to forget.

It was nearly dark when we set off for our final destination, Kurt and Traude's home not far from the East German frontier. As we came up the hill out of Prague we passed the spot where Reinhardt Heydrich, the Nazi Protector of Moravian Bohemia, was shot by Czech patriots. As a result the village of Lidice was burned and the population martyred.

Kurt had warned us that the road was bad. It was indeed, it was absolutely awful; how we survived without broken springs we shall never know. It was necessary to fill up with petrol; at every garage we came to the man in charge shook his head sadly, he had sold the last litre hours ago. We made a détour to one where Kurt thought we might be lucky; it was closed but the owner spotted our GB plate and came hurrying out. Kurt told us afterwards that he had been so thrilled to see a British car that he had sold us all that remained in his pump.

Very late and very tired we crossed the River Elbe and came to rest at last outside the home we had waited so long to see. There to welcome us was not only Traude but her mother, known to us ever since the war as *Tante Irene*. *Tante* was an important politician in her younger days; she spent the war years as a refugee in London and now, at over eighty years of age, she is still remembered and beloved by the Czech people, especially the children, to whom she continues to broadcast inspiring little messages.

We could spend only three days with Kurt and Traude; they were three very precious days, packed full with nostalgic memories, with exciting discoveries, with delightful music, and best of all, with long, long periods of talk such as only the closest of friends can enjoy.

Our first duty was to register at the police station; this somewhat solemn occasion passed off peacefully and we were free to enjoy ourselves. We had no idea how much Czechoslovakia is bound up with the musical traditions of Europe. We found the little village of Nelahozeves where Dvorak was born in 1841. He was the son of the village butcher and became a butcher's assistant until his musical genius was discovered by an organist named Zlonice. The New World Symphony is a great favourite of mine and became even more important after I had seen something of the composer's background. We went to an old twelfth century castle standing high above the Elbe with views reminiscent of those from the Lorelei. It was in this castle that Wagner planned his opera Tannhauser – the only Wagner opera I really appreciate – and here, through the open lattice windows, he heard played on a shepherd's pipe the motif that is incorporated in the overture and the song from the Venusberg.

Not everything that we discovered gave us so much pleasure; we drove through the town of Terezin. Before the war it was a small place with a population of 4,000 people. In 1942 it became a ghetto, where between forty and sixty thousand people were incarcerated before being dispatched in cattle trucks to the gas chambers of Auschwitz in Poland. Among the victims were Kurt's parents and all his relations. Today there is a great cemetery at Terezin, dedicated as a national shrine.

One afternoon we went shopping for glass and ceramic jewellery; Kurt and Traude took us to the best shop and left us to enjoy ourselves. Occasionally, while we were there, young Russian soldiers came in – presumably for presents to send home to their girl friends. Immediately all assistants vanished from the shop; we went on with our choosing feeling vaguely uncomfortable. After a while the Russians looked at each other sheepishly and wandered out again. They looked so bewildered that one felt convinced that they did not know where they were or why they were there.

We enjoyed the country better than the town. Kurt and Traude have a tiny summer cottage up in the nearby hills. Here there are fruit trees and flowers; the birds sing; rabbits scuttle in and out of their burrows; great graceful hares leap across the meadow. Kurt and Traude spend much of the summer here; there is peace and beauty undisturbed; nothing reminds them that their lives were shattered in 1939 and have never been rebuilt. It is possible to forget wars and politics here and live only for the instant present as winter melts into spring and the summer fruit succeeds the spring blossom. We entered into their contentment and were thankful that they had at least this respite. We finished the afternoon by going up into the Erzgebirge, where we could see the winter ski slopes and, incidentally, the distant watch towers on the East German border.

Back home for a cosy evening we consumed frankfurters and cheese while we listened to *Noye's Fludde* and *The Seekers* on the record player and talked far into the night about Peter, their only child and my godson. Peter is studying for a PhD in England; what the future holds for him none of us knows.

The day of departure came all too quickly. We found crowds of Czech boys gathered round our car, waiting to see us set off; the presence of a four-year-old Ford Zephyr was an event of importance in their uneventful lives.

We were leaving Czechoslovakia by a different checkpoint in order to see as much of the country as possible; Kurt and Traude came with us to Karlovy Vary, pointing out to us wide stretches of the Böhmerwald on the way.

Karlovy Vary is the old German spa of Karlsbad and was the most cheerful and lively spot we encountered. It lies deep down among forested hills, and hot springs shoot up for many feet from the pavements in streets and squares. A sparkling stream patters through the centre of the town with smart hotels and gay shops lining its banks. Everyone was 'taking the waters' from cups equipped with a special, narrow spout to prevent burning the mouth with the steaming water. Of course we had to buy one and it now decorates our dresser.

We had an excellent lunch served again by waiters in dinner jackets; they seemed slightly less out of place in this smart spa.

We drove Kurt and Traude to the station; it was here we had to part. We longed to take them with us into the freedom of our country. But this cannot be – we could only promise to come again as soon as possible.

From the personal point of view it had been a perfect visit; they had showered kindness upon us. The only way we can return it is by returning ourselves, bringing with us a breath of freedom to this unhappy country.

We reached the border over appalling roads but once again we had no difficulties at the frontier; we were bidden goodbye with complete courtesy; nevertheless we breathed a sigh of relief and shook hands with each other as we crossed into Western Germany. We had fulfilled our promise; we had completed all we intended to do; we had emerged unscathed but with our eyes wider open than ever before.

The miserable minority in our country who grumble and protest and demand their so-called rights should spend a week behind the Iron Curtain; they would soon rethink their own situation. The West is far from perfect; there is much to be done and much suffering to be alleviated; but life is lived out in an entirely different context. Perhaps we need to go east to know how lucky we are.

We travelled back across Germany and Holland with pauses in Wurzburg, Cologne and the Hague and arrived home greatly refreshed and bursting with health. There were special problems awaiting us at home and an enormous backlog of work. But it is all part of the job – and to us at least it is the most wonderful job in the world.

CHAPTER X

'Tho' much is taken, much abides'

I LOOK back over the decade which has passed since I wrote
my first book; at such a time one tends to sit back and try to
assess the losses and the gains in one's personal circle of
friends and relations. Inevitably much has been taken, but this is
no cause for complaint; it is part of the pain of life, which is the
price of its exquisite joy – the price of that happiness which at
times is so perfect that it is almost frightening. I have had my fair
share of this kind of happiness – perhaps more than my fair share
– and when a part of it has been taken I have suffered accordingly,
but seldom finally. I come gratefully to the conclusion that 'much
abides'.

It so happens that this decade in my life coincides almost
exactly with the decade of the sixties, now undergoing a public
post mortem as we gallop full tilt into the seventies. It is tempting
to look more deeply into one's own mind and conduct a private
inquest as to how far the judgments and values of earlier years are
still valid – at least for oneself.

Life lived to the full is very satisfying; it can be very intense.
The more deeply one loves, the more eagerly one enjoys, the more
firmly one believes in certain ideals and attitudes, the more vulner-
able one is. But very little of real worth is ever completely and
irretrievably lost; there is usually something that can be salvaged
and treasured. In these ever-changing days one has to strike one's
own balance sheet in order to remain solvent spiritually and mentally. Life has to be lived in the present and the future. The best
of the past must be built into both.

Courage, honesty, chivalry, courtesy, consideration for others
seem to count for little in some quarters, but they are not less alive
because they are less talked about; they will blossom abundantly
when the winter of materialism and violence has died a natural

death. Flag-waving is out of fashion but most of us still love our country – and I mean 'our country' and not 'the state'. We know other nations need us, as we need them; for the sake of the whole world we have to believe in ourselves:

'Pray God our greatness may not fail
Thro' craven fears of being great.'

Drink, drugs, sexual licence, controversial scandals sometimes seem to be the blueprint for the affluent society. The moral code, faithfulness in marriage, national honour are all so much grist to the satirical mill. However in a short letter printed at the beginning of one of his programmes the popular David Kossof writes:

'None of my material is sick ... no four-letter words are used ... I remain clothed throughout; no ministers of the crown are mentioned; there are no fellow actors on the stage to beat up, give drugs to, betray or discuss sexualities with. No dirty songs are sung, no kitchen sinks, unmade beds or lavatories are seen. No comments are made on the week that was or what the papers said ...'

If I were a protest-marching, banner-bearing type – which I am not – I would willingly display that slogan among the ranks of the pornographers. It is good to see men like David Kossof and Christopher Booker coming into the lists in support of things that have contributed to the stability and sanity of our society. Advocates of the permissive society are not going to have it all their own way.

The 'Naughty Nineties' and the 'Roaring Twenties' have become bywords in the history of society; until recently one wondered if the present decade would go down to posterity as the 'Sexy, Satirical, Slovenly Sixties'. But already it seems that this may not be so; people have become tired of the confusion and unreality of a counterfeit society; there is a turning towards truth and beauty and genuine worth. There is a growing feeling that obligations and duties are more important than rights and that life depends not on what you can get out of it but on what you put into it. Above all there is a longing for inspiring leadership, for a clearer attitude towards right and wrong, even for authority – of the right kind. The wholesale casting aside of all conventions has produced a situation which shows only too clearly that a few, at least, are necessary; their limitations and restraints are essential to any healthy civilization.

It seems incredible to me that anyone like myself, who is by nature more interested in private than in public affairs, should get so much caught up in matters that are of national and world-wide importance in contemporary society. This arises from the age in which we live and for all its pressures and confusions I, for one, would not have wanted to live in any other. It is exhilarating, if nothing else, and keeps one on one's toes. I used to imagine that in middle age it would be only too easy just to settle down comfortably; that is impossible today if you are in any sense a keen and caring kind of person. If you really believe in the survival of certain ideals and principles you have got to do something about it or take the consequences.

But this is as it should be – it is all part of the 'poetry and problems' of life. We all have moments of supreme contentment offset by, or more often resulting from, occasions of difficulty, perplexity, anxiety, perhaps even danger. So often for me these moments have occurred on the mountains. There are days when everything seems to go wrong, rain pours down your neck, the next handhold always eludes you, the wind all but blows your rucksack off your back. And then, still struggling painfully, you suddenly emerge on the summit. Miraculously the rain stops, the wind drops, the sun sweeps up the clouds from the cauldron of the valley and dispels them beyond the horizons. You see the world as God sees it – and you know that life is good. Such satisfaction belongs to the poetry of life; it sheds light on the problems and gives more meaning to them. It is to moments of inspiration like these that I turn when banner headlines and dramatic announcements depress me; something in my subconscious tells me that God will see to it that truth will prevail.

And so, after all these reflections and ruminations I come back to the realities of daily life more than ever convinced that Hilaire Belloc was right:

'There's little worth the wear of winning,
Save laughter and the love of friends.'

I printed these words at the beginning of *Bishop's Wife – but still Myself* and they still ring true. Work in the diocese and in the wider context of the Church becomes more complex and absorbing. We have been in Leicester fifteen years now; we have never been bored and we never expect to be; our only trouble is that there are never enough hours in the day to do everything we would like to do and feel we ought to do. When we hear complaints about dioceses that are too large and too time consuming in travel we realize how lucky we are to have one that is so compact and full of variety.

We are immensely rich in friends; of the very special ones who put their signatures on the end-papers of my first book only Dick and Bernard are gone – the rest remain, more like brothers and sisters than friends. We have shared many of life's great experiences and we hope to continue to do so for many years yet. Our circle grows larger as our travels take us to more distant parts; among those nearer to us the quality of friendship deepens as the years lengthen.

From time to time readers whom I have never met write to me asking for news of our household – this paragraph is written specially for them! Here at home in Bishop's Lodge life goes on – a blend of happiness and contentment with a sufficient supply of problems and anxieties to make it real. Changes sometimes have to be and as I started this last chapter our dear Mr and Mrs Bell, who have been with us so long, finally retired – with a promise to return whenever we need them. Our driver, Mr Green, with his wife have moved in as welcome successors; we are grateful that friends, not strangers, occupy the flat. Mrs Perrott has been helping us now for six years; she is the 'oldest inhabitant' and remains faithful and loyal as ever. Cheerful Arthur Eccles still works three days a week in the garden and enlivens 'elevenses' with his fund of stories. Secretaries come and go; Audrey Gibbons has filled the bill now for three years and we never had a more faithful or devoted helper. She is the wife of a parson and the mother of a fine teenage son – long may she reign in the secretary's office. Martin, the little wire-haired terrier, is our loved and constant companion; he accompanies us about the diocese and is well-known to every visitor to the house – fortunately most of them are prepared to receive a vigorous doggy welcome.

We are lucky too that we still have a bit of 'family' left; Ronald has his sister; I have my brother Geoffrey, whose elder son John has now provided us with a great-nephew – Duncan James. We regard this as a luxury in spite of the fact that it makes us sound terribly venerable. Our chances of meeting are not very many but when they do occur we go right back to the shared experiences of 'first beginnings' and turn the pages that have led up to the present, culminating in the birth of the youngest member of the clan.

And now this book of highlights, reflections and reminiscences comes to its end; many things have been taken, so many more abide – above all the priceless gifts of home and husband; friends, the magic of the hills and all the lovely, simple things.

'These things must live, whate'er may pass –
The trees; the dew upon the grass;

The starry skies; the glow of dawn;
The songbirds' choir in early morn;

The scent of brown earth after rain;
The flowers in an English lane:

And memory with us to the end
Of English hearth and home and friend.'

GEORGE ALLEN & UNWIN LTD

Head office:
40 Museum Street, London, W.C.1
Telephone: 01-405 8577

Sales, Distribution and Accounts Departments
Park Lane, Hemel Hempstead, Herts.
Telephone: 0442 3244

Athens: 7 Stadiou Street, Athens 125
Auckland: P.O. Box 36013, Northcote Central, N.4
Barbados: P.O. Box 222, Bridgetown
Beirut: Deeb Building, Jeanne d'Arc Street
Bombay: 103/5 Fort Street, Bombay 1
Calcutta: 285J Bepin Behari Ganguli Street, Calcutta 12
Cape Town: 68 Shortmarket Street
Dacca: Alico Building, 18 Motijheel, Dacca 2
Delhi: 1/18B Asaf Ali Road, New Delhi 1
Hong Kong: 105 Wing on Mansion, 26 Hankow Road, Kowloon
Ibadan: P.O. Box 62
Karachi: Karachi Chambers, McLeod Road
Lahore: 22 Falettis' Hotel: Egerston Road
Madras: 2/18 Mount Road, Madras 6
Manila: P.O. Box 157, Quezon City D-505
Mexico: Villalongin 32, Mexico 5, D.F.
Nairobi: P.O. Box 30583
Pakistan: Alico Building, 18 Motijheel, Dacca 2
Philippines: P.O. Box 157, Quezon City, D-502
Rio de Janeiro: Caixa Postal 2537-Zc-00
Singapore: 36c Prinsep Street, Singapore 7
Sydney: N.S.W. Bradbury House, 55 York Street
Tokyo: C.P.O. Box 1728, Tokyo 100-91
Toronto: 145 Adelaide Street West, Toronto 1

BISHOP'S WIFE—BUT STILL MYSELF

Cicely Williams

Cicely Williams tells in her first full-length book, a fascinating story of adventures with an ice-axe and the pen; of thrills and horrors experienced as a war-time driver in the London blitz, of post-war days as Principal's wife in a Durham College and finally of her painful adjustment to the life of a bishop's wife in circumstances far removed from those of Mrs. Proudie. She writes with a disarming sincerity and simplicity and introduces the reader to a varied and interesting circle of her friends.

Those who are interested in mountains, free-lance journalism, colleges or the Church, will be enthralled by her keen observation and sensitive approach to life. Laughter and tears are as close to each other in these pages as they are in life itself.

DEAR ABROAD

Cicely Williams

Here she shows how 'abroad' became '*dear* abroad' for her from a very early age, and has remained so up till now. Readers of her earlier books will find the same enthusiasm for Switzerland and the Alps, but will also be able to travel with her to more distant horizons, to the Gulf of Mexico in the west and to the Dead Sea in the east. The author's adventures, by land, sea and air, will be vividly shared by her readers as a result of her keen observation, photographic memory and thoughtful reflection. Often laughing at herself she encourages others to laugh with her. Here is a book for those who still like beautiful things and beautiful places, and whose zest for enjoyment has not been finally stifled by the cynicism of the times.

LOUISE MOUNTBATTEN, QUEEN OF SWEDEN

Margit Fjellman

Born Princess Louise of Battenberg, Louise Mountbatten was a member of one of the most intriguing families in Europe. Her father, Prince Louis of Battenberg (later first Marquess of Milford Haven), was First Sea Lord at the outbreak of World War I but resigned because of his German origin. Her mother was Princess Victoria, the grand-daughter of Queen Victoria.

Shy, vivacious, talkative, quick to anger and to forgive, unfailingly generous and kindhearted, Louise was also critical of waste and stupidity, possessed radical views, a keen interest in politics and a live social conscience. During childhood and youth her parents moved from home to home, alternating between the gaiety of Malta, the castles of Barmstadt and Heiligenberg, and a succession of English houses; and there were visits to cousins in Hesse, in Russia, at Osborne and Windsor. With World War I, Princess Louise nursed French soldiers on the Front, afterwards returned to social and charity work. Then at the age of thirty-four, she fell in love with Crown Prince Gustaf V Adolf of Sweden – and they married despite her vow never to wed either a widower or a King.

The book includes the diary that Princess Louise kept during a cruise in the Russian imperial yacht in 1914 and a selection of her letters; extracts from the memoirs that her father and mother penned for their children; Louis and Louise's description of how their father 'stood the Fleet fast'; the special account of the sinking of the *Kelly* that Lord Mountbatten wrote for his sister; many of Lord Mountbatten's letters to her from every corner of the globe; and the enchanting letters that the children of the Russian imperial family sent their cousin Louise.

REBEL DAUGHTER OF A COUNTRY HOUSE

Francesca M. Wilson

Much has been written about the Save the Children Fund, but little about its founder, Eglantyne Jebb, though in the field of relief and welfare work she was one of the most remarkable pioneers of our time. She was no humourless do-gooder: she was passionate, witty, adventurous yet always tormented by a sense that she had some mission in life. This she found only in her last ten years. Born in a country house in Shropshire of a family distinguished for their intelligence and social conscience, she rebelled not against them but against the feudalism which surrounded her youth. All the Jebbs were great letter-writers and from these Miss Wilson has constructed a lively picture of Victorian house life.

SAILOR HAT IN THE HOUSE OF THE LORD

Theresa La Chard

The reason why the author has not written a full-length work until her present ripe age is, she says, because life has been too full. Life with its stately beginning: a Victorian cageling *par excellence*, the motherless child of a wealthy Anglo-German family living on the rural fringe of London, a home in which 'system' was the only ogre, involving obsessions with health and music which became a tyranny and caused her to revolt. Midway through youth came a sudden decline into biting poverty, with a lovely young stepmother and a clamorous brood. Teaching in a series of 'Church' and 'Board' schools was the only way to independence, all else having failed for lack of qualifications, and her picture of the lives of children, students and teachers seventy years ago is especially vivid.

There are wayward stories of the heart, too: of war and helpless involvement on two sides: of adventurous strides into political freedom of the new voter after 1918, and constantly in the background the fine old Bremen family, woodcarved and almost stylised in its social rigidity, but ever kind and open-hearted.

ROME'S HISTORIC CHURCHES

Lilian Gunton

This book is a record of a love affair. Not with persons but with places and those places the churches of Rome. For here Lilian Gunton sets out to pass on to the reader a lifetime's study of Rome's most ancient and most beautiful churches.

In this book, Lilian Gunton has had the original idea of describing the 'stational churches' in the order in which they are traditionally visited. In each case, the author lovingly tells the history and associations of the church and describes the exterior and interior in detail. Often she points out features of art and architecture that the visitor can easily miss and which sometimes even experts will not know. This book is intended both for the person visiting Rome for the first time, for those who have made the art and architecture of Rome a special study and also for any student or lover of art or architecture who has never had the chance to visit Italy.

LONDON · GEORGE ALLEN AND UNWIN LTD